FAMILY BUSINESSES

THE ESSENTIALS

PETER LEACH

Foreword by Roger Pedder

P

PROFILE BOOKS

First published in Great Britain in 2007 by
Profile Books Ltd
3a Exmouth House
Pine Street
Exmouth Market
London EC1R 0JH
www.profilebooks.com

A CIP catalogue record for this book is available from the British Library.

ISBN-10: 1 86197 861 8
ISBN-13: 978 1 86197 861 5

Consultant editor: Simon Perry
Illustrations by Belle Mellor
Text design by Sue Lamble
Typeset in Stone Serif by MacGuru Ltd
info@macguru.org.uk

Printed and bound in Great Britain by Clays, Bungay, Suffolk

BDO Stoy Hayward is the UK member firm of BDO International, the world's fifth
largest accountancy network, with more than 600 offices in 100 countries. We specialise
in helping businesses, whether start-ups or multinationals, to grow. Through our own
professional expertise and by working directly with organisations, we've developed a
robust understanding of the factors that govern business growth. Our objective is to use
this to help our clients maximise their potential.

The paper this book is printed on is certified by the © 1996 Forest Stewardship
Council A.C. (FSC). It is ancient-forest friendly. The printer holds FSC chain of custody
SGS-COC-2061

FSC
Mixed Sources
Product group from well-managed
forests and other controlled sources
Cert no. SGS-COC-2061
www.fsc.org
© 1996 Forest Stewardship Council

FAMILY
BUSINESSES
THE ESSENTIALS

In fond memory of

Neil Crawford, Leslie Lewis, Jonathan Davis and Paul Bates

Contents

Foreword

Roger Pedder

For those interested in family business this is a must-read book – not a prescriptive manual, more a dramatised documentary. Here is the proper distillation of experience that Peter Leach has gleaned over 25 years of advising family companies. It is also a work of scholarship.

I am impressed by the understanding that every family business situation is different. Nevertheless, a well-considered interpretation of the established principles of good family management is essential for any family business. My experience of working in a major family-owned company for over 40 years, and chairing it for 13 of those years, echoes Peter's insightful analysis. If, when I was learning, he had been writing about how to conduct a major family enterprise, I would have had a reliable text to guide me on issues which, frankly, I had to address on a trial-and-error basis. It would have saved me and the family time and anxiety.

Much modern management writing is full of jargon, takes a unifocal point of view and is presented as a panacea for all management ills. It is a pleasure to read a book that is written in plain language, is well ordered and is not dogmatic. Any family member of any family business will find something relevant which, if they think about it, will improve not only their understanding of the enterprise and their relationship to it, but also how they can help and improve the conduct of the enterprise itself.

Family members in a family business often suffer emotional pain and anguish. They may be neglected and even abused by both family owners and non-family managers, and their lives may be blighted by insensitive or hostile treatment. Active understanding and implementation of Peter's advice on the treatment of family members in family businesses should ameliorate the worst aspects of the problem, but it remains the dark side of the family business experience. Family members are often trapped in a frustrating or demeaning situation, because moving on from a family business without any external experience is difficult. Our management culture seldom recognises family company management as valid and professional experience. Perhaps this should be the subject of Peter's next book.

The importance and contribution of family businesses to our society and economy are increasingly being recognised, so Peter's insights and sound recommendations appear at a propitious time. My hope is that families in business take note and act on them.

Roger Pedder
Chairman, C. & J. Clark (Clarks Shoes), 1993–2006
November 2006

Preface

My fascination with family businesses took hold some 25 years ago. From the early 1980s, as a partner with the accountancy firm Stoy Hayward (now BDO Stoy Hayward LLP), I worked with owner-managed businesses and some older family companies in the UK. I noticed the way that business and family often overlap and depend upon each other in these firms, and I kept seeing the same issues cropping up – what to do about Dad; brothers finding it hard to work together and so on. But at that time no one in the UK had really studied the issue. In contrast, on my travels in the USA (from the mid-1980s) I saw the way that conceptual thinking about family companies was taking hold among both advisers and family business people, spurred on by focused academic research into the unique issues faced by these companies.

Influential figures working on researching and analysing family businesses in the USA at the time included Peter Davis (then at Wharton Applied Research Center), Ivan Lansberg (at Yale School of Organisation and Management) and Harry Levinson (at Harvard), with more practical input from established consultants like Benjamin Benson and Léon Danco. During my US visits I was fortunate enough to have the opportunity to shadow Davis on his assignments advising some major US family businesses, and I also attended many family business seminars and conferences, which, by the late 1980s, were becoming increasingly popular across the country. Witnessing all this interest and enthusiasm, I decided to organise some activities and events in the UK.

The first step was to commission two studies, supervised by the London Business School, designed to review and quantify family business activity in this country.[1] These included the key finding that 76 per cent of UK businesses are family controlled. Next I wrote the first edition of *The Stoy Hayward Guide to the Family Business*, which was published in March 1991, and invited Davis to help launch the various UK initiatives – he was the keynote speaker at a series of sell-out seminars (organised in conjunction with venture capital group 3i) which took place around the country. Family business people at these seminars spoke of a new sense of belonging, based on the realisation that what they were experiencing was not unique to them, and that all family businesses faced the same sorts of issues.

It rapidly became clear that taking a fresh look at family businesses was an idea whose time had come, and in 1992 the Stoy Centre for Family Business was established (recently rebranded as the BDO Centre for Family Business). The launch of the centre created a stir – it was recognised as the first attempt to do some joined-up thinking in this country about family systems theory, family psychology and business – and, teaming up with the CBI, it became a powerful lobbying group, supported by a publishing programme and nationwide seminars.

Encouraging trends

Some 15 years have elapsed since these events, and over that period the family business community has become firmly established in the UK and Europe as an independent, dynamic and increasingly well-researched study discipline. Many universities and colleges have set up courses for family members, and the value of family business consulting too is now coming to be fully recognised. This is not consulting in the traditional sense of client-visiting, fact-gathering and report-writing. Family business advising and consulting offers families expert facilitation, trust-building, support and guidance services that help them arrive at their own solutions and their own consensus as to the best way forward.

Reflecting these developments, and the raised profile of the sector, family businesses themselves have become much more knowledgeable and sophisticated – much more willing to embrace a fresh outlook and policies that start to counter some of their in-built disadvantages. For example, 15 years ago the hallmark of most family firms I encountered was their unstructured (often chaotic) approach to decision-making and organisation, but it is noticeable that family businesses today for the most part have adopted what could be termed a structured but flexible model, with much more thought being given to building family and corporate governance, more efficient decision-making processes and accountability. Similarly, it used to be rather unusual to find female family members employed in the family business, but today it is much more common – and many women have joined after collecting an MBA from a top international business school (with executive education itself another example of a field that has been transformed since the early 1990s). Other examples abound. Favouring the eldest son in family business succession today is often regarded as an anachronism, and attention, quite rightly, now focuses on competence. Similarly, equal remuneration of family members is giving way to merit-based reward systems; secrecy is giving way to more openness; and family business values, rather than being assumed ('We've always done it this way') are more likely to be embraced, with families making special efforts to define and articulate their values in the belief that values, vision and culture can make their businesses more competitive, resilient and sustainable.

Encouraging as these trends are, they should not disguise the fact that a great many family businesses still face huge challenges coping with the dangerous overlaps between family and business systems, organising responsible family ownership, working productively with non-family members, developing the next generation (and future leaders), creating policies to manage the roles, remuneration and rivalries of family members, implementing successful generational transitions, and establishing best practice in family and business governance. So the family business adviser's job is far from over. Also, there is no obvious sign of improvement in the key mortality statistics for family firms that fail to make it to the next generation, nor do we expect to escape the US trend towards more and more family businesses being run by groups of siblings rather than a single leader[2] – the problem being that we have only limited experience of how to make this team-based family business model work well.

During my career I have come to understand that a key aspect of an adviser's role is finding out what is really happening both with the family and at the company. Plagued by selective amnesia, procrastination, paranoia and a few other syndromes, family businesses are generally very good at concealing what is actually going on. I have developed a number of techniques to help me (and the family) get at the truth, including compiling my own *Family Business Phrase Book*. Some examples of translations from 'what is said' into 'what is actually meant' will serve to give the flavour of the phrase book and of many of the scenarios discussed in this book:

❋ On a pay package for the kids – 'I know it's less than the going rate but we can't be seen to be overpaying family' translates to 'You're going to own the business someday, and a bit of hardship along the way will help remind you of the fact and keep you in line.'

❋ Reasons for joining – 'I mainly joined the business to continue the family traditions' equals 'I can't really explain why I joined, and now I'm not quite sure what my long-term plans are.'

✳ Succession – 'Someday, all this will be yours' equals 'I really don't know what's going to happen and I want to keep my options open.'

Some important lessons I have learned – courtesy of the many families who have generously shared with me their setbacks and successes – are summarised in the following golden rules:

✳ The key questions family members must address are 'What do we want to achieve by being in business together?' and 'What do we hold dear to our hearts in terms of values and our vision for the future?' When families are able to come up with a clear consensus on answers to these fundamental questions, normally everything else will drop into place.

✳ The issues that present themselves in family businesses can almost always be divided into three categories: personality – such and such a person is impossible, unreasonable, illogical, irrational; structural – something is malfunctioning in the structure of how the family relates to the business; business – the business may be going downhill and nobody is quite sure whether commercial or family factors are causing the underperformance. In the great majority of cases, the real issue affecting the company is found to lie within the second category (structural), even though the case is presented as concerning the first (personality) or the third (business).

✳ Linked to the previous point, because structural issues in family businesses are to a large extent predictable, such businesses enjoy a special advantage relative to their non-family competitors – they have the opportunity to solve tomorrow's predictable problems today. In other words, they can effectively resolve such problems before they arise. For instance, the development and mentoring of next-generation leadership can be planned in detail ahead of time, in a calm atmosphere, under an agreed process, thus reducing the potentially disastrous impact of unexpected yet predictable events.

✳ The money that people are paid in a family business is often a tell-tale sign as to what is really going on. For instance, if the next generation is wildly overpaid for the job they are doing, stakeholders will not respect them because they will see their pay package as a special perk attaching to family status. Similarly, if they are grossly underpaid, stakeholders will conclude they do not have the respect of their family and are unlikely ever to take over.

✳ Lastly, when family business people find themselves making business decisions for family reasons, all sorts of alarm bells should start ringing.

Objectives

Family firms face complex dilemmas that affect not only the destiny of the business, but also the destinies of owners, their families and their employees. How do owners reconcile their own and their family's aspirations with the commercial goals of the firm? Can they motivate family and non-family employees alike? Should they try to solve problems themselves or take independent advice? There is the major issue of who is to succeed to management and ownership control – when should planning for succession begin and who to choose? Other concerns include whether to sell out, raise external finance, diversify, de-merge, bring in more family members or more outside management, and so on.

All these dilemmas affect most family businesses sooner or later – that is, to a greater or lesser extent they are all predictable – and the aim of this book is to help family business people approach them in the right way and arrive at the right decisions. Depressingly, in many cases, by the time the problems associated with the issues arise it is too late to take action and the business is well down the road to distress and upheaval, and sometimes on the brink of failure. The chances of success for a family business are greatly increased by ensuring that the major, life-threatening questions are tackled at an early stage and plans are developed for the future. In the same way that the company's commercial activities and opportunities must be continually examined and evaluated, the development of its relationship with the family needs to be constantly assessed, managed and reviewed.

Family business owners and managers often fail to consider these crucial issues in sufficient detail. Too involved with the day-to-day activities of their company, they put off getting to grips with them until a later date. Reluctance to face the problems and to take external professional advice often stems from family business leaders' inability to gain knowledge (and in some cases self-knowledge) concerning the systems-based and psychological forces that are at work. How, for example, have others tackled the problems and with what consequences for the firm? What might happen if the issue is ignored – will it go away or will a major crisis arise?

This is not a how-to book for family businesses. Indeed, there can be no such thing because each family business is different, and there are really no success and longevity rules that can be applied from firm to firm without serious qualification and adaptation. Instead, what are proposed in the pages that follow are some broad frameworks, mindsets, processes and best-practice principles to help shape problem-solving perspectives for family business people, as well as some tools and working guidelines designed to contribute to the efforts of these firms to achieve long-term continuity, growth and prosperity.

Structure and organisation

First, an explanatory note about my approach to and treatment of the subject. The need to discuss family businesses in a coherent fashion has meant that the book structure in many ways reflects the development and life cycles of family businesses themselves – that is, a progression from straightforward owner-manager beginnings through to third-generation and multigenerational family companies; from clear-cut simplicity through to significant complexity. The book (and to an extent each chapter within it) reflects this evolutionary process, starting with personal, hands-on management and governance, which then benefits from integrating outside expertise. Next, family membership becomes broader and more inclusive, although family activity in management becomes more restricted based on objective competence. Finally, management and ownership succession become more planned.

On occasions, the need to progress through the subject in this way has required that certain topics be introduced and explained in one part of the book and then re-examined in a different context in another part. For example, most family businesses benefit from having what is called a family council, the principal role of which is to ensure that the values, vision and aspirations of the family and the business are aligned. But a family council in a small-scale second-generation business (the sort of firm discussed in Chapter 3, where family councils are first introduced) bears only passing similarity to that same body at work within a sixth-generation, multifamily business with hundreds of shareholding cousins (so, in the light of this, we revisit family councils again in Chapter 7, which is devoted to the special factors affecting these more mature businesses).

The book is divided into ten chapters. Chapter 1 represents a broad-based introduction, covering the economic importance of family businesses, what factors make them special, and the dilemmas and challenges they need to overcome. Attempts via research to test whether these advantages and disadvantages have a measurable impact on commercial performance are reviewed. Although family firms are to be found in every sector of commercial activity, their special strengths mean that they flourish best in fields in which their advantages can be fully exploited. These sectors are examined, together with supporting cases and examples.

The special status of family businesses, introduced in Chapter 1, derives from their structural form. This structure is characterised by complexity – a family system, a business system and an ownership system linked together through wealth, legal arrangements, employment relationships and emotional/relational bonds. Understanding the interaction of these systems is crucial to understanding family business dynamics, and this is the central topic in Chapter 2. The other feature that makes family businesses special is the people who are involved in them; the background and perspectives of each of the major participants are examined. The chapter also introduces some of the main causes of conflict that can arise – particularly father–son conflict and sibling rivalry.

Families learn to build a shared vision by aligning individual and family values and goals, and that vision becomes a guide for planning, decision-making and action. A good starting point is the simple question: 'What's our business for?' Developing a consensus on this most basic of questions helps families improve their chances of success when they move on to establishing ground rules for their relationship with the business (the main subject matter in Chapter 3) and in defining the responsibilities of family members. The aim is to formulate and adopt policies that strike a good balance between the best interests of the business and the well-being of the family, and then to design and establish effective governance structures that help the family develop a cohesive approach to the business and provide organisational focus and accountability.

Chapter 4 discusses the next generation – to join or not to join the business, the importance of outside experience, and issues surrounding relationships with the senior generation. It goes on to highlight how conflicts arising between the family, business and ownership systems are particularly acute and troublesome in relation to human resource management practices. Clear and explicit management criteria must be drawn up relating to personnel issues and family members. Guidelines designed to help control and manage the contradictory forces are proposed. Family employees should be rewarded and promoted in line with their contribution to the business; their performance should be evaluated regularly and objectively within a system that applies to all staff.

Family businesses have a dangerous tendency to introversion that needs to be countered by the effective use of external talent. Chapter 5 discusses making the most of outside resources under three headings: employees, non-executive directors and advisers. Family companies must endeavour to attract and motivate high-quality, non-family employees and (under carefully designed incentive schemes) reward their contribution. Non-executive directors can be especially valuable to family-owned companies, providing seasoned guidance, specialised expertise and networking connections. Lastly, skilled family business advisers and consultants are able to probe difficult family business issues and develop discussion of a family's problem areas in a subtle and sensitive way that minimises the possibility of friction and confrontation. Their selection should be based on competence and their performance periodically reviewed. Possible conflicts of interest need to be thought about and avoided.

The role of the board of directors in the governance structure of a family-controlled company – the topic addressed in Chapter 6 – is critically important. Establishing a board that includes independent outsiders is probably crucial for the vast majority of family businesses if they are to achieve long-term success. Such a board brings objectivity and experience to operational and policy deliberations, and imposes important disciplines. When a family introduces board diversity it sends a positive and motivating message to customers, shareholders and employees. In larger, more mature family companies there is a balance to be struck between the interests of the family as owners of the business and the managers entrusted to run it. No single model works for all, and, instead, a solid set of principles and processes must be drawn up and applied in the unique circumstances of each company.

Chapter 7 is devoted to family governance in multigenerational family firms. By the time a family business reaches the third generation there may be several dozen or more family members who have some sort of stake in it. Ownership is generally in the hands of many cousins from different sibling branches of the family, with no single branch having a controlling shareholding. Some of these owners will work in the business, but probably most will not. There is significant potential for friction and dysfunctional behaviour if the large-scale complexity arising with these family and shareholder groups is not controlled and managed. Governance architecture must be tailored to meet the unique needs and circumstances of particular families.

A well-structured and systematic approach to succession planning is required to overcome all the forces that favour doing nothing. Chapter 8 explains why preparation and planning for succession are so difficult and important, analyses the options, and aims to provide practical guidelines on ensuring that transitions are accomplished as smoothly and as advantageously as possible. Whether the transition is from a single owner to a sibling partnership, or from a sibling partnership to a cousin company, an important point is that it is not just changing the guard – it is more like a system change, a transition to a different type of business structure with a different culture, different procedures and different ground rules.

The words 'retire' and 'retirement' crop up a lot in this (and the next) chapter, and I should explain here that I have trouble with these words. My problem is based partly on current dictionary definitions – which centre on concepts like withdrawing from work/business, retreating and becoming a recluse, and singularly fail to define and explain retirement as it is understood today – and partly on confusion about the concept of retirement at a time when most people in their 50s and 60s are healthier and more vigorous than previous generations. But my main difficulty concerns the fact that family business leaders do not retire, and never have done! Where families are in business together it does not matter whether leaders receive a monthly salary or indeed whether they ever cross the threshold – their name is above the door and they will always be attached to their family and the business.[3] What retirement means for these people is not withdrawing from the business, but reorganising and reshaping their attachment to it.

Family business leaders remain an important resource to the family firm, even when they have passed on day-to-day operational responsibility to their successors. Many leaders, as part of their succession plan, assume new roles in the company, such as managing special projects, acting as roving ambassadors for the firm and/or helping to foster management continuity by connecting new managers with individuals and organisations that may be important to the future success of the company. Experts are more or less unanimous that this phase is most likely to be successfully negotiated if business owners are retiring to a new life of interesting activities, rather than from their old one, which implies that their useful and productive days are over. So, at the risk of repetition, the idea of leaders severing their connection with the family business is neither desirable nor possible because the business is part of the fabric of the family. Family business leaders must think, therefore, about how best to reshape their attachment to the business and to plan their future work activities, while readers of this book are asked to reject dictionary negativity and to construe the words retire and retirement in the constructive sense described here.

Chapter 9 starts from the premise that building financial security is an important element in preparing for a successful retirement. This can be achieved either inside or outside the family business, or, if there are no viable succession options, by selling it, and various sale structures are examined. Insurance and share purchase agreements can be used to resolve many of the complications arising from multifamily ownership of a business. When passing the family company on to the next generation, continuity of the business, liquidity and family needs are the cornerstones of estate planning. Ensuring ownership ends up in the right hands in the next generation may require treating heirs differently depending on whether or not they are active in the business. Ways of passing on voting control to selected heirs are examined, as are the uses of trusts.

Finally, once larger family businesses have established the family governance structures and mechanisms they need to manage complexity and the relationship between family and business, they often look for other ways to help foster their family commitment and vision and to perpetuate their family's legacy. Opportunities to achieve these objectives can be provided by the family office and philanthropic initiatives, and these subjects are examined in Chapter 10.

Peter Leach
February 2007

Acknowledgements

Finally I would like to make some important acknowledgements. First, to all my colleagues at BDO Stoy Hayward who have given me an enormous amount of support in the preparation of this book; however, I single out in particular Juliette Johnson, who works closely with me on many complex and challenging cases from which many of my examples are drawn, and Don Williams and Rupert Merson, who have been tremendously supportive throughout the project. In addition, I have had the privilege to work with inspiring people from other cultures and would like to thank in particular Mr P. M. Kumar from Bangalore for the insights and inspiration I have learned from him when working in India.

My day-to-day work has brought me into contact with many different families over the years, and I would like to take this opportunity to thank them for their willingness to let me share their experiences, problems and successes, especially those who have permitted me to refer to them by name in this book.

Last, but by no means least, I gratefully acknowledge the contribution of my wife Antonia. Her advice, enthusiasm and patience during the preparation of this book has been invaluable.

P.L.

1

Why family businesses are special

Family businesses comprise the predominant form of enterprise around the world, yet, until recently, little information or guidance has been available on the unique and complex issues they face. This is because it is only in the past 20 years that we have started to study and understand two fundamental ideas: that family businesses differ in a variety of critically important ways from non-family businesses; and that business families function quite differently from non-business families. These two distinctions lie at the heart of this book and, if a family business is to achieve its full potential, it is essential that its management understands them and the challenges they create.

As well as making the right decisions on the commercial problems that beset all enterprises, family business people have to be able to analyse the special dynamics that surround their businesses and their families. They need to develop special skills that enable them to identify and manage the unique difficulties and dilemmas that these dynamics introduce, and to adopt constructive strategies to foster growth of the business and the transfer of power and control within it.

So understanding the characteristics that distinguish family and non-family businesses and entrepreneurial and 'normal' families is the first step, and highlighting these distinctions is the main aim of Chapters 1 and 2. However, it should not be concluded from this that there are any general panaceas: every family business is idiosyncratic, shaped by its own set of distinctive personalities, their concerns, objectives and relationships, and by a host of other personal and commercial characteristics. But there are some common patterns of experience, and developing an appreciation of them is important so we can avoid repeating everyone else's mistakes.

Definitions

Before introducing some of the characteristic strengths and weaknesses of family businesses, and commercial sectors in which they have proved especially successful, it is important to propose a working definition of what is meant by a family business. Criteria that are too rigid should be avoided – just looking at share ownership or management composition often leads to an inadequate picture and the wrong conclusions. In this book, therefore, a family business is one that, quite simply, is influenced by a family or by a family relationship, and that perceives itself to be a family business.

In the clearest example, the family as a body may effectively control business operations because it owns more than 50 per cent of the voting shares, or because family members fill a significant number of the top management positions. But there are also less obvious cases where a firm's operations are affected by a family relationship – enterprises in which the relationships of father and son, brother and sister, in-laws, cousins and so on have an important impact on the future of the business.

Note also that for larger, more mature family businesses where the number of shareholders may have multiplied down the generations, or where the business has obtained a stock exchange listing, effective family voting control can be maintained with significantly less than 50 per cent of the shares.

Economic impact

A great many books and research studies try to provide educated guesses of the proportion of business enterprises worldwide that are family controlled, and the figures vary a lot. Data shortages, different definitions of family control and other statistical issues make this a tricky area, but even the most conservative estimates place the proportion at between 65 per cent and 80 per cent.[1]

It is fair to say that many of these enterprises are small-scale sole proprietorships that will never grow and be passed down the generations, but it is also true that the figure includes some of the world's largest and most successful companies. John Ward, a professor of family business at IMD, Switzerland, and clinical professor at Kellogg School of Management in the US, has calculated that approximately one-third of the 1,000 largest companies in the world are controlled by families and, of these, half are traded publicly and half are privately held.[2]

Family enterprises dominate commercial life in the emerging markets of Asia and Latin America and, many believe, play a larger role than is

Irrational and inappropriate patterns of emotional behaviour can emerge in family businesses

generally acknowledged in developed markets, particularly the USA, Germany and Italy.[3] In the UK, family firms are the dominant form of ownership of companies in the private sector, accounting for around two-thirds of all enterprises and half of the output of the private-sector economy, and they employ about half the workforce. The constituency where they are best represented is the small business sector. According to research published by Barclays Bank, around 60 per cent of UK firms with turnover of £5 million or less are owned or managed by related family members.[4] The same survey records that, across England and Wales, such family businesses are most prominent in the north-west of England and East Anglia, with around three-quarters of all businesses owned and managed by the family. By contrast, in London, family businesses account for less than half of the business population.

Moving up the size scale, family firms are also a common form of ownership within the small and medium-sized enterprise (SME) sector, but this is one of the areas where detailed statistics are in short supply. More data are available on both large private firms and the quoted sector. Indeed, family firms comprise over one-third of the UK's biggest private firms listed in *The Sunday Times* Top Track 100 survey.[5] In the stock market quoted sector, 6 per cent of the companies in the FTSE All Share Index are family businesses, but the UK stands out in terms of international comparison, with the smallest percentage of listed family companies relative to the quoted sector overall. In contrast, around half the companies quoted on the French stock market have a significant level of family ownership.[6]

Special strengths

The overriding characteristic that distinguishes most family businesses is a unique atmosphere that creates a sense of belonging and an enhanced common purpose among the workforce. Sir Terry Leahy, chief executive of Tesco, has neatly encapsulated some of the factors underpinning this:[7]

> In family firms ... ownership and management are in the same hands, so they tend to have a far longer time horizon. ... As a result, they do not have to float with the tide of market sentiment. They can be braver about what they do and say. They can dare to be quirky. Or they can dare to be traditional. They can stick to the long-term values established over many years, building up loyalty and trust in their customers and staff. A good illustration of that is the language they tend to use to describe their values. A family-owned business will use words such as courage, loyalty or authenticity to capture what they stand for. In a public company you are more likely to find management speak – words such as efficiency, innovation and added value.

Family business culture and values

These issues relating to long-term values and vision will resurface in a variety of guises throughout this book. Families who are able to define and articulate their shared goals, and the guiding values and principles that will help achieve them, give their businesses a strong foundation for long-term competitive advantage and sustainability.

A family business can be seen as the external manifestation of a family's value system. Put simply, values, or rules for living, underpin a code of behaviour that builds and supports family vision and business mission. Typically, it is the founder who articulates the mission he or she sees for the business, but these values – sometimes called lived rather than espoused values – transmit down through succeeding generations, often without the family even recognising that this is occurring. A common way of behaving is created, which helps to explain and reinforce what the family stands for and why they are in business together. During periods of challenge and transition their business is supported by the belief in a set of shared values, but where there is no relevant vision to unite the family, opportunities for conflict can arise.

The family's value system may need to be reinterpreted and revitalised by succeeding generations. Each new generation of the Rockefeller clan, for example, re-examines the family's core ideals and values, redefining and renewing them as is felt appropriate to help reinvigorate the sense of connection between family members and the organisational mission.

Predictable problem resolution

The next special strength of family firms is the unique opportunity they give to the people owning and running them to resolve a range of predictable issues before they become serious problems.

The world's most successful entrepreneurs sometimes seem to be blessed with 20/20 foresight. Their insight into what the future holds enables them to deliver commercial solutions that take advantage of this prescience, and that is how fortunes are made. This, of course, is difficult to achieve, but in a family business it is always possible to resolve a range of tomorrow's problems simply because, for the most part, they can be identified in advance.

Time and again, three types of issues present themselves in family businesses: personality – such and such a person is impossible, unreasonable, illogical, irrational; structural – something is malfunctioning in the structure of how the family relates to the business which undermines family dynamics and decision-making; business – the business may be going downhill and nobody is quite sure whether commercial or family factors are causing the underperformance. In the great majority of cases, however, the real issue affecting the company is found to lie within the second category (structural), even though the case is presented as concerning the first (personality) or the third (business problems). Herein lies the key: because structural issues are to a large extent predictable in family businesses, they have the opportunity, not enjoyed in other businesses, to effectively resolve these problems before they arise.

Succession provides a classic example. Rather than waiting till the reading of the will to resolve questions like 'Who gets the shares?' or 'Who is best suited to take on managerial leadership?', in a family business it is possible to address such issues ahead of time, in a calm atmosphere, under an agreed process, thus reducing the potentially damaging impact of unexpected yet predictable events.

Commitment

People who set up a business can become passionate about it – it is their creation, they nurtured it and built it up, and for many such entrepreneurs their business is their life. This strong bond translates naturally into dedication and commitment, which extends to all the family members who come to have a stake in the success of the business. They feel they have a family responsibility to pull together and, provided there are no conflicts, everyone is happy to put in far more time and energy working for the company's success than they would dream of devoting to a normal job. Family enthusiasm develops added commitment and loyalty from their workforces – people care more and feel they are part of a team, all contributing to the common purpose.

Knowledge

Family businesses often have particular ways of doing things. They may have special technological or commercial know-how not possessed by their competitors; knowledge that would soon become general in a normal commercial environment, but which can be coveted and protected within the family.

This idea of knowledge is also relevant in relation to the founder's sons or daughters joining the business. The next generation grow up learning about the business, infected by the founder's enthusiasm, and when the time comes for them to consider joining they may already have a deep understanding of what the business is all about.

Flexibility in work, time and money

Essentially this boils down to putting the necessary work and time into the business and taking out money when it can be afforded. A further aspect of commitment is that if work needs to be done and time needs to be spent in developing the business, the family puts in the time and does the work – there is no negotiating of overtime rates or special bonuses for a rushed job.

The same flexibility applies to money, and here is another important distinction between entrepreneurial and non-business families. Most families have a set income derived from wages or salaries paid by an employer and the only decisions they take concern how this income is to be spent. But for families in business, income is not a fixed element in the domestic equation: they must decide how much money they can safely take from the business for their own needs while at the same time preserving the firm's financial flexibility and scope for investment. Sometimes one aspect of commitment to the family business takes the form of dismay at the idea of removing money from it – draining the business of its lifeblood can be how the family sees it, even if the business has been trading profitably for decades. Some of Britain's wealthiest families do not have any ready money because their company, often established generations ago, has hardly ever paid a dividend. All its profits have been reinvested to finance future growth.

Flexibility in time, work and money once again creates a competitive advantage for family businesses. Generally, they can adapt quickly and easily to changing circumstances. If, for example, the firm needs to switch into a new product to capitalise on a developing trend in the market-place, the decision will rarely involve lengthy discussion by a hierarchy of committees and its implementation will be equally speedy: 'We are going to stop doing this, start doing that, and the move will mean we have to put in six months of extra hard work and not take any money out of the business for the next two years.' This would be a tall order for many companies, impossible for others, but a typical, flexible agenda for a lot of family firms.

Long-range thinking

Family businesses are better than other enterprises at thinking long term – the next generation is often a higher priority than the next quarter's financial results. They generally have an instinctive preference for patient capital (leaving the investment intact for the long term in the hope of better rewards than the short term could offer). Strategic planning reduces risk, enabling a business to cope more effectively with unforeseen events, and is also the hallmark of a great many successful new ventures and of long-term survivors. The fact that families usually have a clear view of their commercial objectives over the next 10–15 years can therefore represent a considerable advantage.

Energy services group Hunting provides a case in point, with the company tracing its origins back five generations to the last quarter of the 19th century. Charles Samuel Hunting entered the oil business in the 1890s, but he was already expanding on a successful ship-owning company set up by his father in 1874. Today the group is chaired by Richard Hunting, who is a firm believer in taking the long-term view. 'People aren't constantly looking over their shoulder in case we will be bought,' he says, citing 130 years of trading history and experience. 'During that time the business has been through many cycles, so one doesn't panic when one hits another. We don't assume that when we are in an upswing it is necessarily going to last.'[8]

An interesting contrast between the family preference for patient capital and stock market expectations has been highlighted by recent developments at troubled US car giant Ford. The company's North

American unit made a $2.9 billion loss in the first three months of 2006 as it implemented plans to cut 30,000 jobs and close 14 plants by 2012 to reduce costs. By mid-2006, Ford's shares had lost more than half their value since the founder's great grandson, William Clay Ford Jr, took over as CEO in 2002, and the non-family shareholders (Ford is an NYSE-listed company) were beginning to lose patience. Holders of Ford's Class B stock, however, have a different agenda (various Ford heirs control 40 per cent of the company's voting shares, and each of them has 16 votes per share compared with one vote per share for the other shareholders); they operate on the assumption that wealth is being created for the long term, not quarter by quarter. Craig E. Aronoff, an American family business consultant, has summed up the perspective disparity:[9]

> The family has been through up and down cycles over the last 100 years – they understand these things well. Most shareholders are just hoping their $6 stock will turn into a $10 stock, but because Ford is a public company and a family business, you're seeing normal shareholder expectations and family views of expectations clash. But the family remain the dominant force at Ford, and they are going to remain patient.

But while family shareholders and family members working in the business are good at thinking long term, they are not always so good at formalising their plans – writing them down, analysing the assumptions they are making, testing past results against earlier predictions. In short, the strength means that the long-range thinking is there, while the potential weakness is that this thinking is undisciplined.

A stable culture

For a variety of reasons, successful family businesses are stable structures. They are generally durable, low-profile, profitable niche enterprises that shun publicity – the types of firms that Hermann Simon describes as 'hidden champions'. In his book of the same name, he characterises these companies as taking a long-haul view of their business; focusing on narrow markets; retaining long-term stable partnerships with employees, customers and suppliers; and emphasising value, not price.[10]

The chairman or managing director has usually been around for many years. The key management personnel are all committed to the success of the business, and they too are there for the long term. Relationships within the company have usually had ample time to develop and stabilise, as have the company's procedural ethics and working practices. Everybody knows how things are done.

Exemplifying stability and continuity, Christopher Oughtred is the fifth-generation chairman of Hull-based food manufacturer William Jackson & Son, established in 1851. The company's products include frozen foods under the Aunt Bessie brand name, chilled ready meals for Kwok Foods and bread for many of Europe's sandwich-makers. It remains a private, family-owned business. With generation six comprising 19 individuals, the fifth generation currently running the business is taking a proactive stance on family governance issues to help ensure the sustainability of the company. However, the family members are also very conscious of their history, regarding themselves as custodians of the firm's culture, ownership and management. As Oughtred explains:[11]

> We are proud of something which William Jackson's has that few of our competitors can copy or invent: namely a great heritage. Part of understanding where our business is today comes from knowing where we have come from. ... Our task is to harness the efforts and dedication of previous generations and to take our business forward so that an enviable, reputable and successful company may be available for a sixth generation.

Like some of the other factors working in favour of family businesses, however, a strong, stable culture can be a two-edged sword. A stable business environment can become a dangerously introverted atmosphere in which the attitude is 'We do it this way because we have always done it this way', and nobody is thinking about change and looking to see whether doing things differently might introduce more efficiency. So stability in the family business is one of its unique and valuable assets, but business owners need to think about whether a stable business culture has become an obstacle to change and adaptability.

Speedy decisions

In a well-managed family-controlled business, responsibilities are usually clearly defined and the decision-making process deliberately restricted to one or two trusted individuals. In many cases this means that such firms have an advantage over their competitors in that they are more nimble and, therefore, capable of making faster, better operational decisions (or, if necessary, of quickly adjusting or reversing previous decisions). However, when it comes to other areas – for example, long-term change and transition management – the speed and quality of decision-making can erode significantly (see Dilemmas and challenges for family businesses on page 11).

An interesting aspect of this decision-making issue has been the return to the private sector of a number of high-profile family business companies. For example, Pentland Group (a sports and leisure apparel firm founded in 1932 by the Rubin family) returned to private, family company status in 1999. Similarly, steel and engineering group Caparo, controlled by the Paul family, went private in 1991, buying back the public's 20 per cent stake in the business. Although a wish to return to speedier and less bureaucratic decision-making processes was not the prime motivation, it is clear from company management's comments at the time that it was a significant contributory factor.

Reliability and pride

Commitment and a stable culture are the basis of family businesses' generally solid and reliable structures – and are perceived as such in the marketplace. Many customers prefer doing business with a firm that has been established for a long time, and they will have built up relationships with a management and staff that are not constantly changing jobs within the firm or being replaced by outsiders. What can be called the 'My name is on the door' factor, even when not trumpeted by the person concerned, often contributes to a competitive edge. Also, the commitment within the family business, discussed earlier, is not just a hidden force – it reveals itself to customers all the time in the form of a friendlier, more knowledgeable, more skilful and generally much higher standard of service and customer care.

Closely connected with reliability is the notion of pride: the people who run family businesses are generally extremely proud of the business and of their achievement in having established and built it, and their staff are proud to be associated with the family and what they are doing. This pride, which in some circumstances can work to almost institutionalise the business, is often translated into a powerful marketing tool. For example, Coopers Brewery in South Australia advertises its beers with the slogan 'Taste the difference that four generations of brewing tradition makes'. The following extract from its website powerfully illustrates the marketing value that can be attached to family tradition:[12]

> 'We are now engaged in the brewery business.' So wrote Thomas Cooper to his brother John in England, after establishing his brewing business in the new colony of South Australia in 1862. ... Today Coopers is Australia's sole remaining family-owned brewery

of stature, so it's still an everyday occurrence to meet a Cooper at Coopers Brewery. Dr Tim Cooper is the Managing Director of Coopers Brewery and still keeps a keen eye on the brewing. Mr Glenn Cooper is Executive Chairman and Marketing Director. Mr Bill Cooper remains on the Coopers board of directors, having retired from the position of Managing Director in February 2002. Maxwell Cooper retired from his Chairman's position at the same time. Melanie Cooper and Matthew Cooper also work at the Brewery in Financial and Sales positions. Many other family members also keep an eye on things from the boardroom. So rest assured, Coopers Brewery is in the hands of those who have the same values as Thomas Cooper and who believe in the product that Thomas himself began brewing all those years ago.

Dilemmas and challenges for family businesses

As well as having valuable advantages, family businesses are prone to some serious and endemic problems. In the same way that family business strengths are not unique to family firms, neither are their challenges, but family businesses are particularly vulnerable to these potential short-comings. Many of the problems hinge on the inherent conflicts that can arise between family and business values (this crucial area is discussed in Chapter 2).

Resistance to change

Walking through the doors of some family businesses can be like entering a time tunnel. Sentiments such as 'Things are done this way because Dad did them this way' and 'You can't teach an old dog new tricks' reflect the ways in which behaviour patterns can become ingrained and family businesses can become tradition-bound and unwilling to change. Many examples of this came to light in researching this book (see, for instance, the case highlighted under Modernising outdated skills on page 12).

It is all too easy to find ourselves doing the same thing, in the same way, for too long, and in a family business it is easier still. This is because change not only carries with it the usual disruption and an array of commercial risks, but it can also involve overturning philosophies and upsetting practices established by relatives.

Business challenges

The business challenges that particularly affect family firms fall into three categories.

Modernising outdated skills

Often the skills possessed by a family business are a product of history and, as a result of developments in technology or a change in the marketplace, they can quickly become obsolete. Problems in this area are not necessarily triggered by drastic changes such as the effect of word-processing technology on typewriter manufacturers. They can also arise from subtle changes of emphasis in product manufacture or marketing that can be just as damaging if they catch an unresponsive, tradition-conscious family business off balance.

A second-generation family metal-bashing business in north-east England illustrates this well. Run by three brothers, the company was highly profitable, but everything was done manually – across a 200,000-square-foot factory they employed a human army of metal-bashers, welders and finishers to make the company's products. The brothers, now in their 60s, realised they had to make a choice: to continue with their traditional production methods, or to upgrade their entire plant with state-of-the-art, robot-controlled technology. As one of the brothers explained:

> We see the logic when people talk to us about the need to modernise, but we're making money here, and we're doing it using methods and work practices that have been tried and tested across 50 years. Robots would transform our business, but we're worried they'll transform it into something we won't recognise or be able to control.

Managing transitions

This represents another major challenge for family businesses and can often make or break a family firm. A typical example in many companies is that the founder is getting on in years and a son or daughter, the heir apparent, is convinced that things need to be done differently. The merest hint of this potential conflict can be disruptive, causing uncertainty among staff, suppliers and customers. In many cases the disruption becomes even more serious when the successor begins to introduce his or her programme of radical change. So managing transitions is a difficult challenge to the business and, because of the added dimension of possible intra-family upset and conflict, it is a much bigger challenge for family businesses than for others.

Raising capital

In comparison with the wide range of funding options open to publicly held companies with a diversified shareholder base, family businesses obviously have much more limited options when it comes to raising capital. But over and above this, family businesses commonly have a problem with the very concept of raising money from outside sources. This occurs most frequently in relation to longer-term capital for significant projects, such as opening a new plant or creating a new division of the business, but it also shows itself in a reluctance to go to outsiders for bank overdrafts or other short-term funding that would help the firm through minor cash-flow shortfalls. If funding from the family's own resources means skimping on important projects or inefficiently struggling through short-term crises, the healthy development and even the survival of the business can be threatened.

The growth of private equity and a much more accommodating and flexible approach to debt financing by banks do not alter the underlying issue: behind these overcautious attitudes to external finance there are usually fears about loss of control – fears that will turn up in a variety of guises and contexts throughout this book. The fear can take the form of a mild aversion to outsiders acquiring influence over how the business is run, but – and more often – deep-seated and intense paranoia is the description that most readily springs to mind. On a day-to-day basis families tend not to want to be answerable to anybody for how they run their businesses and the idea of the family losing control is usually unthinkable. Family business people can feel that control is inextricably linked to the love of freedom and independence that has often been the principal driving force behind the establishment of the business and its subsequent success.

Succession

The passage of a family business from one generation to the next, and the change of leadership it involves, is a process that can be fraught with difficulty.

When changing the managing director of any company, as well as the obvious managerial considerations, there is a set of emotional issues that have to be settled at the same time. For example, where there is a defined management hierarchy, decisions have to be made about people's competence to assume new responsibilities after promotion, and what their reaction will be if an outsider is brought in to take on the top job. Again, this is a situation where, on the face of it, family businesses encounter identical problems to those experienced by other firms, but underlying their problems is a minefield of psychological, family-related, emotionally charged dilemmas that transform the change of leadership issue into one that can threaten the survival of the business.

Here is a real-life case example that illustrates the point. It does not involve a world-famous family and it is not hugely dramatic, but it represents a story that comes up all too often. The founder of an electrical business had a flair for practical innovation and a real love of the business, which he ran for 30 years, almost as an extension of himself. To customers and the workforce he was the business. He could not conceive of anyone else being able to run it in his place. Then in his 60s, and still very much in control of the company, he fell ill unexpectedly and died soon after. There was no natural successor. His two daughters had little involvement in the business and his two sons (the youngest just out of university) felt unprepared to take over. They had no experience at a senior management level in the company, nor did they have a clear picture of how the business worked. As a result the company was sold. If the founder had been able to plan for succession the result would have been very different.

Selecting a successor can often mean choosing between sons or daughters who, until now, have all been harbouring their own secret ambitions of succeeding when the founder retires; and founders themselves are often ambivalent about succession because they are worried about their children's abilities and how to approach favouring one at the expense of the others. But, more fundamentally as far as the business is concerned, almost always the change is not simply a move from one generation to the next – it is a revolution in which the culture of the organisation is reconstructed by the next generation, who bring with them new ideas about how the business should be run, how it is to develop, new working practices, new staff, new loyalties and so on.

So succession represents a major transition, with the fortunes of the firm resting on how successfully it is negotiated (and this is why considerable attention is devoted to succession planning later in the book – in particular in Chapters 4 and 8).

Emotional issues

The hazards of succession lead on to and are an aspect of the next family business pitfall: the emotional issues that limit the firm's scope for commercial action. This will be discussed in a broader context and in more detail in Chapter 2, but this is a good place to introduce the important idea that family and business are two distinct domains.

The family domain is emotion-based, emphasising care and loyalty, while the business domain is task-based, with an emphasis on performance and results. The family business is a fusion of these two powerful institutions and although it provides the potential for superior performance, it is not surprising that it can also lead to serious difficulties. These can mean patterns of emotional behaviour emerging within the business, which, in a commercial context, are deeply irrational and inappropriate: the marketing director does not trust his brother, the finance director, because he used to steal his toys in the nursery – an extreme illustration perhaps, but indicative of the sort of emotional undercurrents that can be at work. Making matters worse, the root of the trouble can lie many years in the past: 'Your side of the family swindled our side out of its shares in 1927.'

When competency yields second place to family needs, or business decisions start to be made for family reasons, warning lights come on for the family business.

Leadership

One last difficulty for family businesses worth highlighting early on concerns leadership, or rather the lack of it, in situations where there is no one within the organisation empowered to take charge. This becomes especially critical when the business has reached the second generation, and even more so when it reaches the third.

In the second-generation scenario, for example, the board of directors may comprise three brothers, all of whom have inherited equal shareholdings, and none of whom has been empowered to take ultimate control – no one has the last word. It is a common weakness among family businesses that there is great reluctance to allocate power. The situation where business founders are unwilling to plan for succession and choose, when they eventually bow out, which of their children they want to do which jobs was discussed earlier. To a large degree, the predicament of the three brothers may be the founders' fault, but for them it is too late to dwell on this. It is the responsibility of each generation to resolve its own conflicts so that it is able to empower and legitimise the next generation, and the brothers must define where power lies between themselves before they can start to think about where it should lie in the future. If they do not, the arrival of the third generation with its increased cast of characters may well herald catastrophe.

A competitive edge and outperformance?

Because of the often anecdotal flavour of some of the advantages and disadvantages of being a family business, there has been a lot of research recently to try to provide some hard evidence of the impact of these factors on the commercial performance of family firms. In other words, do advantages such as commitment, stability, flexibility, long-term planning and so on, translate into tangible commercial returns, or do the disadvantages like resistance to change and the conflict between family values and business values carry the day, serving to provide non-family firms with a competitive edge compared with their family counterparts?

In a UK study carried out in 1996–97 by Warwick Business School,[13] information was gathered from a cross-section of 427 unquoted companies and the performance of family and non-family firms was compared using nine criteria, including percentage growth in sales and employment. Some commentators suspect that the relative advantages and disadvantages of family status (while frequently critical on a company-by-company basis) may cancel out when examined across a broad sample of family firms; and indeed the main finding of this research was that there are no statistically significant differences in the performance of unquoted family businesses when compared with non-family businesses.

Quoted family businesses fared better in a 2006 study conducted by Manchester Business School and CIIM Business School.[14] In the period 1999–2005, shareholder returns of UK quoted companies where families held a significant stake outperformed the FTSE All Share Index of companies listed on the London Stock Exchange by about 40 per cent. This outperformance mirrors recent US findings where quoted family firms financially outperformed their S&P 500 Index counterparts.[15]

Continuing this international perspective, John Ward has reviewed the growing body of evidence now tending to support the case that, on a range of measures – including return on capital, profitability and growth – family ownership does indeed lead to superior financial business performance. He also believes, however, that family companies often appear to be unaware of their special advantages, and suggests that three strengths in particular may lie behind the identified outperformance.[16] First, he notes that family businesses often pursue different strategies from those normally followed or recommended, choosing these instinctively and implementing them successfully. Second, he cites the positive contribution of the family business culture, and third, a focus on continuity and risk-aversion at family firms, which, he argues, changes attitudes and mindsets, leading to a prudent outlook and avoidance of certain types of mistakes.

Successful sectors for family businesses

Although family firms are to be found in every sector of commercial activity, their special strengths reviewed in this chapter mean that they flourish best in fields in which their advantages can be fully exploited. Family-controlled enterprises therefore are more likely to be found in industries and technologies that demand a long-term perspective, and are less likely to be found in fast-growing industries with high capital requirements.

Furthermore, family businesses often do well in sectors in which the personal, owner-manager feature is important, particularly in services industries; for example, most hotel chains in the UK (and indeed throughout the world) were originally family owned. Family firms are also strong in activities where entrepreneurial drive remains a principal ingredient of success in the business. There is a great tradition in the retail sector, for instance, of businesses being passed on from one generation to the next (such as fashion groups River Island and C&A, and Musgrave supermarkets).

The Barclays Bank survey quoted earlier[17] found that, among a sample of UK family enterprises with turnover of £5 million or less, family firms are most common in the agricultural sector (94 per cent) and in retail (73 per cent) and least common in financial services (40 per cent) and business services (38 per cent). In general, the survey authors noted, family businesses are prominent in people-centric sectors, such as tourism, or those where manual skills are important. Nearly all agricultural businesses (94 per cent) are family owned and managed (helping to explain their other finding that East Anglia, an important location for agriculture, is home to the greatest proportion of the country's family businesses).

Another example in the small-firm sector where family firms play a major role is the franchising industry. Some 80 per cent of UK franchises involve married couples, and most franchises are being run as family businesses, with many next-generation family members viewing the franchise business as a good opportunity to gain practical work experience.[18]

An above-average representation of family businesses is also to be found in sectors where cash flow is good. Cash is critically important in the financing of family companies – in food processing, for example, which has traditionally been a good cash generator, long-established companies such as Associated British Foods in the UK and Campbell Soups in the USA are still in family hands. (The Weston family owns 54 per cent of ABF, and descendants of John Dorrance, who invented condensed soup, own 43 per cent of Campbell.) Similarly, family businesses do well in niche sectors, often still trading on the genius of someone who founded the company many years ago, or where the business is based on some specific knowledge or trading secret that represents the key to success.

Lastly, family businesses are relatively successful in supply industries where the business involves supply relationships with other larger companies that appreciate and value the owner's presence. Thus a lot of family firms are distributorships, especially in the automotive sector, for example the £1.7 billion turnover Reg Vardy, which traces its origins back to the 1920s, when the founder Reg Vardy began a haulage business at Houghton-le-Spring near Durham.

2

Family business dynamics
People, systems and growing complexity

S pecial dynamics set family businesses apart from other enterprises. These dynamics are at work at three levels: they affect the people who participate in family businesses; they affect the way in which such businesses are organised and operate; and they lie behind the way family firms become more complex with the passing of time, especially with the transition from one generation to the next.

Family business people

Family businesses are unique because of the people who are involved in them. Rather than a random cross-section of employees, managers, directors, advisers and investors, they are family members and they are all related to one another. Sometimes, particularly in the early stages, the family involvement is confined to just a few individuals, but whatever the size of the business, each family member has his or her own set of attitudes, opinions, objectives and problems. As a result, an important aspect of understanding how family businesses operate involves an awareness of the background and unique perspective of each of the major participants.

Founders

Dr Peter Davis, an American family business researcher, has drawn a helpful distinction between entrepreneurs and founders:[1]

Though all founders of family businesses are entrepreneurs, not all entrepreneurs become founders. Founders are typically intuitive and emotional people. They obviously have the drive and ambition to build a great business, but they also have a feeling about the place, a love of what they have created that makes them want to perpetuate it through the generations.

He goes on to identify three types of founder, calling them proprietors, conductors and technicians. Because the personality, attitudes and behaviour of founders colour all stages of the development of family businesses – and in many cases their influence persists long after they are dead – some of the main characteristics of founders in these categories are worth highlighting. (Health warning: most family business founders fall into one of the three categories described but, as with all such attempts to pigeonhole human personality, it is important to emphasise that the groupings, although helpful, are to an extent arbitrary in that many founders will exhibit some characteristics of all three types.)

Proprietors

For proprietors, ownership of the business (as opposed to mere control of it) is central. Their identity is usually wrapped up with that of the company, they have little trust in anyone else's ability to make decisions, and they dominate their children and other members of the family involved in the business in the same way that they dominate everyone else.

Proprietor founders want simply to control their children, not to develop their talents with a view to ensuring a smooth succession. The children may become dependent and submissive in the face of the founder's behaviour, seeking out a quiet existence in some part of the organisation; alternatively, they adopt a rebellious strategy. The classic result of the latter course is a turbulent saga of resistance and fighting back against the founder's authoritarian regime, generally resulting in a steadily deteriorating relationship and a parting of the ways.

Another aspect of a founder wanting to dominate the organisation, to the extent that others are excluded from any genuine power or responsibility, is that family businesses under the control of proprietors are hardly ever professionalised. Professionalising involves, as a minimum, strategic management of planning, directing, controlling and staffing, and it places emphasis on the importance of properly motivated, talented people within an organisation. This type of cool-headed, rational analysis based on trust and delegation of responsibility is anathema to most founders in the proprietor category.

Understanding the psychology of father–son conflict is the first step in learning to manage it

'Proprietors', in Davis's classification of family business founder types, are often the legendary characters of family business, with perhaps the most famous example being Henry Ford and his dictatorial control of the Ford Motor Company. In the first 30 years of the 20th century he built the company into the most successful industrial enterprise the world had ever seen, but then, during 15 years of paranoia and obsessive behaviour, he reduced it to virtual bankruptcy. Edsel, his only son, became president, but throughout his tenure Henry Ford remained alive and wielded the real power in the company. Edsel was admired for his creativity, his consensus approach to management and his good judgement, but his presidency was purely nominal. All his important ideas were blocked by his father, who belittled him in public, portraying him as incompetent, weak, and 'too fond of cocktails and decadent East Side living'. Edsel became a pawn in a huge and destructive power struggle, eventually emerging from the process an ill and broken man.[2]

Conductors

Like proprietors, conductors are also firmly in control, but they are much more willing to build up a good staff, delegate responsibility, and foster efficiency and harmony in the organisation. Conductors like the idea of a family business, and they like the idea of their children joining the company and working with them. Thus they invite and orchestrate the involvement of the children and, to preserve harmony, often encourage them to take over different areas of the operation – so one may assume responsibility for marketing, another production and a third financial administration.

Conductors are proud of the family and of the family business. They work to engender a sense of common endeavour, loyalty and family warmth within the company and their offices are often full of family photographs. But this portrait of sensitive amiability should not obscure the fact that conductors are firmly in control, and much of their behaviour is directed towards bolstering their own paternal role and ensuring that they are the ones conducting and organising the firm's development. As the business matures, the conductor avoids facing the dilemma of succession and of having to favour one child at the expense of the others. Tensions begin to build up below the surface, but a business culture has been created that is not well equipped to take stress, and the fabric of both the business and family relationships is put at risk.

Technicians

Davis's third category of family business founders build companies based on their creative or technical skills and are often obsessive types, most at home in drawing offices working on designs and products that only they fully understand. Technicians generally dislike administration and the day-to-day details of management. Thus, unlike conductors, they are not orchestrating and usually will have brought in non-family managers to whom they delegate the organisational role in the business.

While technicians are relaxed about giving up control over administrative details, they are usually less willing to pass on their special knowledge to their children, who may lack the same technical skills.

> Their knowledge and skill is like a magical sword, an Excalibur endowing them with the prestige and power they want. The last thing they want to do is to give it away, especially to their children, who might eventually usurp their position.[3]

The children thus move into administrative positions in which they will not be competing with the founder (or receiving much respect from him for their efforts) and, as a result, often find themselves in conflict with entrenched non-family managers.

Despite finding it difficult to let go, and a reluctance to turn over the business to the children, technicians, as they get older, often discover they have little room for manoeuvre because they may be so vital to the success of the business it is worth little to outsiders without their presence. In the end, what usually forces them round is the realisation that unless their technical skills, which are at the core of the business, are passed on, the company will not survive.

Having looked at examples of types of founder (all of whom are entrepreneurs, although not necessarily vice versa), a brief review of some other relationships and players in the family business drama will help throw light on the complicated people dynamics involved.

Women in family businesses

It would be refreshing to be able to exclude a section under this heading on the basis that there are now no distinctions to be drawn between the roles of men and women in family firms. But although 'bastions of sexism' is no longer an appropriate description of most family businesses, it remains true that gender issues still cause tension.

Part of the problem is that there is little in the way of quantitative evidence in this area, and descriptions of what is going on are often based on observed and anecdotal evidence. Clearly, women have come a long way in family business, in step with increases in the scope of women's independent activity and personal ambition over the past 40 years. At the same time, however, we still see the wives of family company owners playing traditional, behind-the-scenes roles as confidante and business adviser, acting as a sounding board for their husbands, often on issues of character and human perception, and, more prominently, as family leader and a symbol of unity, fostering teamwork and communication. As wives and mothers, their first priority is generally the preservation of the family, and often, when there is conflict in the business between the father and the children, the owner's wife (sometimes known as CEO – for 'chief emotional officer'!) is the mediator who works at calming the situation and keeping the peace.

It is clear that more women in the UK than ever before are now business owners. During the past 20 years, a rising trend in female ownership has been a highlight of new business development, principally in the sole trader sector, but also among partnerships and limited companies. Businesses that are wholly or majority female-owned now account for between 12.3 per cent and 16.5 per cent of the UK business stock.[4] In the UK and across western Europe generally, however, growth has been low and slow in comparison with the spectacular expansion of women's enterprise in the USA.

In family businesses, the treatment of sons and daughters provides an example of how (often in subtle ways) the sexes continue to be treated differently. Regarding entry, for instance, because women are still not usually in the picture their fathers have painted of the business, they typically have to ask to join it. More generally, women rarely view entering the family business as an entitlement. Once working in the firm, daughters usually find learning from their fathers is easier for them than it is for their brothers, because of the absence of psychological-based father–son conflict and the fact that they are able to have a more sensitive and respectful disposition towards their fathers' needs. On credibility, it used to be that a daughter had to work harder than her brother to earn respect in the business, but although there is still a predisposition towards sons, merit and competence are now much more important factors than they used to be.

On passing down the business to the next generation, gender differences seem to remain more ingrained, with the common assumption being that the boys will have the business and the girls will get the cash, and that they are not likely to be interested in working for the family company. Keeping shares with the male blood line is still of course a pronounced preoccupation in some parts of the world. In the Indian culture, for example (although things are rapidly changing there too), it was not so long ago that children were moved around respected families to make sure there was a male in each of the branches. It has also been known for an elder brother, unable to have children of his own, to adopt his younger brother's male child.

In the West, it is probably fair to say that the days of sexism in family businesses are numbered as such businesses have become more knowledgeable and sophisticated. Whereas it used to be unusual to find female family members employed in the family business, today it is much more common – and many women have joined after collecting an MBA from a top international business school. Similarly, favouring sons in family business succession is often regarded as a historical anachronism, and attention now focuses much more on competence.

Husband and wife teams

Husbands and wives in business together is not a new phenomenon, but what is new is a greater degree of business equality between the partners.

As with so many other aspects of family businesses, there are few hard-and-fast rules. For some couples, being together all the time can be a recipe for disaster and divorce; for others, shared business experiences, like shared personal experiences, can strengthen and enrich their marriage. What does seem clear is that while complementary temperaments and talents are particularly important, the couple must also be able to work together as a team. This means that they have to decide how they are to share the workload, allocate power and divide up the rewards of their efforts.

Especially difficult problems arise in relation to decision-making and role definition. Some husband and wife teams find that making joint business decisions can be the key to success, while others divide decision-making responsibilities either according to agreed strengths and weaknesses or with reference to previously agreed roles, so that the partner with authority in a certain area makes all the decisions in that area. Clear role definition is crucial, as is conscious separation of business and family issues so that criticisms or conflicts about business decisions do not become personal.

Couples planning to go into business together should realise that they are entering a potentially disastrous emotional minefield. It has to be a step they are both determined to take, but even then it may be best to include an outsider in the company structure from the start – someone who will be able to offer a balancing viewpoint (or even a casting vote if conflict arises), defuse tension and help the couple to avoid the slippery slope to rivalry, jealousy and blame.

In a family publishing business established by a husband and wife team, the couple each owned 50 per cent of the company. After an initial period of profitable trading, the firm began to falter because of marital difficulties. Advisers drew up a scheme to strengthen management by the appointment of a non-executive chairman with a casting vote, and a suitable candidate was found whose personality enabled him to cope with the couple. He was able to guide the husband and wife team into a separation of roles within the company, with each performing functions for which they were particularly suited – the wife in a creative role and the husband in administration.

As a result, the business began to thrive again, and the clearly defined organisational system helped in the recruitment of extra management talent. The couple obtained a divorce, but they were able to carry on working together in the business, which was maintained intact by the presence of the strong chairman – a neutral outsider who enjoyed the couple's respect. This case illustrates, once again, that getting the structure right generally provides the key to unlocking family business problems.

In-laws

Marrying someone whose parents own a business has some clear benefits: the family is likely to be wealthy, close knit and exceptionally strong, and in-laws may often have opportunities to work in the business and even eventually share in its ownership. But the marriage will also involve a range of potential difficulties that need to be managed carefully.

The principal problems relate to the spouse's new family and the business, and range from feeling like an outsider to being treated like one. Even when the spouse does not work in the family business, he or she is likely to be involved in many discussions and meetings about it and may feel excluded. Business families share a common, often all-encompassing passion about the family firm, and they are usually forceful and extremely energetic. Newcomers, with no prior experience of such families, may feel overwhelmed and under intense pressure to conform to the family norms. New in-laws are frequently seen as a threat to the status quo: 'The difference between in-laws and outlaws', somebody once wryly observed, 'is that outlaws are wanted.' Their arrival on the scene forces the family to examine how they are likely to fit in and whether they should eventually have any claim to ownership in the business. There are areas, as we have seen, that many business families prefer not to anticipate, plan for or even think about. The increasing incidence of divorce – in the USA, for example, females born after 1965 will have more husbands than children – and therefore of families with children from more than one marriage, further complicates the determination of who is in and who is out.

Approaches to the issue vary, and there are interesting cultural differences around the world. At one extreme (common in some Mediterranean countries and in Latin America), in-laws are fully accepted and effectively enjoy family member status in relation to the business. At the other extreme (especially in the USA), in-laws are often excluded, not just from share ownership, but also from any involvement in the business or its family governance architecture.

A middle course has been taken by a fourth-generation US pharmaceuticals company, which has adopted a formal entry process to the family covering both young family members and their prospective spouses. They are invited to annual meetings (before which they sign confidentiality agreements) at which they receive a detailed briefing from family leaders on financial and trust arrangements in place, along with the opportunities and roles available for new family members. The main aim of the briefings is to ensure that each new family member finds out what their new family can expect and what is expected of them. With benefits balanced by obligations, the positive message is clear – that new members are welcomed into the family, but they are required to respect rules and traditions that have developed across the generations.

For in-laws, coping strategies include avoiding establishing a relationship with the family and the business exclusively through their spouse, and developing family friendships quietly and sensitively to encourage acceptance and trust. They should never take sides in family conflicts or try to act as a family therapist – however good their intentions, they will inevitably be misunderstood. Aside, however, from a general strategy that incorporates preparation, patience and calm diplomacy, special problems arise for sons-in-law and daughters-in-law, especially in deciding whether to join the family business, and these may require a different approach.

Some families put pressure not only on their children but also on their children's spouses to work in the family firm. Their contribution may prove to be a disaster or a tremendous success – usually there is no halfway house and the outcome is at one of these extremes. One factor contributing to this polarisation between very bad or very good is that in-laws working in the business usually find themselves in a situation in which, almost regardless of their performance, family members treat them as outsiders, and non-family employees believe they have got the job solely because they have married into the family. They thus find that their deficiencies swiftly become the focus of attention, and if they are to be accepted they must prove themselves to be very good indeed. To help overcome both types of opposition, new in-laws should try to acquire outside experience before they join the family firm. With their contribution under the spotlight, there is no substitute for competence.

Some male owners find that they are able to enjoy a better relationship with their son-in-law than their son because of the absence of father–son conflict. Others are not willing to risk the consequences of discovering whether this is true for them and, like the Rothschild family, impose an inviolable rule that sons-in-law are not permitted to work in the business.

Another possibility relates to prenuptial agreements, which are particularly popular in the USA. Business families often insist that all family members contemplating marriage enter into a prenuptial agreement with their spouse, stipulating that specified assets – principally shares in the business – remain the property of those who owned them before the marriage. The device is designed to avoid any part of the family enterprise falling into the hands of the new in-law. Prenuptial agreements are not legally binding in the UK, but their pros and cons are the subject of continuing debate, and the likelihood is that they will be given legal force in the not too distant future. At present, in a UK divorce case the courts will take such an agreement into account if it was based on a complete disclosure of income and assets, each party took separate legal advice, the agreement has regard for existing children and it was signed at least 21 days before the marriage.

Multifamily ownership

The majority of family businesses consist of a single family unit comprising parents and children. As if the dynamics of this structure are not complex enough, the problems multiply exponentially when more than one family unit becomes involved. This is generally what happens if the business survives through to the second and third generations.

Consider the case, for example, where the owner bequeaths the business to his or her two children. If they each have two children who inherit their parents' shares, the single owner in the first generation is replaced by two in the second and four in the third and, while the second generation comprises siblings, the third consists of both siblings and cousins. If the business is started by unrelated partners, the problem of proliferating ownership can become more acute more quickly. If two partners bequeath their shares to their respective families, there are likely to be five or six shareholders in the second generation and 12 or 15 in the third.

These examples concern numbers, but consider also family dynamics. Say two brothers start a business, and each owns 50 per cent of the share capital. Brother A has two boys and brother B has two girls. Once the founders have left the scene, each of the four children owns 25 per cent of the business. Perhaps the boys work in the business and the girls do not, in which case, with the company prospering, the brothers are likely to begin thinking: 'We're doing really well, but in large part we're working for our cousins who are not even interested in the business. Why are we doing this?' Conversely, say the company starts going downhill, and the girls have married lawyers who look at the annual accounts and say: 'We own half this business and these cousins of ours look set on ruining it. We'd better find some new, more talented people to take over who will be able to stop the rot.' Both eventualities represent predictably troublesome scenarios.

Siblings often end up working together, especially in second-generation family businesses. Because of its destructive potential, sibling rivalry is examined later in this chapter, where it will be seen that the best solution involves agreeing strictly defined roles and responsibilities for siblings in family firms. It is worth mentioning here, however, that some experts believe siblings, despite jealousy and rivalry, have a better chance of forming a working business relationship than people who have not grown up together. By the time they are in business together, brothers and sisters, even if they do not necessarily love and trust each other, do know how the others think, how they respond to pressure and what motivates them, and they will usually have developed conflict resolution skills. Cousins have no such historical bonds – they originate from different families and may have different values. Indeed, because they are the co-product of in-laws from outside the family, their values may be radically different.

Multifamily ownership requires a unique combination of people, skills and attitudes, so it is not surprising that few family businesses survive beyond the third generation. Those that do have usually taken steps to avoid intra-family conflict by, among other things, enabling family members who are not interested in the business to sell their shares and making sure that the family members who remain are competent.

Others will have decided that the wholesale transfer of management to outside professionals is the only answer, although leadership may still come from key family members. However, if voting control is spread around the family, there is still the risk of the differing needs of family members causing disagreement or, indeed, outright warfare (as, for example, memorably broke out at C&J Clark, a sixth-generation footwear manufacturer and retailer; see page 46). In practice, the best way to avoid chaos in these circumstances is through some form of centralised share ownership.

The governance of multigenerational family firms is discussed in Chapter 7.

Non-family employees

This discussion of people dynamics and family businesses would not be complete without mentioning the under-researched role of non-family employees. Successful non-family employees in family businesses are often interesting characters with a distinctive psychological make-up that helps them fit into an unusually demanding work environment. The job will not suit everybody, and there are many instances of talented managers who have resigned because they have run out of opportunities, or because the politics and emotional cross-currents in family-owned companies have become too much of an interference in their work. But managers who are able to cope with such factors are often very good indeed.

Non-family employees, particularly their role in the management of family businesses, are discussed further in Chapter 5.

Managing conflict in family firms

Later in this chapter, the family and the business are analysed as two distinct, essentially incompatible systems. Family behaviour is based on emotion and powerfully influenced by the subconscious, whereas the business system revolves around accomplishing tasks and generally entails behaviour that is consciously determined. Family businesses undoubtedly have a lot going for them, but when family emotional issues and subconscious needs (frequently expressed in the form of aggressive and/or destructive behaviour) turn up and are played out in the context of the family business their impact can be devastating.

There are, however, two particular types of family conflict that can seriously disrupt the operation of the business: the relationship between fathers and sons, and sibling rivalry. Their impact need not take the form of an outburst of suppressed emotions that suddenly makes it impossible for family members to continue working together (although there are famous instances of such spectacular debacles). More often, these conflicts find expression in constant bickering, with the process of arguing usually much more important than the subject matter of disagreements. Battles are fought time and time again over the same ground in a war of attrition that can carry on for years, draining the company of its strength, vitality and, eventually, its life blood.

Father–son conflict and sibling rivalry can never be entirely eradicated, but gaining an understanding of the nature of the psychological factors that underlie them is a vital step in being able to limit their corrosive impact and destructive consequences.

Father–son relationships

Unlike father–daughter relationships, the majority of which are relatively trouble-free, the complex relationship between fathers and sons has been the subject of much study by psychologists and family therapists. A general review of current knowledge would be both impractical and inappropriate here, so what follows represents a summary of important research conclusions, related as closely as possible to those aspects of father–son relationships that especially influence not only the emotional health of the parties but also the welfare of the family business.[5]

It is worth emphasising that father–son relationships are not always bad news. There are many fathers and sons who love and respect each other, and who find that working closely together, far from causing tension, is the most natural and easy thing in the world. Indeed, their relationship is often a source of unique strength and, as a result, they are able to form an effective and formidable business partnership. Unfortunately, however, such fruitful teamwork is relatively uncommon, and it is important to examine why problems arise.

A helpful approach is to look at the relationship between fathers and sons from the point of view of the psychological needs of each, and a good starting point is the perspective of a father who has established a family business. It has already been noted that many entrepreneurs see the business they have created as an extension of themselves – a device or instrument that represents, above all else, their source of personal fulfilment and even masculinity, as well as the symbol of their achievement. The people who work with and for the founder are characteristically his tools in the process of shaping the organisation that will become his monument when he dies. Consequently, he guards power jealously and has great difficulty in delegating authority. Consciously, he may want to ease his son's entry into the business, planning gradually to transfer responsibility to him and, in due course, to pass control of the business on to him. Subconsciously, however, he needs to be stronger than his son: he feels that to yield the business to him would be to lose his masculinity, and that if he lets his son win he will be removed from his centre of power. These contradictory influences often lead the father to behave in erratic and inexplicable ways, sometimes appearing as if his sole motivation is the welfare and development of the business, sometimes as if he is hell bent on its destruction.

The son develops his own feelings of rivalry that are a reflection of his father's. Psychologists tell us that rebellion against parental authority is a natural phase of a child's development, and when the parent is also the employer and source of economic sustenance for an adult child, this phase may be repressed. Also, as he gets older the son needs and seeks increasing independence, responsibility and executive power in the organisation, but finds that he is denied it by his father, who refuses to cede authority. Often the son, desperately eager to take on running the business, is left on the sidelines for years – way beyond the age when others of comparable ability and experience in non-family businesses would expect to take over. The father, not infrequently, refuses to retire despite repeated promises that this is what he wants to do, and the son's frustration is made worse by this type of contradictory signal. The discrepancy between what the father says and what, by his actions, he apparently really means becomes ever more irritating. Harry Levinson, an American authority on business administration, illustrates the dilemma well:[6]

> The father often communicates to the sons that he is building the business for them, that it is going to be theirs, and that they should not be demanding of either appropriate salary or appropriate power because they are going to get it all anyway in due time. Nor should they leave the father and the business because it is self-evident that he has been good to them and is going to give them so much. Thus they are manipulated into an ambivalent position of wanting to become their own persons with mature, adult independence on the one hand, and the wish to take of what they are being offered on the other. If they leave, seemingly they will be ungrateful. If they threaten to depose the father or demand to share his power, then they will indeed destroy him. If they don't do as he says, then they are disloyal and unappreciative sons.

So we have a situation characterised by mounting tension as the father looks on his son as ungrateful, potentially even treacherous, while the son sees himself the victim of emotional blackmail and feels both hostile to his father and guilty about his hostility.

The history of IBM is well worth reading for an insight into the torments of father–son conflict. Together, Thomas J. Watson Sr and Thomas J. Watson Jr built IBM, one of the largest and most profitable businesses ever created, but the story is of two men who loved and fought each other with equal ferocity. In his 1990 book, *Father Son & Co.*, Thomas Jr reflected on their relationship:[7]

> During the ten years after World War II, Father taught me his business secrets as we worked together. It was a stormy relationship. In public he would praise me lavishly … But in private Father and I had terrible fights that led us again and again to the brink of estrangement. These arguments would frequently end in tears, me in tears and Dad in tears. We fought about every issue of the business … I never declared myself the winner in the contest between us, but I hope I was successful enough that people could say I was the worthy son of a worthy father.

As Levinson explains, within the family business father–son conflict can manifest itself in many different ways. The father often actively cultivates an atmosphere of ambiguity which allows him to call the shots as events occur, rather than being bound by clearly defined rules; the son wants and needs clear direction. Similarly, the father is generally most comfortable deferring decision-making until the last possible moment; the son wants decisiveness. These behaviour patterns foreshadow the types of problem the son is likely to face when, and if, he eventually does take over. Often the father has retained obsolete management principles and techniques, or the company may have grown beyond the capacity of one man to control it effectively. The son finds himself faced with the task of repairing an organisation full of previously concealed weaknesses, and the job may well prove too much for him, with the company joining the ranks of family businesses that cannot survive (or at least survive independently) beyond the tenure of their founders.

In one case, a family business consultant became involved in a dispute between a father and son at a medium-sized packaging company. It was September, and the son approached the consultant because his father had just announced out of the blue that he wanted to retire at Christmas and had asked the son to give him a cheque for the business. The son explained that he had been working in the business for 23 years, most of its growth was a result of his efforts, and being asked for a cheque was unreasonable and unfair.

The consultant quizzed the son further and asked him what was the original deal agreed when he first joined the business. 'Funny you should ask that,' replied the son, and he produced from his pocket a four-page letter written to him by his father 23 years before, imploring him to join the business and explaining the opportunities; in three separate parts of the letter the phrase 'Someday son, this will all be yours' came up The son's understanding of this had always been that he would work in the business and that some day his father would pass it on to him. The consultant asked the son if he had raised the matter with his father since the original letter, and the son replied: 'My father has always seemed to tense up when talking about ownership of the firm, so I've avoided raising the subject with him.'

The consultant then went to speak with the father and asked him his interpretation. He said the letter was purely administrative and that the words in question were not intended as a promise to make a gift of the business to his son. Twenty-three years ago, he explained, he had no idea whether they would make a lot of money, or just a little, or none, and he had wanted to keep his options open.

In the end the dispute could not be resolved and father and son fell out. The latter resigned from the company, took an MBA and started a new career. As well as illustrating a typically awkward father–son relationship, this case emphasises that in family businesses it is vitally important to manage assumptions and expectations. When a son joins his father in the family business, both sides need to rethink their relationship. In particular, the son regards his father as 'Dad', not as 'Boss', and while he knows what his father is like at home, he has no experience of his business persona. It is up to the father in this situation to take on extra obligations and responsibilities. In this case, for instance, the young son responding to his father's pleading and joining the business is not going to ask for a proper legal agreement with his Dad covering the terms of his employment and the long-term future plans for the business, so the onus is on the father to take the initiative (although we shall see in What to do about these problems on page 35 why this does not often happen).

Some strategies for trying to cope with the psychological elements that underlie father–son relationships are examined later. First, however, we will look at the second main source of family conflict that can jeopardise the efficient functioning of family businesses.

Sibling rivalry

Rivalry between siblings represents a potentially crippling obstacle to the successful development of many family businesses, and it is critical to understand why and how it comes about before looking at some of the ways in which it can be contained and controlled.

Psychologists believe that sibling jealousy is rooted in the deep desire of children for the exclusive love of their parents. Underlying this is the child's concern that if a parent shows love and attention to a sibling, perhaps the sibling is worth more, and the child is worth less.

An older brother, dominant as a child by virtue of age, size and competence, is resented by his siblings. A sister is jealous of her sister's perceived beauty or is forced to be 'the good one' in order to compensate and redress the balance for her sister's bad behaviour.[8]

Sibling rivalry is normal and, in a family context, can be seen as a useful competitive ingredient in relationships that stimulates the healthy development of well-adjusted, coping adults. But there is an assumption in this interpretation that adult siblings will take their separate paths in life, leave the parental home, establish separate families, follow separate occupations, and so on. With family businesses, this normal growing apart of families is inhibited and we have a situation where childhood rivalry between, for example, brothers for their father's affection is perpetuated in adult life as a result of the necessary day-to-day contacts between them arising from their roles within the business. Thus we find the rivalry exerting an adverse influence on how the business is run, colouring management decisions and, if left uncontrolled, eventually paralysing the organisation.

The legendary feud between the Gucci brothers provides a graphic example of escalating sibling rivalry in a family business. The Gucci empire, known around the world for luxury fashion goods and accessories, has its origins in a humble saddlery store in Florence, opened in 1905. Second-generation brothers Rodolfo and Aldo each ended up holding about 50 per cent of the shares in the family empire. At first their rivalry, while fierce, was contained; each had different ideas about how to expand the business and the role to be played by their own sons. But arguments and resentment about slights, real and imagined, increased, and by the 1980s they had boiled over into well-publicised boardroom fist-fights. In the handover to the third generation, Aldo's 50 per cent shareholding was divided unevenly among his children, while Rodolfo's shares passed as a block to his only son, Maurizio – an imbalance that only served to fuel dissension and anger. Along with boardroom violence, other highlights of the feuding included Aldo's son, Paolo, shopping his father to the tax authorities (and later suing him) and the murder of Maurizio in 1995 – an assassination financed and organised by Maurizio's estranged wife, Patrizia. The back-stabbing brought comparisons with the Borgia family in medieval Florence, and, well before the killing of Maurizio in Milan, the company had been disabled by conflict and was sold.

On occasions, often without realising they are doing it, owners intensify sibling rivalry by fostering a competitive spirit among family members in the business, effectively reinforcing and magnifying the rivalry that already exists. More commonly, yet just as problematical, the family tenet of parents treating their children equally will probably have been applied to the family business, with the result that children own equal shares in the organisation and are members of the board – thus sibling rivalry is locked in place.

What to do about these problems

Only rarely can the difficulties that flow from father–son, sibling and other forms of family rivalry be completely avoided. By their very nature these rivalries are facts of life in a great many family businesses, and the issue therefore is whether they are allowed to dictate behaviour and become a destructive force that threatens the survival of the business. In other words, can family members learn to manage the conflicts rather than be managed by them?

On the positive side, business families do have a head start when it comes to conflict resolution and conflict management. Possession of these skills is generally one of the hallmarks of strong, coping families (discussed in Chapter 3), and lasting family businesses are usually owned by strong families. In general, 'optimal families', as they are often dubbed, demonstrate those skills that are crucial in dealing with the tensions between individual choice and group needs – between the need for individual freedom and the need for belonging and togetherness.

First and foremost, it is essential for family members struggling with the debilitating consequences of both father–son and sibling rivalry to appreciate and understand the psychological basis of their dilemma. Without this, there is an inevitable tendency to believe that the aggression, the destructive and irrational behaviour, and the guilt involved are a result of purely personal or unique family defects. Once it is realised that what is being fought out is a series of primeval rivalries that affect not just individuals but most of the human race, this cannot fail to begin to defuse some of the intensity of the emotions generated by the problems, thus making it easier both to analyse what is going on and to begin thinking more clearly about ways of coping.

Regarding father–son discord, unfortunately, experience shows that most entrepreneurial fathers, even when they understand the processes that are at work, are not good at getting to grips with their dilemma. Their fears over losing control and suffering rejection seem to make it difficult for them to grasp that there may be other valid points of view that they can accept without appearing to be irresolute and weak. This means that much of the responsibility for taking positive action falls on the son's shoulders.

A father who pressures rather than invites a son to join the family business is sowing the seeds of future conflict, and the son's recognition of why he chose to join is often very important. As Levinson explains:[9]

> Most sons will say that it is because of the opportunity and the feelings of guilt if they had not done so. Often, however, the basic reason is that a powerful father has helped make his son dependent on him, and so his son is reluctant to strike out on his own. He rationalises his reluctance on the basis of opportunity and guilt. Struggling with his own dependency, he is more likely to continue to fight his father in the business because he is still trying to escape his father's control.

A son should also recognise how his own feelings of anger and rivalry naturally lead to defensive measures on the father's part and to increasingly entrenched positions on both sides.

Communication between father and son is crucial. The son should explain that he recognises how important running the business is to his father, and how much of his personality is wrapped up in it, but that it is just as important that he has an independent area of opportunity in which to develop his own skills and responsibilities. One possibility is for the son to establish a new venture, either a division within the existing company framework or a new subsidiary, over which he has managerial autonomy. A variation on this might be a corporate restructuring under which the group creates a core operating division to be presided over by the son, while the father controls the remaining activities and pursues new ventures. Approaches such as these have the advantage of providing the son with space to grow and mature while avoiding the possibility of appearing to desert the father.

Serious cases of father–son conflict may require third-party intervention. The neutral third party – perhaps a business friend or a specialist mediator or counsellor – should understand the nature and intricacies of the problems that father and son are grappling with. The intermediary should begin by talking at length with both parties privately to build up a picture of the history of their relationship and a clear view of their feelings. Father and son should then discuss the situation together in the presence of the intermediary, who must try to ensure that the real issues are debated – the father's fears over losing control, the son's rejection of him or dependence on him, and so on. An agenda should be drawn up of agreed ways in which the parties plan to try to change their behaviour, together with possible organisational changes of the type already mentioned that will reduce the potential for conflict.

If all these measures are unsuccessful, the son is faced with a choice of learning to tolerate the situation until events arise that change it, or leaving the business to seek opportunities elsewhere. In either case, it is not uncommon for the passage of time to heal divisions between fathers and sons, especially after the son has established his own family and reached a level of maturity at which he no longer sees his parents as omnipotent, but feels genuine compassion for them as individuals with real needs, fears and dreams.

Turning to rivalry between siblings, once again, a path needs to be followed that starts with gaining an understanding of the psychological nature of the posture each sibling adopts towards the other and continues with them talking together about their mutual feelings and behaviour and, if necessary, enlisting third-party help. If possible, however, the siblings themselves should try to prevent their rivalry becoming destructive by acknowledging its harmful potential and agreeing on a code of behaviour that recognises their mutual dependence and puts in place a procedure for resolving disputes, perhaps with the assistance of independent board members.

It is worth noting that sibling rivalry can sometimes be more of an issue for other family members than it is for the siblings themselves. For example, when two brothers working in a family business have an argument, they typically go home and report the row to their respective wives. The following day the siblings may well have forgotten the dispute because they are brothers, used to doing things together and solving problems, and enjoy a bond that has served to smooth over yesterday's differences. But their wives will often be oblivious to the reconciliation and will have dwelt on the reported argument, discussing what happened with family allies, generating and spreading bad feeling. Thus collateral damage from sibling rivalry can sometimes be more destructive than the rivalry itself.

As well as talking through and thus demystifying their feelings of anger and guilt, siblings need to consider how they can divide their roles in the family business in a way that enables them to demonstrate competence, reduces the potential for competitive conflict and increases their chances of finding ways of working together in a complementary relationship. If the organisation is large enough, rivalry can be minimised by siblings taking responsibility for separate areas, defined operationally or geographically (or preferably both). The aim is to help them focus on their own jobs and not on those of their siblings.

It helps if remuneration and job titles are defined in advance according to objective criteria. This will reduce the emotional repercussions should one sibling perform better and achieve more than another. Again, independent directors are potentially valuable because they can help to contribute objectivity to (and remove some of the emotional sting from) important decisions involving siblings, such as performance evaluation, promotion and management succession.

Family business systems

The second area in which special dynamics set family businesses apart from other enterprises concerns the way in which such businesses are organised and operate.

The main way in which the family firm is different from any other business is that its directors, managers and employees share a family relationship, the values, ethics and behaviour patterns of which are, to a greater or lesser extent, carried over into the workplace. This section looks at the effects that this family relationship can have on the business – on how it is organised and how it operates – and particularly the inherent tensions that exist between the emotional factors that govern family life and the objective nature of business management.

A helpful framework for looking at the relationship between the family and the business is to think of the family as a system and the business as a system. The initial concern is not with the characteristics of individuals within the two systems, but rather the features that define the relationships between individuals in each system. The emphasis of these features within the two types of system is distinctly different, as shown in Figure 2.1.

The family system is based on emotion, with its members bound together by deep emotional ties that can be both positive and negative. These ties, and indeed a great deal of behaviour in family relationships, are influenced by the subconscious (the need for sisters to dominate sisters, fathers to be stronger than their sons, and so forth). The family system tends to be inward-looking, placing high values on long-term loyalty, care and the nurturing of family members. It is also a conservative structure operating to minimise change, keeping the equilibrium of the family intact.

The business system is based on the accomplishment of tasks. It is built around contractual relationships in which people do agreed jobs in return for agreed remuneration and, for the most part, behaviour is consciously determined. It is also oriented outwards towards producing goods or services for its marketplace, while emphasising performance

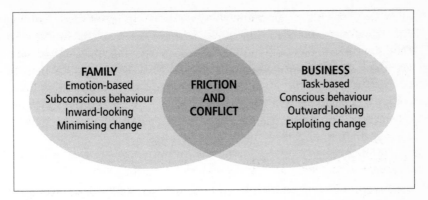

Figure 2.1 Overlapping systems

and results – that is, the competency and productivity of its members. To help ensure its survival, the business system operates to make the most of change, not to minimise it.

In the non-family business these two basically incompatible systems operate independently, but in the family business they not only overlap, but they are also interdependent. Their differing purposes and priorities produce the special tensions that exist in family firms, some of which create at the point of overlap operational friction and value conflicts for the founder and other family members.

Concentrating on family involvement as a source of weakness in firms should not be allowed to obscure the many advantages of the family relationship discussed in Chapter 1. There are interesting theories developing which suggest that what successful families in business do best – and what it is that gives them their unique culture and superior performance (see Chapter 1) – is to reconcile these differences and contradictions with counter-intuitive thinking and unconventional actions. Here, however, the concern is to highlight the undeniable negative impact of an excessive transfer of either family values to the business or business values to the family.[10]

Seeking a balanced approach

The answers to questions such as how to evaluate the business performance of family members, how to transfer power, and whether and how to share ownership of the business can be very different depending on whether things are looked at from a family or a business perspective – that is, from a standpoint of family first or business first.

There are many examples of family-first solutions. Next-generation family members may be expected to join the family business and commit their working lives to it regardless of their aptitude, talent or inclination.

Once they have joined, family members may dictate that they must all be paid equally, regardless of their abilities and how much they contribute. Family members may be paid more than they are worth or, alternatively, less than they are worth on the basis that they have an obligation to contribute to the family enterprise and money should be the least of their concerns. The family tenet that children must be treated equally may be reflected in owners leaving children equal ownership shares, regardless of their position in or contribution to the business.

The incursion of the business system into family life can be just as damaging as the reverse situation. Building a business often becomes an obsessive preoccupation for the owner, and this single-mindedness can undermine the quality of family life. Similarly, although at a later development stage when other family members have joined, families can find that they are never free from the business because its influence pervades all aspects of their lives. A particularly important golden rule, for example, is no business talk at the dinner table. Yet a surprising number of cases of serious family unhappiness and conflict arise where children and other family members who are not involved in the family firm have come to feel marginalised and isolated as every evening meal turns into a sort of board meeting at which that day's family business successes and problems are top of the agenda.

If there are business conflicts, the problems become much more serious. With some families, differences over business policies become so intense, and there is so much proximity both inside and outside business hours, that normal family life simply becomes impossible.

The answer is to seek a balanced approach. Conflict arising from the overlap of family and business systems cannot be avoided entirely. However, successful families devise strategies that help them keep the overlap under control and minimise the possibility of the major problems that arise when one set of values engulfs the other.

Attempting to separate family and business life completely is the first response of many people when they begin to see the danger signals. But as well as denying the reality of family and human behaviour, this strategy jeopardises the sources of commercial strength that flow from the family relationship: family vision and values, loyalty, commitment, sharing in a common enterprise, flexibility, and so on. A much more effective approach is to develop strategies that assist in recognising and analysing family and business issues, and then to address them in a direct way to ensure the correct degree of balance between system components. The correct degree of balance is one that allows the business to be run properly while not disrupting family harmony. The main steps that can be taken to achieve this objective are as follows:

✱ **Professionalise the business.** Introduce strategic management within an organisation that has thought through its goals and introduced systems for monitoring performance in relation to a strategic plan. This is an important step towards being able to manage the overlap of family and business systems. It focuses attention on a number of human resource areas that are particularly problematic for the family business, and it begins to strip out many of the emotional factors that obscure and confuse a proper appreciation of how the business is really operating.

✱ **Be proactive and pre-emptive.** Do something about the range of problems that can afflict family businesses before they take hold. Two approaches that can be particularly useful in helping families to anticipate and avoid these problems are the development of a written constitution for the family business, reflecting both family and business values, and the holding of regular family retreats and communication sessions (see Chapter 3).

✱ **Distribute power and resources thoughtfully.** The most important long-term issues in a family business concern power and resources, including who has, or should have, power within the business and control its resources today, and how power and resources can be transferred to the next generation in a way that safeguards the future of the business. Too often, the potential consequences of these critical decisions are not understood by the founder or controlling shareholders.

✱ **Manage transitions effectively.** As well as the normal business and industry life-cycle transitions, in a family business the ability to manage the complex problems of management succession between one generation and the next may be critical for the firm's survival.

Introducing the ownership dimension

The two-circle conceptual model (Figure 2.1 on page 39) depicts the underlying tensions affecting family companies, but a more subtle representation is needed to portray what is going on in the full range of family enterprises (especially the older, third-generation and beyond, more complex family businesses). Rather than just looking at family versus business, a further distinction – owners versus managers – sheds useful light on the dynamics of what is happening in family businesses, leading to the three-circle model, in which the independent but overlapping and interlocking subsystems comprise the family, ownership and the business (see Figure

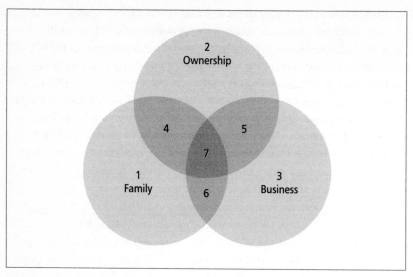

Figure 2.2 Interlocking systems: the three-circle model

Source: Adapted from Renato Tagiuri and John Davis (1982) 'Bivalent attributes of the family firm'. Reprinted (1996) in the 'Classics' section of *Family Business Review*, Vol. IX, No. 2, Summer, pp.199–208.

2.2). Understanding the ownership structure in a family business is often fundamental to understanding the forces at work within it.

Everyone involved in a family business falls within one (and only one) of the seven sectors created by the three circles:

1–3 Individuals in these sectors have only one connection with the business – they are family, or they are owners, or they are employed by the business.

4 This sector is within both the family and ownership circles and therefore comprises family members who own shares in the business but who are not employees.

5 Owners who work in the business but who are not family members.

6 Family members who work in the business but who do not own shares.

7 Inhabiting all three circles are owners who are also family members and employees of the business.

This model helps identify and clarify the different perspectives and motivation of family business people, as well as the potential sources for interpersonal conflict and role confusion. For instance, owners-only individuals (that is, investors in sector 1 of the diagram) will be principally concerned with return on their investment and liquidity, while owners who are also managers (in sector 5) will have the same concerns but with an extra layer of self-interest relating to issues such as job satisfaction and autonomy. Similarly, when taking a view on the appropriate level of dividend payments, non-owning family members who work in the business (sector 6) often take a different view from their relatives who own shares in the business but are not employed by it (sector 4). The former may want to cut dividends to boost reinvestment in the business (and, by the by, improve their career prospects); the latter may want to increase dividends to provide a better return on their investment.

Other potential sources of tension and conflict are reflected in questions like who should lead the business, who should work in it, how they should be remunerated and who should own shares in the family firm. Because business life and family life represent distinct cultural domains with different behaviour patterns, these questions are often the cause of emotionally troublesome predicaments for those who have to resolve them. Too often, families resort to short-sighted and dysfunctional approaches, trying to keep a lid on tensions, as seen in classic family business syndromes such as:

✳ procrastination – always putting off discussion of potentially difficult family matters;

✳ selective amnesia – forgetting some discussions and decisions that do not suit their own perspective, but enjoying a clear recollection of others that do;

✳ taboos – certain subjects are not talked about at all in the interests of family unity;

✳ fear – raising certain issues risks provoking unpleasant confrontations;

✳ divide and conquer – excluding some family members, shareholders or employees from certain decisions as part of a generally secretive management style.

Note the common thread in all these syndromes – a lack of communication, and, in some cases, miscommunication. As discussed in Chapter 3, effectively managing the problems arising from overlapping systems requires transparency and open communication and decision-making within and across the family, the business and the ownership groups.

The three-circle model in Figure 2.2, although helpful in isolating and identifying the range of concerns and motivations operating in a particular family business, is a static model – a snapshot in time. Family businesses, however, are constantly changing and evolving across all three dimensions of the model. This leads on to the last of the three areas in which special dynamics set family businesses apart from other enterprises.

Family business life cycles: a story of growing complexity

A strong desire to safeguard and perpetuate the family business is a primary motivating force for many of those who lead family firms. The reasoning behind this will be different for different families. Sometimes it rests on the way in which the company has come to be seen as the guardian of family values, so that safeguarding the existence of the business becomes a way of preserving strong family values and traditions. Alternatively (or as well), keeping the business in family hands from one generation to the next is regarded as the most effective way of protecting the family's wealth and long-term security. Sometimes there are concerns that disposal of the business may risk the livelihoods of employees who have worked loyally for the company for many years.

Life-cycle stages

So the survival of the business between generations is often a more powerful factor than the one-off financial gain that could be acquired by selling it. But the family business tends to become more complex with the passing of time, and especially with the transition from one generation to the next. John Ward first drew attention to the fact that, in broad terms, ownership of family businesses tends to progress through a sequence, reflecting ageing and expansion of the owning family: owner-managed business; sibling partnership; cousin consortium.[11]

Owner-managed business

This is how most family businesses start life, and they receive a lot of attention from analysts and commentators. At the owner-managed stage, where an individual typically has voting control and makes all the key decisions, governance is not really an issue. The board of directors, for example, is usually something of an illusory entity; if it exists at all, it often comprises mainly family members rubber-stamping the business founder's decisions rather than carrying out any serious advisory role.

To perpetuate the family firm, the owner-manager may well be counting on his or her children to come into the business. If this is not what they want to do, outsiders must be brought in to run the firm (the best ways of approaching this decision are discussed in Chapter 8). Assuming that the next generation are keen to enlist, their joining brings a new set of questions – What role are they expected to play? What will they be paid and how will their performance be evaluated? How will their employment affect loyal, non-family employees? Do they have sufficient business ability to take over the business? How should a future leader be selected from among them? Who should inherit the shares in the business?

These questions are made more complicated by the founder's dual role as parent and employer, as well as by his or her probably ambivalent attitude concerning relinquishing control and coming to terms with the realities of age and mortality. For the first time, succession has become a major issue.

Sibling partnership

Assuming the transition is negotiated successfully, the evolution in second-generation family firms is generally therefore from a single, all-powerful owner to a partnership of brothers and sisters in which power and authority must now be shared. There may be additional owners – sometimes from the parent's generation, sometimes among the siblings' children – but ultimate ownership authority and influence will rest with the siblings. Developing processes for sharing power and control among siblings and avoiding sibling rivalry are important challenges for family firms at this stage of development.

At this point it is useful to define the role of non-employed owners (individuals in sector 4 in Figure 2.2, page 42). Because of their different perspective in relation to the business and the consequent potential for friction, a workable relationship, based on good communication and clear, effective governance structures, needs to be established between these people and their sibling owners who are employed in the business.

When they come to consider succession, they must face a similar type of problem to that with which the founder had to grapple, but on a much larger scale. There will usually be more succession candidates when the second generation comes to decide who in the third generation should take over the business – a situation often exacerbated by equal second-generation voting power and sometimes by a history of unresolved conflicts.

Cousin consortium

By the time the third generation is in place, there is a well-established business and there may be several dozen or more family members who have some sort of stake in it. Ownership is generally in the hands of many cousins from different sibling branches of the family, often with no single branch having a controlling shareholding. Some of these owners will work in the business, many will not. It is easy to imagine the potential for friction and dysfunctional behaviour if the large-scale complexity arising with these family groups is not controlled and managed, and there are many real-life cases that prove the point.

For example, trench warfare broke out in the early 1990s between family shareholders and management at Clarks Shoes, one of the UK's oldest independent family-owned businesses. Now back on an even keel, thanks largely to the successful operation of its family council, the company's improved fortunes are discussed in Chapter 7. The aim here, however, is to highlight how it was that, from mid-1992 onwards, years of private family feuding came to a head, fuelled by a breakdown in communication on a scale such that family shareholders' perceptions and aspirations bore little or no resemblance to those of management.

The business had prospered during the 1950s and 1960s when 'Clarks' entered the language as a byword for well-fitting, comfortable footwear. Although a public flotation was considered at various points in its history, the company remained resolutely private and family owned, under the control of an ever-increasing number of the descendants of Cyrus and James Clark, who founded the business in the 1820s. By 1992, with the fifth generation on the board, around 1,000 family members controlled 70 per cent of the equity, with a further 10 per cent in family trusts.

In the late 1980s Clarks, like the UK shoe industry as a whole, found itself under mounting pressure from the dramatic increase in cheaper imports. Pre-tax profits tumbled, which resulted in drastic dividend cuts, angering many shareholders who, with no day-to-day involvement in management, had come to rely on the family company for a steady income. As well as dividend income, another festering issue centred on demands that shareholders be able to cash in their shares. A procedure was set up whereby shares could be traded once every six months, but this proved ineffective. With the feud developing into a much more general debate about how family owners could extract the full value of their shares, not surprisingly potential bidders for the company began to emerge.

In the end, after a long period of acrimonious debate conducted via press statements, proposals to sell the company were rejected by shareholders in May 1993, but only by a narrow margin (52.5 to 47.5 per cent). The bitter arguments had come within a whisker of ending the independent existence of this long-established business, and the lessons from this period of Clarks' history are clear. Business managers can find themselves in serious peril in the face of angry family owners suffering an income cut with no prior warning or communication, and having no proper share-sale escape route. Surprisingly rapidly, pride in the family inheritance, a stable family business culture and so on can turn sour, and the pressures on everyone to end the feuding and sell up may prove hard to resist.

Unlike siblings brought up in the same family, cousins (especially the more remote cousins who proliferate once a business has reached the fourth generation and beyond) often have little in common, and some may never have met. The powerful family connection that worked for the business in the first two ownership stages may now be significantly weakened. Even more than with sibling partnerships, therefore, there is a fundamental need for cousins to develop a shared vision about the future of the business which provides vitality and a sense of purpose and direction.

Many family companies find it useful to introduce special governance systems and mechanisms to manage the diversity of interests and demands, and to let everyone have their say. In building a common and workable vision together, it is often useful at this point to allow those family members who do not buy into or believe in that vision to exit as shareholders. There are no one-size-fits-all solutions, and the importance of tailoring governance architecture to meet the unique needs and circumstances of particular families is discussed in Chapter 7, which examines family governance in multigenerational family firms.

Lastly, on the subject of family business life-cycle dynamics and growing complexity, it is useful to understand a little more about the factors at work in the transition process from owner-managed business through sibling partnership to a cousin consortium. The process is far from straightforward – and sometimes it can even go backwards.

Ownership transitions

Not all owner-managed family firms are first-generation businesses. There are examples of family businesses where the single-owner model is recycled, and the company is passed to just one owner (usually from father to son) in the succeeding generation. This distinctive type of succession is often found in farming businesses, where families do not want to split land among siblings. Also, third-generation buy-outs can lead to the re-establishment of an owner-managed business or sibling partnership, where one cousin or one branch buys out all the others and takes control.

The important point is that whether the transition is from a single owner to a sibling partnership, or from a sibling partnership to a cousin company, it is not just changing the people, it is changing the system and the ways in which things are done. It amounts to introducing a different type of business structure with a different culture, different decision-making, different procedures and different ground rules.

New system, new culture

In the first generation, the culture celebrates the heroic achievements of a founder who, usually against all the odds, has built a substantial business from nothing, and who continues to guide it through adversity. The culture of a sibling partnership (and, more so, a cousin consortium), in contrast, celebrates the achievements of the team working together, and no individuals are seen as heroes. So what works in one structure tends not to work (and can indeed be a recipe for disaster) in another. Moreover, it is easy to overlook the huge challenge that this implies – in effect family business leaders are being asked to forget what they learned through decades of observation and example, despite the fact that they have masses of data proving that what they learned worked very well.

Another point about these changes in system and culture is that they do not take place overnight. In most successions there is a transitional period (illustrated in Figure 2.3) during which the business is effectively between systems. Depending on the spread of ages within generations, these periods of overlap can last anything from a month or two up to 20 years. During transitions, there is a hybrid business that is in neither one camp nor the other, and this can be extremely confusing and frustrating for everybody.

One reason for the confusion is that behaviour, strategies and methods that used to work (and work really well) in the outgoing system no longer work (or do not work as well) in the incoming system. This creates a need to define and retain what used to work and will still work; to forget or unlearn what used to work but no longer does; and to define and then master what used not to work in the old scenario but now does in the new. Not surprisingly, it is generally hard for people deeply involved in succession to understand and get to grips with these counter-intuitive ideas.

The need to recognise that it is the system, not just the personnel, that is changing applies particularly in transitions to the third generation, when a sibling partnership is passing to cousins. Siblings cannot assume that what worked for them in growing the business will also work for the cousins. Neither can they assume that the cousins will behave as they have done; siblings generally forget how little the cousins will have in common and that they will operate within a different system that has different values, rules and methods. In sibling-to-cousin transitions,

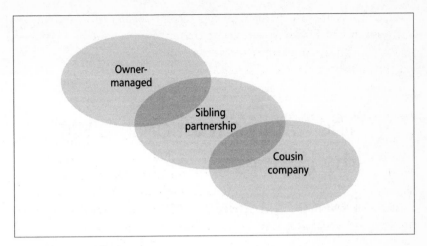

Figure 2.3 Transition phases

Source: Adapted from Kelin Gersick, John Davis, Marion McCollom Hampton and Ivan Lansberg (1997) *Generation to Generation: Life Cycles of the Family Business*. Boston, MA: Harvard Business School Press.

siblings also often overlook the added complexity with which cousins will have to cope and fail to appreciate the extra structure, formality and governance systems that cousins will need to introduce to help manage this extra complexity.

So different ingredients make for success in the three stages of family business ownership: the heroic entrepreneur in owner-managed businesses; teamwork in sibling partnerships; and effective corporate governance systems in cousin companies.

3

The family's relationship with the business

Developing a strategic vision and building teamwork

F amilies learn to build a shared vision by aligning individual and family values and goals, and that vision becomes a guide for planning, decision-making and action. A starting point is the simple question: 'What's our business for?' Often this enquiry produces a range of answers from different family members: some may see the business as jobs for the kids; others may see it as a pension fund, or a lasting family legacy, or a Ferrari, or a charitable foundation, and so on. Developing a consensus on this most basic of questions helps families significantly improve their chances of success when they move on to establishing clear ground rules for their relationship with the business and defining the responsibilities of family members. The aim is to formulate and adopt policies that strike a good balance between the best interests of the business and the well-being of the family, and then to design and establish effective governance structures that help the family develop a cohesive approach to the business and provide organisational focus and accountability.

Articulating values and a shared vision

Values are what a family and its business stand for; vision is a shared sense of where each is heading. Together, values and vision provide a major source of strength and resilience for the family firm, and are central to long-term family business success.

Founders are usually the source of values and vision. The foresight and sheer ambition to succeed of individuals who start family businesses often represent a powerful force with an enduring impact that can inspire succeeding generations. Indeed, family businesses have their own personalities, often deriving from the personalities of the founder and/or subsequent leaders, who still make their presence felt. Many of the most successful family businesses have managed to bottle these qualities and convert them into their organisational values by keeping the family involved and united, and by managing transitions and succession carefully.

Even when such an enterprise becomes a publicly owned and operated corporation, the family's values can remain an integral part of company culture. Such is the case with the Kikkoman Corporation, whose roots stretch back to the 17th century when the Mogi family (one of eight founding family branches) began soy sauce production in Japan. A company creed (or constitution) sets out many family traditions and values, in part based on Buddhist beliefs and philosophy. Among the ideals it articulates are peaceful behaviour, faith, mutual respect and discipline. Kikkoman's vice-chairman, Kenzaburo Mogi, explains that although members of the founding families now own only a small percentage of the company, the creed provides a continuing family influence as it 'formalises many of the traditions and habits long observed by the families, and these concepts are often referred to among management even today'.[1]

A family's values often reveal themselves in less formal ways – via a complicated tangle of customs, anecdotes and unwritten codes of conduct – but this informality should not be allowed to disguise the deep-rooted power of the perspectives and behaviours involved. It does, however, mean that some work and effort are generally needed to explore and define more precisely the nature of personal and family values and what they encompass. Of course, values should not and cannot be fabricated, or chosen because a family feels they should have them; they are not statements of aspiration. True values arise from a family's real experiences, history and traditions.

In examining and documenting the values they share, a good starting point for family discussions will be to explore some open-ended statements based on the family's experience, such as: 'Our most important priority as a family is …'; 'Our family has responsibility to ensure that …'; 'When faced with conflict our family …'; 'Our family legacy is …'.[2] In many cases this will involve a heated and lengthy debate, and it may be necessary to note agreement on certain core values while reserving decisions about others for later family meetings. However, it is important for the family to approach this exploration process from a serious and mature standpoint, and with honesty, remembering that core values form a compelling rationale for family unity as well as the foundation for meaningful family and business plans.

Other reasons why values are so important in a family business are not hard to pin down. As rules for living they create a code of behaviour that builds and supports the shared vision and mission. Values also encourage the development of knowledge and trust in the family and in the family business, and they create a legacy. A family member who does not share the family's core values would do well to bail out, avoiding the inevitable conflicts they will face. However, even the most distant relative who is not involved in the business in any way may believe in the family's values and thus remain fully committed to the business in the long term.

Real-life family values that have emerged from the sort of family meeting described are often grouped under headings such as 'honesty and integrity', 'care and share', 'respect' and 'unity'. Statements of principle under these heading have included the following:

✳ Honesty and integrity – 'We will always strive to be just and fair' and 'We will not judge people by their wealth or social standing.'

✳ Care and share – 'We will put the welfare of the family and the company ahead of our own individual welfare' and 'We will share all setbacks and our successes alike.'

✳ Respect – 'We will show fairness, respect and understanding to family and to employees alike.'

✳ Unity – 'We will remain together and protect the family from harm.'

Over time, statements like these often evolve beyond a mission for a single business into a set of values about how business should be conducted and guiding principles for the family's emerging role in community activities.[3]

Many family businesses have achieved competitive advantage through a values-driven approach. For instance, under the banner 'A family company', Sweden's Axel Johnson heads up its website with the message:[4]

> The name on our door is a daily reminder of our heritage as a family-owned company. Antonia Ax:son Johnson is the fourth generation to lead the worldwide group of enterprises launched in Stockholm in 1873 by her great-grandfather, Axel Johnson. In her leadership and in her life, our owner provides the moral compass that guides every member of the Axel Johnson Group. She continues the long tradition of ethical entrepreneurship that has won respect for Johnson companies for 130 years.

Families need to work hard building a shared vision that helps them develop a unified approach to the business

Another example of tangible rewards came in a case involving a family-owned manufacturing company, which also had some property interests. The company had taken a loan from a bank, but because of a real-estate downturn, the amount of the loan came to exceed the value of the property portfolio on which it was secured. The management team came up with a plan to dispose of the property, which, because of the shortfall, would have left the bank holding about £1.5 million of debt to be written off. The non-family managing director of the group went to the family with the message: 'We've lost money on the property, but don't worry about the bank, they can afford to take their share of the loss.' To his surprise, the family response was: 'Sorry, one of our core values is "our word is our bond". Please write a cheque to the bank repaying the full amount they lent us, and tell them that this family business always pays its debts.' The bank was also taken aback because it had already written the money off. Two years later the bank decided to sell one of its businesses following a change of strategic direction. Because of the history, it gave the family first refusal on an excellent deal, which the family took up, and that business is now worth a fortune.[5]

Of course, times change, families expand and markets and business cycles move on, so it is important that values and vision are periodically re-examined. If the family's reaction is along the lines of 'It worked well enough for grandfather when he was building the company', it is probably time for a change, or at least for a review. If values and attitudes remain static and entrenched in the past, the family risks creating a vacuum in which – with no relevant vision to unite them – disconnection, communication failures and conflict are likely to flourish.[6] Renewal of a coherent ownership vision is required with each generational transition of the family business.

Patrick Peyton, the non-family chairman and chief executive officer of Minnesota-based Despatch Industries, explains how, when he joined the business, family values turned out to be firmly rooted in the present and with a direct impact on his take-home pay:[7]

> Minnesotans have incredible work ethics, so values are incorporated into our mission statement … When I joined the family company 11 years ago I found this out firsthand when we discussed my compensation package. In my annual incentive plan, 25 per cent of the payout is a subjective review by family members, when they would ask whether I had led the business in a manner that reflects the values of the family. It has been surprising what things have been raised as an issue. While it was maybe the right business decision, it wasn't the way they thought it should have been handled from an employee standpoint, or from a public disclosure standpoint. So it is interesting to incorporate those values in the way I do my job.

A final thought is that a well-established set of values generally underpins a healthy organisational culture. In the words of Nigel Nicholson, a professor at London Business School: 'The only sustainable source of competitive advantage a firm can possess is its culture.'[8] A precise definition of family company culture can be difficult to pin down, but there is agreement on its importance and on many of its principal ingredients. It encompasses, for example, ideal leadership style (autocratic versus consultative), proper decision-making authority (hierarchical versus individual), the role of the family in the business, norms of secrecy versus openness, and the company's time horizons (focusing on the past versus the future, or on the short term versus the long term). Family business authorities place significant weight on the power of corporate culture in the family business sector, according to Kelin Gersick and colleagues (1997):[9]

> Company cultures can endure for a long time without major changes when there are reliable methods for faithfully transmitting their essence. That is certainly the case in family firms; the family is perhaps the most reliable of all social structures for transmitting cultural values and practices across generations.

Effective business families

Research on family functioning highlights that a strong base of common values and shared vision underpins a number of the main characteristics that distinguish strong, healthy families. In general, optimal families, as they are often dubbed, demonstrate those skills that are crucial in dealing with the tensions between individual choice and group needs – between the need for individual freedom and for belonging and togetherness. More specifically, their common qualities can be summarised into five categories:[10]

✳ Commitment. This manifests itself in the importance that family members place on family unity, sharing the same goals and concern for each other's welfare. Family members are encouraged to pursue their individual goals, but the commitment to family would preclude pursuits that threaten the best interests of the family.

✳ Appreciation and communication. The research highlights that members of strong families have the ability to recognise each other's positive qualities and to share open and frequent communication. An important aspect of these qualities is that such families establish clear boundaries between, and emotional space around, members. There is an acceptance of differences and respect for personal choice while working towards shared goals.

✳ Time together. Strong families enjoy time together, in terms of both quality and quantity – not allowing outside pressures to pull them into going separate ways, yet not stifling individual identities – closeness without coercion. There is usually joy in relating, and this can include organising time together at regular family gatherings, family meals or family attendance at religious services.

✳ Spiritual health. Reinforcing the conclusions from the previous point, strong families often share a unifying force that encompasses integrity, honesty, loyalty and high ethical values – attitudes that may be categorised as spiritual health. Whether this spirituality is expressed in terms of organised religion or through a moral code, many such families gain strength through a belief in a higher power that can influence their lives.

✳ Coping with crises and stress. Strong families are good at keeping problems in perspective and handling them by focusing on the positive elements and by pulling together, seeking outside help when it is needed. Their ability to communicate freely, their respect for individual choice and a strong base of spiritual health are important assets in dealing with crises and in enabling them to resolve conflicts among themselves.

Exploring and recording personal and family values helps individual family members relate to the group and develop a sense of shared purpose, and a family's core values provide the foundation for meaningful family (and business) plans. The next section goes into more detail and looks at how other qualities of strong families – especially open communication – contribute to how they plan their relationship with the business.

Ingredients of successful planning

A family can significantly improve its chances of success by planning its future together, establishing clear policies governing its relationship with the business and defining the responsibilities of family members. The process of developing a family strategic plan helps families approach their businesses in a committed, unified way, rather than as a group of individuals who just happen to be related. The chances of misunderstanding are greatly reduced when the objectives and rules are clear, and the rules are much more likely to be adhered to if they are arrived at through consensus rather than imposed by edict.

Planning is more complicated for family firms than it is for other businesses. As well as business strategy, plans are needed for leadership and ownership succession, financial planning for family members, and what John Ward calls 'the family continuity plan', which he describes as 'the glue that holds all the other plans together':[11]

> It is the core plan. It comprises the family's vision for itself and defines the family's mission. It answers such questions as 'What do we want to accomplish together as a family? How will we get there? How does owning a business together help us to get to where we want to go as a family?' A strong and compelling commitment to preparing a future for the family makes all of the rest of the pieces fall into place. It gives family members the motivation and energy to do the work as well as the purpose for which to do it.

Establishing open communication

Members of family businesses often think they are communicating in a full and frank manner, but on many occasions they are not. A strategic plan for the family is essential if misunderstandings are to be avoided.

The importance of direct communication between family members is impossible to overstate. The ability to share open and frequent communication has been highlighted as one of the hallmarks of strong, coping families, and indeed family businesses are often owned by such families.

Unfortunately, however, quality communication can be in short supply in family companies. The problem has been described well by business leader Sir John Harvey-Jones in relation to a number of the firms he examined in the *Troubleshooter* series of television programmes:[12]

> Family businesses, where everyone enjoys working together and where there is a great deal of mutual respect for each individual's contribution ... can suffer from a lack of frankness. It can sometimes happen that the bonds of love and respect are so strong that individuals are constrained from saying what they really feel, for fear of treading on someone else's cherished aspirations.

Sir John made these comments in the context of discussions with real families which may account for the measured and diplomatic flavour of his analysis. The reality is often rather different, in that family business people generally dislike the idea of working through family issues and difficulties – they find it hard to talk about them, let alone analyse what is going wrong and what needs to be done to ensure that problems do not interfere with the efficient functioning of the business. There is often a forbidden agenda covering a variety of potentially sensitive family issues that might generate unpleasant conflict. Despite the fact that many family conflicts can only be truly resolved if they are tackled early enough, the unspoken understanding is to let sleeping dogs lie. This is why family businesses have survival problems – the weight of unresolved, unacknowledged conflict can be so heavy that the business suffocates beneath it.

Furthermore, the secretive management style of many owners can further inhibit communication. The origins of this desire for secrecy are difficult to unravel: some owners say they feel guilty about accumulating a disproportionate amount of wealth compared with their employees; with others it relates to their excessive need for control which, at least in part, can be maintained by severely rationing information. Yet it is the owner who usually suffers most as a result of this secrecy. Rather than sharing family-related business problems with the family and gaining their support in resolving them, the owner bears the burden alone, while an atmosphere is created that fosters rumour and speculation, allowing frustrations and tensions to build.

It is possible for families to improve their communication skills. Tips include organising thoughts before speaking, listening, not rushing to judgement, practising give-and-take, using paraphrasing to confirm understanding, asking for and providing feedback. Because families know each other so well, relatives are especially attuned to relying on non-verbal cues to meaning, such as body language, so, in the words of Jean Kahwajy, professor of organisational behaviour at IMD, in family businesses 'it's not what's said that's important, but what's heard'.[13] (As the *Talmud* says: 'We do not see things as they are; we see them as we are. We do not hear things as they are; we hear them as we are.') It is also worth taking particular care to avoid miscommunications, such as hidden messages (skirting around the issue), misattributions (hearing hidden messages) and projecting ideas and values on to other people. Remember to tailor communications to be appropriate to both the message itself and to the receiver – that is, a different approach is needed depending on your assessment of who you are dealing with. Also, giving thought to the appropriate times and places for communication often pays dividends.

The blend of family and business is demanding and complicated in the best of circumstances, and impossible in the worst. However, if family members can learn to communicate and share with each other their thinking about the important issues the family must face up to, and if the next generation have a forum in which they can express their opinions openly and take part in policy-making, it is possible for the family to develop a cohesive approach to the business. In seeking to achieve this aim, establishing organised procedures and a formal framework in which dialogue can take place is an important step[14] (this is discussed from page 64).

Creative versus destructive conflict

Developing a strategic family plan will touch on many sensitive and difficult issues for family members and working towards a consensus is likely sometimes to lead to heated debates. At these moments it will help to bear in mind the distinction between constructive conflict, where different perspectives are accepted and appreciated, and where debate can lead to positive, creative outcomes, and destructive conflict, which generally centres on disputes about personal identity, relationships and history, and where debate leads nowhere. The most effective families focus on methods to manage differences rather than deal with conflict *per se*.

Take rivalry, for example, which is encountered in many families. With constructive rivalry, people challenge and confront each other, but they still listen to and respect each other. They usually have complementary skills and they also bring in humour, which can ease tension and rebuild the family bond. But when rivalry becomes destructive no one is really listening, ideas are not developed, and fighting takes over from co-operation and problem solving.

We saw in the section on characteristics of strong families (pages 54–6) that they often exhibit an acceptance of differences and respect for personal choice while working towards shared goals. An important aspect of this is that conflict is not necessarily viewed as an obstacle to communication. Indeed, Kahwajy sees conflict as a necessary prerequisite to 'a conversation':[15]

> People ought not to wish for the absence of conflict, but rather to realize that conflict is the mechanism that invites discussion; it provides a basis for conversation by offering the potential for updated understanding. ... Communication boils down to the understanding of difference – in knowledge, in intimacy. Conversation truly begins when two people hold their own views but maintain an openness to hearing new ideas and potentially have these new ideas update their understanding. ... Healthy, productive communication merely requires the willing participation of both parties who must want and struggle to achieve mutual understanding.

The goal for the family's planning process is consensus, but, unhelpfully, dictionary definitions of 'consensus' do not to go much further than 'agreement'. The notion is so central to developing effective communication and teamwork in family firms, and for implementing a successful family plan, that it is important to try to pin down some ingredients of what consensus adds up to in practice. During his time at the University of Pennsylvania's Wharton School, Peter Davis interviewed leaders of the US Quaker religious community, asking them what consensus – obviously an important tenet for this peace-loving movement – meant to them. The main responses included:

✳ an understanding of, and unity with, the ideals of the organisation that make consensus rather than majority rule preferable;

✳ an understanding of group individuals and their idiosyncrasies;

✳ a deep commitment to listening;

✳ a sense of trust in the validity of each member's contribution;

✳ an openness to learn from those who may be better informed;

✳ a conviction that individual knowledge untempered by group wisdom is often shallow;

✳ a willingness to undertake self-examination, particularly when a compromise between an individual's own point of view and the point of view of the group has the potential to lead to consensus.

Building family teamwork

Another helpful perspective on the components for successful planning by the family concerns the need for families to work hard on improving their team effectiveness. Amy Edmondson, a professor at Harvard Business School and a member of the Families in Business Program, had some interesting thoughts on this issue when she addressed a recent UK family business conference.[16]

The big challenge is that the conditions that are generally prescribed as helpful for achieving effective teamwork are not always found in family teams. For example, the ideal conditions for teamwork include goal clarity, role clarity and members having complementary skills and experience. But for families in business the family goal is not always clear, members have multiple roles (such as management and ownership), which often leads to role confusion, and the mix of skills and experience is not selected into a family by deliberate design.

Research shows that when teams face challenging situations – meaning situations where there are differing viewpoints, high stakes and uncertainty (such as when families sit down together to plan their relationship with the business) – their responses fall into five advocacy-oriented categories:

	Question	Advocacy orientation
1	How to play the game	Win by gaining converts to your point of view
2	How to win	Forcefully and confidently advocate your point of view
3	Spontaneous view of team members who disagree	They are competitors
4	Strategy for dealing with gaps in your argument	Hide them
5	Response to dissent	Find it annoying and suppress it

In a typical team where these advocacy dynamics are going on, the result is that team members become frustrated and start to become personal, progress grinds to a halt, and people begin to withdraw and give up on the team and the whole process of teamwork.

Edmondson went on to propose an alternative to this advocacy approach – an enquiry orientation. Team members, alone and collaboratively, explore other points of view. The shared goal is to collectively arrive at the best possible solution rather than implicitly to get converts to 'my solution'. Note the contrast with the previous table:

	Question	Enquiry orientation
1	How to play the game	Propose your point of view as a point of view; explore others' views; experiment with different points of view
2	How to win	Collectively arrive at the best solution
3	Spontaneous view of team members who disagree	They are collaborators
4	Strategy for dealing with gaps in your argument	Reveal them
5	Response to dissent	Seek out and welcome it; examine its implications

So team members need to explain and explore their own and each other's reasoning, including the information they regard as more important or less important, their interpretations of that information and their conclusions. These skills, academically termed 'advocacy and enquiry', are more colloquially called 'explaining and asking' or 'explaining and exploring', and along with one extra ingredient – acknowledgement – they underpin a more effective approach to teamwork in the face of challenging situations. Balancing advocacy with enquiry and acknowledgement involves:

✳ Enquiry: What is the other's story?
 – What do they see?
 – What are you missing?

✳ Acknowledgement: Show others you understand.
 – Paraphrase what you have heard.
 – Empathise with their feelings.

✳ Advocacy: What is your story?
 – What do you see?
 – What are they missing?

This change of emphasis is what Edmondson calls a 'shift from certainty to authentic curiosity'. So at family meetings when our inner voice is saying 'They're wrong' (stubborn, manipulative and so on), we must translate this to 'I wonder why they see it differently? What's their data? What's their reasoning?' This engages our internal voice to be motivated to enquire and understand what is going on. Genuine curiosity leads us into effective conversations in challenging situations, and effective conversations lead to more successful family teamwork, improved relationships and better planning and problem solving.[17]

Unifying plans, processes and structures

The aim of the planning process, as we have seen, is to formulate and adopt policies that strike a good balance between the best interests of the business and the well-being of the family, and then to design and establish effective governance structures to underpin these policies.

Policies should cover the critical area of family–business relationships, such as the involvement of family members in the business, share ownership and management succession. A list of the factors that are likely to merit consideration at this stage of the planning process is set out in Table 3.1, and the most important are discussed in detail at appropriate points elsewhere in the book.

Table 3.1 Checklist for developing a successful family protocol or constitution

Factor	Considerations
What is the business for?	✳ Work opportunities for the next generation?
	✳ Wealth creation?
	✳ To build a family legacy?
Values and vision	✳ What are the family's core values?
	✳ What is the family's vision for the future, for family members and for the business?
	✳ What is the family's business philosophy?
Long-term goals	✳ What are the growth aspirations for the business?
	✳ How committed is the family to business ownership?
	✳ Keep the business in the family?
	✳ Sell it eventually?
Management philosophy	✳ Is the business a meritocracy, an autocracy, an ad-hocracy (governed on an entirely ad-hoc basis) or is it run for the benefit of the family?
	✳ A combination of these – and if so what is that combination?

Factor	Considerations
Family members in the business	✳ Do family members want to work for the business, or do they want the business to work for them?
	✳ What should be the criteria for entry?
	✳ Should in-laws be allowed to join?
	✳ How will the roles of family members be determined?
	✳ How should family members be remunerated?
	✳ How should their performance be evaluated?
	✳ What if family members do not perform up to appropriate standards?
	✳ At what point should family members retire?
Share ownership	✳ Do shareholders regard themselves as owners of an asset that they seek to maximise, or as stewards and custodians of the shares (which are perhaps placed in trust) for the next generation?
	✳ If the shares are viewed as a realisable capital investment, is everyone aware of this and are exit procedures in place for owners who want to cash in?
	✳ Are the shares seen as a non-transferable trust for future generations?
	✳ If so, is everyone aware of this and is the company geared up to provide income and pension rights in place of capital asset status for the shares?
	✳ Who will be allowed to own shares in the company?
	✳ Who should have voting control?
	✳ What should the dividend policy be?
	✳ What will happen as regards share ownership in the next generation?
	✳ Should family members who are working in the business be treated differently from those who are not?
Management succession	✳ What should be the criteria for selecting the next leader (or leaders)?
	✳ When will the transition take place?
	✳ What should be done if the choice is wrong?
	✳ What are the owner's aspirations after stepping down?
	✳ How can the family help the owner to achieve them?

Factor	Considerations
Drop-dead arrangements	✳ What happens if the owner/business leader is run over by a bus this afternoon?
	✳ Are arrangements in place to cover this eventuality, and does everyone know about them?
	✳ What effect will the accident have on the business?
Relationships within the family	✳ What responsibilities do family members have towards each other?
	✳ What is the best way to ensure an atmosphere that enhances mutual respect and support?
	✳ How should intra-family differences be dealt with?
Other matters	✳ Should the business have independent directors?
	✳ If so, how should the family relate to them?
	✳ How can the family protect the security of loyal employees?
	✳ What role should the business have in the community?

Designing family governance

Defining policies should be followed by action planning, including the identification of family members responsible for implementing aspects of the plan, timetabling the plan, and deciding how implementation is to be monitored and evaluated. A major next step will be to establish processes and forums whereby family issues can be openly discussed and constructively managed.

This is a complicated area. A variety of concepts, co-ordinating structures and committees can be designed and tailored to help families create organised accountability among the different interests and priorities of ownership, the family and the business. A lot of attention will be devoted to these later in the book – in particular in Chapter 6 on the board of directors and Chapter 7 on governance in multigenerational, cousin-owned businesses. Here, however, the aim is to introduce the basic ideas, principles and structures of family governance in a straightforward way, often with younger family businesses in mind, so as to provide a platform to build upon later.

Family council

The establishment of a family council provides an organised forum for family members to participate in the development of their strategic plan and in future policy-making. They have a chance (perhaps for the first time) to start tackling the forbidden agenda and to lay down some clear ground rules governing their ownership of, and involvement in, the family business.

The principal issues for consideration by the family council will be strategic, including maintaining shared values and vision for the family and the business; creating stronger bonds among family members; inputting into important business decisions; and setting policies for entering and leaving the business. Even if all family members do not agree on every question, they at least have a voice in the process, and in many ways the setting up of this process is the key step – as well as providing a structured opportunity for the family to assess and organise its relationship to the business, it puts needed pressure on individual family members to face up to emotional issues that, uncontrolled, can damage the business.

A good example concerned a long-standing and profitable clothes retailer where ownership was divided between a mother and her six children. The mother owned 76 per cent and the children each owned 4 per cent. One of the siblings had the job description style director, and he was responsible for the design and layout of the company's retail outlets. The way he did his job was a long-standing cause of friction among the siblings. He would turn up at the office at about 11 am, work for an hour and a half or so, go out for a long lunch, get back at about 3.30 pm, stay for an hour and then go home. His siblings, however, were all working 45–50 hours a week and, despite the fact that he was excellent at his job, the style director became a major cause of resentment. The other siblings had discussed this among themselves but had never raised it with the style director.

Following interviews with all the people involved, it was clear to the family business consultant that this had become a seriously divisive issue for the family and that it should top the agenda at the first meeting of the newly established family council. The agenda item came as a surprise to the style director, but he stood up as the meeting got under way and said:

> I should like to make my position clear at the start so that everyone knows where I stand. I'm very happy working in the business and I think I do a good job. I know some of you are upset that I work funny hours and I don't seem to work as hard as you, but let me say this – I'm only prepared to work the hours I work. However, I guarantee I'll do the job to the best of my ability. If I don't achieve the targets you've set me then please fire me. But if my results are OK, I can only

do my work here in my own way, and if that's unacceptable to you I will go and do it for someone else. It is your call.

The style director won over his siblings and secured unanimous support at the family council meeting. This family business problem was therefore solved, not by any change in working practices – supposedly the source of the friction – but as a result of discussing openly at the family council meeting a previously unspoken grievance.

An interesting corporate governance side issue involved in this case was that, with 76 per cent, clearly the mother formally controlled the business. So there was some disillusionment among the children, with their 4 per cent each, about the idea of setting up family council meetings because 'Mum will decide whatever we do or say'. The mother was told about this feeling and at the first meeting she announced to her children that all family council decisions were to be made on the basis of 'one arm, one vote'. Suddenly, the 'elephant' was removed from the room, and the family council became a meaningful forum for all the children.

As regards the composition of the family council, some prefer to limit inclusion to family members who are active in the business. However, unless there are persuasive reasons to the contrary, the general rule is that the council is most effective when both passive and active family members are included. All family members, whether directly or indirectly, have a stake in the business and it is best if everyone is fully involved from the start – the objective, after all, is to establish a unified and cohesive family approach to the business. An exception to the general rule sometimes arises where a family council comprises representatives from a number of different families, as can happen with long-established family firms (see Chapter 7). In these cases the chances of achieving consensus can often be improved by restricting family council membership to just the key players.

Sometimes the best decisions for a business are wrong for the family that owns and runs it. As owners, they may set goals for the business that on first examination run contrary to established business practice. Family councils are the most appropriate forum for discussions of such intangible and possibly idealistic targets. These may include such diverse aims as reinforcing a corporate culture reflecting family values; providing an opportunity to involve other family members – offspring, spouses, and so on – in common family interests and goals; and the maintenance of family tradition, status or craftsmanship.

To sum up, the key benefit of a family council is the contribution it can make to family unity and consensus. Opening the channels of communication and separating the discussions from day-to-day family and business affairs allows family members to focus on positive aspects of family relationships, abilities and successes. There is a tendency in all relationships to allow problem areas to loom large, obscuring what is right and what works. The family council is a chance for the family to correct this imbalance and reaffirm their commitment to each other, to family values and to the business.

Family retreats

An excellent starting point for a family council is a one- or two-day residential retreat, with relatives gathering in a quiet environment away from the everyday surroundings of job and home. A non-confrontational atmosphere will help them to discuss their future in a constructive way, and all the main issues in the family strategic plan (summarised in Table 3.1 on page 62) should be on the agenda, perhaps with the aim of writing up the conclusions of the discussion in a draft of the family's constitution (see below).

The chances of a successful retreat are greatly improved by asking an impartial person from outside the business and the family to act as a facilitator. A facilitator will help the family to discuss the issues in an informed and logical way, guide family members as they seek a consensus, and help them draw together their decisions and codify the results. The process can be painful: indeed it can often be said about such retreats that 'if there's no pain, there's no gain'. But the discomfort usually goes away quickly, especially when those involved discover the liberating effects of discussing and resolving previously taboo issues.

Lastly, and on a practical note, a wise facilitator will ensure that accurate notes are taken of everything discussed and decided at the retreat – as has already been mentioned, selective amnesia is common among family business people. (The role of family business advisers and consultants is considered in more detail in Chapter 5.)

Family constitution

An excellent idea is for families to record the conclusions of their planning in a written family constitution (sometimes also called a protocol or creed) – essentially a statement of intent that spells out the family's policies in relation to the business. In smaller firms (say just three or four family members) this may represent overkill, and indeed 'family constitution' can sometimes be a rather grand title in situations where a smaller-scale 'family action plan' may be more appropriate, setting out policies on just a few fundamental issues. But for bigger family businesses there are serious benefits to be had from a detailed family constitution that lays down ground rules for many years to come. In these cases, the constitution is a powerful tool in helping to ensure long-term ownership.

The constitution should, as a minimum, codify the family's position on the practical issues listed in Table 3.1, such as family jobs, management succession and share ownership. But some families take the opportunity to go further, making their constitution into a much more substantial document – a sort of mission statement that records the family's agreed stance, not just in relation to the business, but also on its values and vision, and on a range of moral, ethical and philanthropic issues.

This extension of the family's original purpose is often the product of a detailed process of examination. Initially, discussion centres on seeking out common ground in relation to business issues. Once this level of consensus has been achieved, however, an appreciation often develops among family members that their ability to agree on business questions reflects the fact that, at a deeper level, they share a common set of ethical, moral and spiritual beliefs and values. This realisation strengthens feelings of family bonding, and helps the family arrive at an agreed constitution that they see as symbolising their commitment and their pride.

Newcastle-based Ringtons Holdings provides a good example of this. In its fifth generation, the group's main trading activity is tea importing, blending, packaging and distribution (including a unique system of door-to-door sales and delivery) and, in 2005, it won the family governance award under the JPMorgan Family Business Honours Programme. The programme case study gives the flavour of the company's stance on family governance:[18]

> Ringtons' approach to family governance is purposeful and well thought through. At the same time, it is organic and does not have formalisation as its prime attribute. Family members have the ability to make changes to the system according to a defined procedure of amendment.

What supports these rules – and arguably drives the company – is a comprehensive, leather-bound *Family Guide*, with 'To be a strong and united family' inscribed on its cover. The mission statement at the start of the guide reads:

> To develop policies, procedures, and activities which provide equality, support and opportunity towards the individual development needs of family members.

After sections on company history and values, it goes on to provide a statement of rules for family members covering succession, a shareholder agreement, a statement of principles, the articles of association, prenuptial agreements and policies regarding philanthropy and education of young family members. Unusually, it also includes separate vision statements for the family and the business, denoting the equal emphasis placed on family values and profitability.[19]

Formulating a family constitution – even a much less elaborate document than the Ringtons' *Family Guide* – is a significant undertaking. It is time-consuming (usually a matter of months, sometimes longer) and, if the process is to be successful, a major commitment is necessary from everyone involved. For GMR Group, an Indian infrastructure business, for example, drawing up the family constitution was an intensive and lengthy exercise. Founded by Grandhi Mallikarjuna Rao in 1976, GMR started life as a single jute mill, and has since expanded into manufacturing (mainly ferro-alloys and sugar) and infrastructure (including power generation, road building and airport projects). GMR now has an asset base of some Rs25 billion ($560 million). Rao's two sons and his son-in-law also work in the business as group directors, and a decision was taken in the late 1990s that, if future generations were to remain involved in a successful group, steps were needed to professionalise the business and build a sound foundation for family involvement.

Guided by a family business facilitator, the process of agreeing the family constitution involved 14 family meetings held over a three-year period. First, the Rao family decided on the list of issues to be addressed in their constitution, which they then prioritised and – depending on subject matter – assigned to three different working groups tasked to develop the detailed content of policies. Regular family meetings were then organised (usually held as retreats outside Bangalore) to discuss the policy recommendations of each working group. The meetings also defined the family's vision for the future and dealt with emotional issues, aiming to help clarify relationships and foster family unity. The result – three years down the line – was a comprehensive family constitution incorporating the family's core values, its governance structure, a family code of conduct, ownership policies, and the family's agreed civil, political and philanthropic agenda.[20] (Further information on GMR's interesting family governance structures and its approach to succession planning are discussed in Chapter 7, page 140, Chapter 8, page 161.)

It is also an all-or-nothing process – to a significant extent the points in the checklist are interlinked and interdependent, and it is not generally possible to formulate policies on some of them while ignoring the others. Another guideline is that, after it has been drafted and before signature, the constitution should be left on the table for six months or so to allow the family to reflect on whether they are comfortable with the conclusions of their work and planning. So immediately signing the document and then tucking it away in a drawer is not enough – the constitution must be lived.

In the end, of course, it is possible that not all family members will agree with every provision of the constitution, but at least the rules have been thought about, discussed, written down and are clear, and the family can avoid the turmoil that so easily results from ambiguity. The retreat, discussed earlier, should be the beginning rather than the end of family communication. A timetable should be set for future meetings, to be held at least annually, at which the constitution can be reviewed and, if necessary, amended.

Family constitutions are discussed in more detail in Chapter 7 in the context of family governance in complex multigenerational family businesses.

Conclusions

That the discussion of family strategic planning in this chapter has centred on process is important. Every family business is different and, for individual firms, there are really no right or wrong answers or hard-and-fast rules. Instead there are certain guiding principles, approaches and problem-solving techniques that need to be applied flexibly. Sensitivity and cultivating a light touch are important for everyone involved in the process because, underlying virtually all the issues, are the goals, values and emotional susceptibilities of the individual people involved.

But a light touch must not translate into an absence of commitment. Indeed, family strategic planning requires a family member at the company to take the lead, champion the process and galvanise fellow family members. Without broad-based commitment and enthusiasm the process will not work. So a straightforward, routine series of meetings will not be enough. What is required is nothing short of a comprehensive plan that allows the family to achieve four large-scale objectives:

1 To establish open, direct and frequent communication between family members.

2 To begin to unravel unresolved or unacknowledged conflicts.

3 To assess and organise the family's relationship to the business.

4 To clarify and define the conclusions of the planning process with sufficient precision for them to be written down in a family constitution.

Families entering into this process need a high level of commitment and a willingness to talk to one another frankly and grapple with taboo issues such as old rivalries. They should also be prepared for a fair amount of discomfort, and sometimes pain. The rewards are substantial, however. Families that successfully negotiate the minefield talk of feelings of personal liberation and a fresh start for the family. More to the point from a commercial standpoint, such families have taken a major step to ensuring the success of their family business and its survival for future generations.

4

The next generation

Human resource management and leadership perspectives

uccession between generations in family businesses is less straightforward than it used to be. Today's generation is growing up in a commercial culture that is radically different from that in which earlier family members took on responsibility. Increasingly well-educated, cosmopolitan and independent, they are less willing to be viewed as the automatic heir apparent. Furthermore, in recent years businesses have come to be seen more as disposable commodities – to be started up, grown and then sold – making it harder for young people to identify with the idea of the family business as a sacred trust for future generations. The advantages and disadvantages of joining the family firm are therefore being weighed much more carefully.

In this chapter we also revisit family business systems theory, which once again provides excellent problem-solving insights. We saw in Chapter 2 how family values and rules of conduct are based on emotional considerations, while business values and behaviour emphasise successfully carrying out tasks. Conflict between the systems is particularly acute in relation to personnel issues in family firms: for instance, employing family members even though an outsider might be brought in who could do the job better, how to judge dispassionately the work performance of family members, and so on. We look at the human resource management problems raised by the clash of systems, and suggest some strategies for coping with them.

To join or not to join?

The next generation joining a family business have a unique opportunity to build a challenging and enriching career for themselves. The advantages of their situation are obvious. The business is already up and running. It offers job security and probably an attractive remuneration package. Working in a family business can be extremely rewarding. These businesses often possess a unique atmosphere that encourages a sense of belonging, there is extra commitment to a common purpose, and they provide a way to perpetuate the family's values, traditions and business heritage. Also, from a personal standpoint, family members enjoy a special status both inside and outside the firm, and it is a distinct possibility that one day they may become owners of the business.

Nevertheless, there is a price to be paid for all this. Family businesses are usually not diversified multinationals that can more easily withstand downturns in some of their markets. There must always be a doubt about whether the business will survive in the long term, and if family members are looking for this type of career security, the family business may not be right for them. If the younger generation join for the wrong reasons – searching for a safe haven, for example, or because they have not thought through the emotional complexities of family business life and the commitment required, or because they have been pressured into joining by parents – it is likely to be a decision they will regret.

Parental pressure to join the family business can be subtle and powerful, and the decision whether or not to enlist is generally the junior generation's first introduction to the emotional dilemmas that arise when business and family values overlap and contradict each other. They generally feel an enormous sense of responsibility to their parents and wider family, who may have devoted a lifetime's work to building the family firm, but at the same time the natural progression is to separate and make their own way in the world. These conflicting options can create emotional torment. Research indicates that most business families do not adequately anticipate the challenges that the next generation will face in balancing responsibility to the family with their own career aspirations. As a result, next-generation members often feel under pressure and are poorly prepared to resolve these issues.[1]

British poet Sir John Betjeman, in his autobiographical poem *Summoned by Bells*, recalls having repeatedly to turn down his father's requests that he should take over control of the family's luxury cabinet-making business. Ernest Betjeman was the third-generation leader of the business and, despite John's decision early in childhood that he would become a poet, he never gave up pressuring his only child to join the business. He told John time and again that all the firm's employees looked to him, as the fourth generation, to safeguard the company's future, and on each occasion John, with growing feelings of guilt and self-reproach, had to turn down his father's pleading. With emotional blackmail high on the list of tactics, this campaign was eventually to see father and son divided and estranged. Some ten years after Ernest's death in 1934, the business he and his forebears had built up was liquidated. During those years John did his best to help out when asked – for example, writing some advertising copy for the firm's products – but there was clearly no question of him taking over. Some of the employees who lost their jobs were bitterly resentful: 'John Betjeman let a great business go to rack and ruin,' said one senior employee.[2] The irony is that it is hard to imagine anyone less suited to a business career, let alone family business leadership, than John Betjeman – the firm would surely have found itself insolvent far sooner with him in control. But, of course, such realities have no bearing on the guilt endured by a next-generation family member, encouraged to feel they are to blame for letting down parents, family tradition, the family business and the firm's loyal employees.

Next-generation family members should ask themselves some serious questions before they decide whether or not to join. What are the reasons behind the decision? Does the business offer the sort of career I want? Will it be possible for me to live up to the senior generation's expectations? Will I be able to establish my own independence and freedom to act, or will I always be operating in the shadow of my predecessors? How will I get along with the senior generation when we have to work closely together everyday? I know my parents as Mum and Dad, not as boss – will they behave differently towards me at work? (This is a particularly pertinent question for second-generation family members working with the founder.) Can I establish working relationships with my brothers and sisters, or will there be too much arguing and conflict? Will the employees respect me?

When family members do decide to join, it is important they make sure their entry deal is at arm's length and covers all the standard points such as remuneration, a proper job description, performance appraisal, and so on. If they were taking a job at an FTSE 100 company, they would expect a comprehensive service contract setting out the terms of employment, and there is no reason to expect less when joining the family business. In fact, because of all the potential for emotional blackmail, procrastination and selective amnesia in family business life, negotiating a sensible and clear entry deal is essential.

It is also important for new entrants to try to plan their career with the senior generation, discussing the latter's ambitions for the firm and how they see the timetable for the future. If next-generation members are unsure about what to do, they should endeavour to get the seniors' support for trying other options. Acquiring some outside business experience beforehand is almost always a good idea, and considering entering

There is evidence that today's senior generation are less likely to count on their children as automatic successors

on a trial basis is another possibility. It is better to have this sort of discussion early on before juniors have invested several years of their lives and seniors have invested time and effort in training. Remember also that founders especially may have been building up their hopes and expectations for many years that their offspring will join the firm, eventually taking over and continuing the dream. If next-generation members think the family business really is not for them, it is much better if this is talked about openly at an early stage to limit the founder's disappointment and to provide time to plan other options. Once again – as with so many family business issues – thinking about how best to manage the expectations of family members is important.

However, there is evidence that today's senior generation are less likely to count on their children as automatic successors. There are also concerns about the long-term welfare of the business in circumstances where successors have grown up believing that they will inherit the shares as a matter of right, rather than having to tangibly demonstrate their level of commitment. One solution to this involves the next generation being given some shares, but only on condition that they purchase the balance of their eventual holding. The need to find, say, £1 million for 35 per cent of the company as a condition for receiving the remaining 65 per cent for nothing could become an increasingly common requirement. It would obviously help offspring decide just how serious their commitment and desire to join the family firm really are.

The importance of outside experience

In advising family businesses, so much depends on the unique history and idiosyncrasies of individual firms that universal truths are in short supply. So on the rare occasions they do crop up they deserve to be highlighted. A golden rule is that before entering the family business, the next generation should take adequate time to work and to prove themselves in the outside world. There are various reasons for this.

Self-esteem and confidence

Succeeding at something alone, away from the family nest, helps individuals build self-esteem and confidence in their own abilities. If the decision later on is to join the family firm, the experience will provide extra role perspective, helping family members to establish their own identity and to succeed on their own merits. And if they choose to leave the firm at some stage, they will have the comfort of knowing they have already proved that they can compete in a world in which the required qualifications extend beyond having the right surname.

This outside experience need not be confined to working in another organisation (although this offers particular benefits that will be discussed later). The new generation should also consider acquiring general business qualifications, perhaps enrolling for a business studies course or an MBA. Nowadays there is no shortage of such courses to choose from, many including specific modules or programmes designed for family business owners.

Wider business experience

Learning how other firms work will almost certainly benefit next-generation family members throughout their business career. A larger, more professionally managed company than their family's should be the target, preferably, although not necessarily, in the same industry. Moving straight from full-time education into the family business can only increase its natural potential to become introverted, whereas outside experience is likely to generate a fund of ideas to bring back to the family firm, helping to make it more extrovert and flexible.

This might include new production or marketing methods, or administrative or strategic planning techniques that will assist in professionalising the business more quickly and more effectively. There is a lot to be said for learning management skills in an objective atmosphere outside the family company.

An aspect of this is the need to ensure that family members aspiring to leadership are growing at least as fast, if not faster, than the business. At one company that matured some 35 years ago with a £3 million turnover, the family chairman realised he needed external help and skills to continue to grow the business. He employed and motivated a non-family professional management team, which in a little over a decade succeeded in growing annual turnover close to £700 million. Both the family chairman, in post for the past 30 years, and the junior generation working in the business (and, early on in their careers, thinking they might one day lead it) watched their company being transformed. It is now so large and complex that family member involvement is limited to non-executive directorships and to being investors rather than managers. In effect, stratospheric business growth left family members behind.

Credibility with non-family employees

A next-generation son or daughter who leaves school or university and straightaway becomes deputy managing director of the family business is likely to generate derision and resentment among non-family employees. This can manifest itself as resentment not only against the individual concerned but also against the whole family. Feelings can run so high in this type of situation that key non-family managers simply walk out, placing the survival of the business in jeopardy.

A family member's credibility will be enhanced if they enter the business with some experience under their belt. The fact that they will need to earn employee respect rather than having it freely given is discussed later. They will have taken quite a few steps along this path if, when they enter the family firm, the employees know that on their own initiative they went out and joined another organisation, gaining first-hand experience of the real world of work.

For some reason, this is one of those pieces of advice that almost everyone agrees with but far fewer take advantage of. Peter Davis tells an interesting story from his time at the University of Pennsylvania's Wharton School. At the start of each academic year, he explained the fundamental importance of outside experience to his new undergraduate class of young people from family businesses. Throughout the course, he stressed the point and explained the advantages summarised here, and at the end of the semester asked: 'OK, of you 25 students, how many of you now are going to get some experience outside before joining the family business?' Usually about three hands went up. Davis then asked: 'What happened to the other 22 – were you not listening?' The response was: 'You don't understand professor, I'm a special case.'

So most people feel that their situation is special, and that they have uniquely important reasons for entering the firm straight away. If next-generation family members find themselves thinking this way, it is well worthwhile to think again.

Systems overlap and human resource management issues

Once again problems arise because of the ambiguous position of family firms, forced to inhabit the dangerous no man's land at the border between two different social systems: family and business. The analysis of these systems in Chapter 2 showed how family values and rules of conduct are based on emotional considerations favouring the care and development of the family, while business values and behaviour emphasise performance and results and are based on successfully carrying out tasks.

Conflict between the systems is particularly acute and troublesome in relation to personnel practices: for example, employing family members even though an outsider might be brought in who could do the job better, deciding whether to pay family members a market rate or a family rate for the job, and how to judge their performance. This section examines the problems family businesses face in the areas of recruitment, remuneration, appraisal, and so on, highlighting the difficulties to look out for and suggesting some strategies for coping with them.

Table 4.1 provides an overview of the clash between family and business values that apply to the main human resource management issues in family businesses. These issues will be looked at individually, but the main point to stress here is that the different behavioural standards that apply in the family and business systems are, to a greater or lesser extent, contradictory. The contradictions, and the conflicts they create, are built into the fabric of family businesses and, as with similar problems looked at elsewhere in this book, there are few, if any, easy solutions.

Nor does the structural nature of the conflicts reduce the personal impact they can have on senior-generation family members (especially founders) who generally suffer their effects most. They come with the job, and the psychological stress they engender can severely reduce such individuals' ability to manage the family firm effectively.

Table 4.1 Overlapping systems and human resource management

	Family values	Business values
Recruitment	Provide opportunities to relatives in need (particularly if they are your children)	Hire only those individuals who are most competent
Training	Provide learning opportunities designed to satisfy individuals' developmental needs	Provide learning opportunities designed to satisfy organisational needs
Remuneration	Allocate allowances in accordance with policies not dependent on the business; for example, need or equality	Allocate salaries/benefits in accordance with market worth and performance history
Appraisal	Do not differentiate between siblings. Regard individuals as ends rather than means	Differentiate between employees to identify the high performers. Regard individuals more as means than as ends

Source: Adapted from Ivan Lansberg (1983) 'Managing human resources in family firms: The problem of institutional overlap', *Organizational Dynamics*, Summer, pp.39–46.

Recruitment

Family principles dictate that unconditional help should be provided to family members and other relatives in need. Thus typically, and regardless of ability or expertise, positions of authority within the family business are reserved for family members who, for their part, often feel they have a right to a job in the company. We have also seen that many senior-generation individuals expect their adult offspring to join the family business and commit their working lives to it, notwithstanding the fact that they may lack the aptitude or the talent, or both, to be successful.

As far as the standards and values that govern business behaviour are concerned, recruitment policies based on heredity or the provision of a safe haven are, of course, anathema. Business principles demand that only people who are the most competent and suited for the job should be employed. Ignoring these yardsticks and hiring individuals according to their family status would seem to represent a clear threat to the firm's effectiveness and, ultimately, its survival.

However, in a recent reappraisal of family business theories, John Ward has suggested that negative assumptions about nepotism and family firms may have been taken too far.[3] He argues that the distinct, concentrated ownership groups of family companies are one of their distinguishing characteristics and sources of competitive advantage, and that the traditional view of family involvement in management as potentially hazardous is conventional wisdom that deserves to be questioned. While conceding that the issues created by nepotism are real, he goes on to argue that:[4]

> ... the direct involvement of owners in management and governance can be viewed positively as well. This close involvement enables the concentrated control characteristic of family businesses, and helps assure that ownership and business are directly linked and mutually informed. This direct, long-term connection enables challenging short-term decision-making, and reinforces a shared long-term vision and alignment of strategic goals.

Indeed, family successors may well have been schooled in the family business since childhood, and are likely to have acquired knowledge, almost by osmosis, about every aspect of its operations. It can also be argued that they often have a special passion for the business, supported by a deep understanding of its values and culture, and that all this idiosyncratic knowledge and passion together represent a key value-added component of family management successors. However, while Ward's rebalancing of the debate as a reminder of the commercial value attaching to committed family ownership and involvement may be overdue, there is a feeling that the argument is stretched perhaps a little too far. Quite a lot of idiosyncratic knowledge and passion will be needed to make an incompetent and ineffective family member into a successful manager.

With nepotism accepted by all sides as a difficult and potentially damaging issue, the fact remains that it is generally senior-generation family members who have to decide whether or not to employ a family member. If their heart is set on establishing a corporate dynasty no matter what, the decision will not be difficult. But if they place rather more weight on trying to safeguard the long-term welfare of the enterprise, they may have to face the dilemma of either employing someone not capable of doing the job or facing the wrath of the family if they choose to employ an outsider.

How to cope, and an approach to a solution

This type of predicament arises in relation to all the human resource management issues discussed in this section. This is a good place, therefore, to look at coping strategies, together with the basis for a generalised approach to family business personnel problems that can be applied beyond just the recruitment issue. First, however, let us look at how not to try to cope.

It is easy to visualise the senior generation trapped between the family system and the business system tenets set out in Table 4.1, facing powerful but conflicting pressures about the best way to resolve family-related human resource management dilemmas. Finding themselves being squeezed in this way, individuals generally opt for one of two strategies. Either they try to find a compromise between the two sets of conflicting forces, or they swing indiscriminately between strict adherence to business principles on some occasions and family principles on others. But the compromise approach often leads to decisions that are bad for the business, and the second seesaw strategy produces arbitrary and unpredictable behaviour that is incomprehensible and unsettling for both employees and family members. The two strategies share a common fundamental defect – neither is based on clear and explicit management criteria.

As mentioned at the start of this section, these contradictory pressures are built into the fabric of family businesses. The most constructive approach, therefore, rather than seeking an essentially unobtainable clear-cut solution, is to settle for trying to develop procedures that recognise and manage the contradictions. An important first step that reduces the stresses produced by the conflicts, and thus improves the senior generation's ability to manage them, is to understand and accept that they are structural, not personal problems – in short, they come with the territory.

Second, as Ivan Lansberg, an American family business expert, suggests,[5] it is helpful to explain and share the problem with both family members and senior management in the business (although beware of overburdening senior managers with family issues). This explaining and sharing shifts the focus of the predicament away from the founder and on to the family business system which, because it is a structural dilemma, is where it belongs. Involving others in this way should stimulate the development of procedures to define and separate family and business issues, encouraging collaborative problem solving among all the parties concerned.

Lansberg goes on to propose that the key to developing effective procedures for managing the contradictions lies in the separation of management and ownership. This involves:[6]

examining the relatives who work in the firm from two distinct perspectives: an 'ownership' perspective and a 'management' perspective. From an ownership perspective, relatives would be subject to all the norms and principles that regulate family relations; from a management perspective, relatives would be affected by the firm's principles.

In recruitment, the distinction would entail:[7]

accepting into the firm only those relatives who, on business grounds, were thought to possess the skills needed to perform effectively on the job. Hence from a management perspective relatives would be treated just as others are treated when they apply for a position. From an ownership point of view, on the other hand, relatives interested in working in the firm would be given the opportunity to acquire the necessary skills required to meet the firm's standards. These opportunities could take many forms, including sponsored apprenticeships in other firms, formal education, training, and so forth. The funds to cover the necessary training expenses would come from the family's assets rather than from the business. In this way relatives could be taken care of in a manner consistent with family principles, without necessarily compromising the company's sound management standards.

Confusion about who can and who cannot join the company can seriously damage family relationships. As in so many other aspects of family business life, agreeing clear criteria and guidelines that specify when family or business principles are appropriate will go a long way towards reducing the potential for conflict and promoting the effective management of human resources in family firms. The family's agreed position on personnel issues provides a clear example of the sort of policy statement that should be included in the family strategic plan (see Chapter 3).

In the light of this constructive approach to human resource management issues generally, let us briefly examine how it can apply to the other personnel practices listed in Table 4.1.

Training and development

Under family principles, family members should be trained according to what is best for them as individuals. Business norms, however, are less concerned with the flowering of well-rounded individual personalities – they demand that training and development should be based on learning experiences that improve the individual's ability to contribute to the achievement of organisational objectives. What is best for the individual and what is best for the business do not always coincide.

Moreover, the business may suffer when founders invest the company's resources to provide their offspring with an opportunity for promoting their individual well-being and development. Such laudable family projects can range from paying for a training course through to buying a company for the next generation to run, and, in either case, the exercise may at best be unrelated to promoting business goals and at worst completely incompatible with them.

Applying the ownership–management distinction, from a management viewpoint it is important that the training and development of relatives should depend on and fit in with the firm's needs. If a family member's ambitions are inconsistent with the firm's needs, he or she must choose between employment in the family business or following personal plans using family assets. In other words, from the ownership perspective family members would be entitled to draw on family assets to invest in pursuing their professional objectives outside the family business.

Remuneration

What to pay relatives who work in the family firm also creates problems. In the family system, the guiding norms are that family wealth should be distributed either according to need or according to principles that are transparently fair. In the case of siblings, for example, fairness is generally taken to mean that resources be allocated equally. But in the business, remuneration should be based on the individual's contribution.

Common causes of pay problems in family businesses include the financial carrot, where pay is used to lure family members into working for the family firm, and confusion over business and personal funds, where pay or perks are used a means of transferring money from the family business to the family. Motives often get mixed up, leading to confusion about whether payouts to family members are in return for the job or as recognition of their status as family or their role as owners. Another issue is pay substitutes – relying on perks to top up family members' pay, either all the time or as a means of placating family members who feel they are not being paid enough.

On top of all this, the British are not comfortable with discussing money generally, and personal salary or wage levels in particular. For senior-generation family members required to talk about remuneration terms with their relatives (especially their children), the word discomfort does not adequately describe the trauma involved. As a result, what relatives should be paid is generally decided on the basis of an ambiguous combination of principles – some from the family system, some from the business system – and they generate all sorts of tension and inefficiency in the company. So we find that some companies pay family members significantly more than the market rate or, more commonly, less than this rate, on the principle that they have an obligation to help out. Other firms pay all family members at the same rate, regardless of their contribution, with the likely result that incompetent relatives stay and competent ones leave the company to earn a fairer salary elsewhere.

In the case of remuneration, the problem-solving approach based on the separation of management and ownership entails rewarding relatives strictly on the basis of business principles. If desired, the ownership route can be used to boost family members' earnings independent of their role within the company – for example, by way of share dividends rather than a higher salary. Such an arrangement acknowledges the privileges of ownership but preserves a merit-based reward system in the business.

Market value of jobs

With rewards for relatives based strictly on business principles, it is important to pay family members a market rate, rather than a family rate, for the job. But how do you determine the market rate? It is possible to unpick a job to establish what it comprises, then to carry out an evaluation exercise – called salary benchmarking – involving checking what rates are paid for such a job in the wider marketplace. Issues to consider when deciding on a job's market value include the industry the company operates in; the size of the company; rates of pay for people in similar jobs; the number of people overseen by the individual; the person's contribution to turnover and/or profitability; and the cost of living in the location concerned. This can be a lengthy analytical process, and for smaller companies a more practical approach may be to establish an internal set of comparative measures for each part of a job's responsibilities.

Although quantitative market value criteria are crucial in evaluating a job, qualitative criteria are also often taken into account, covering, for instance, leadership qualities; ambassadorial qualities (that is, the extent to which a manager is required to represent the business to the outside world); mastery of the big picture; and the number and calibre of contacts the manager is required to work with, both inside and outside the company.

Whatever the remuneration policy details that are finally chosen, they should be clearly spelled out so that they are understood by all family members inside the business, as well as by those who might be contemplating joining. It is also worth considering the establishment of a remuneration committee of the board. If the committee deals with everyone's salaries, this encourages the feeling that remuneration is being approached in a systematic, even-handed way – a perception that will be reinforced if the committee includes some non-executive directors among its members.

Performance appraisal and promotion

Most employees want to know what is expected of them and want feedback on how they are doing. If this is carried out constructively, areas that need improvement can be identified and areas of good performance can be reinforced. This, indeed, is the rationale for appraisal in business activity, where individuals are judged on their ability to contribute to the achievement of organisational goals. But, to put it mildly, it is against family principles to apply an objectively derived set of criteria to evaluate the worth of family members.

It is hardly surprising, therefore, that senior-generation family members, facing the unenviable task of having to assess the managerial competence of their offspring or other relatives, suffer serious psychological stress. It is simply not possible for them to do justice to the requirements and norms of both the family and the business. Once again, the effects of this institutional overlap can at least be minimised by clearly distinguishing family (ownership) and business (management) principles. The separation implies that family members working in the business must be subject to evaluation on professional grounds like all other employees. Modern management techniques emphasise the value of self-assessment – individuals evaluating themselves against their own predetermined performance targets, and discussing the results with employers and colleagues. The process should also include obtaining the views of other employees (peers, superiors and subordinates) to reduce the potential for family bias and promote objectivity. Canvassing opinion in this way is probably best achieved by allowing anonymous responses, perhaps to a regular, standardised questionnaire. Otherwise there is the risk of non-family employees covering for incompetent family members.

At one family business – a medical supplies company – visited during research for this book, the questionnaires used by the firm included measurement scales where a number between one (representing performance far in excess of expectations) and seven (performance far below expectations) were ringed relative to each criterion being evaluated. Two third-generation family members were divisional managers, and it was made known throughout the company that they were subject to exactly the same appraisal process as everyone else (although, because they were family members, their questionnaire was administered by the non-family, non-executive chairman). Their performance evaluation criteria included abilities at developing a clear strategic plan and goals for the division; communicating the division's plan and goals both upwards and downwards within the company, and externally to the company's advisers and customers; showing effective decision-making and delegation skills; and demonstrating sound financial management skills.

If family members are being groomed to assume senior posts in a family business, it is important their performance is evaluated not just in relation to the job they have at the moment, but also against the standards of their target job. In addition, family members aspiring to leadership positions within the company usually need to demonstrate competence as regards family and ownership factors as well as in relation to their job. A daughter may be an excellent performer within the company, but the family may reasonably expect to see evidence that she can also cope effectively with family relationship problems (where diplomacy is a vital skill), or complex financial planning issues (requiring a thorough grasp of shareholder trusts, estate planning, dividend policy, and so on).

A similar type of approach should be considered in relation to establishing a formal policy on job promotion. Decisions on promotion can be entrusted to a special group composed of both family and non-family members where neither side has a majority vote. This group procedure can even be extended to promotion at director level. An objective evaluation and promotion policy brings with it three principal advantages: appraisals are clearly not based on favouritism; the potential for rivalry and jealousy between family and non-family employees is reduced; and it encourages the development of a much more professional managerial climate.

Working in the business

Next-generation family members should plan the progress of their training and education within the business. Early on it is helpful to develop, in consultation with the senior generation, a structured plan that aims to map out a career path designed to develop the family member's talent and abilities for management and ownership.

Much depends on the type of business, but time spent on manual and repetitive jobs just for the sake of doing everything is not very productive. Jobs should represent a progression from what was done last, and a meaningful learning experience in the context of the plan. As well as learning about specific tasks, it is helpful to take a broader view of the company and the industry in which it operates: how well is the firm doing in achieving its core objectives, what are its main strengths and weaknesses, and who are its principal competitors? Becoming a member of the company's industry trade organisation is useful, as is keeping up-to-date with the latest publications about the sector and about business management.

Some other guidelines on working in the business are as follows.

Seek out a mentor

Most people will be willing to help if asked, but going further than this and trying to establish a special relationship with a non-family mentor figure within the organisation is an excellent idea. A high-status manager, who has been with the firm for a long time and is an expert on its business, will often be available to take on this dual role of teacher and friend. Mentors should be involved and willing to share their expertise with the junior family member so as to promote the latter's self-development, and should have a genuine interest and pleasure in their protégé's achievements and potential.

It is difficult to overestimate the importance of mentor relationships for the next generation joining family businesses. Because of the dynamics of parent–child relationships, it is usual to find that knowledge cannot flow efficiently and in a straight line from the former to the latter. As an illustration, take a step back and ask the question: 'Am I the best person to teach my child to drive, or would I be risking us both getting very cross at every lesson and potentially jeopardising our relationship?' The likely answer is yes, there would be such a risk, and employing the skills of someone else to do the teaching would be a much better idea. For a son or daughter joining a family business, a mentor relationship can operate largely free from all the emotional aspects of their family connection, and is almost always very valuable.

Gain the respect of employees

When first joining the family business, the next generation's credibility with non-family employees will probably be minimal. They know what lay behind the job offer, and will be watching events closely and with a degree of scepticism. Some of them may even perceive the family newcomer as a threat to the long-established and familiar ways of the business, and will try to subvert them. Acceptance as a leader will certainly not flow from the family surname – it will have to be earned.

Having some outside work experience will help a lot, but merit and worth will still need to be proved. It is important to avoid seeking special privileges, to be prepared to listen to people and, most of all, to show keenness to learn and willingness to work hard.

John Timpson, chairman and chief executive of niche retailer Timpson, has offered some interesting perspectives on gaining respect, derived from his early years in the family business, which he joined in 1960:[8]

> Father sent me to see the personnel director (causing me to buy my first business suit). I was given a long lecture about company rules and told that my starting salary would be £5.17s.6d per week plus commission ... there was never any doubt that I was going to get the job! But there are plenty of informal interviews. The workforce put you on trial. They take note of everything you do and everything you say. In particular, they notice what you look like (are you smart?) they notice your timekeeping (can you get out of bed in the morning?) and most important of all, they notice how well you get on with people. The big test is whether you are able to work alongside colleagues to the extent that they almost forget who you are. For the first few years you are severely judged by your peers. It is the people on the shop floor that will decide how far you go, not your mother, father or the board of directors. You work alongside some very hard task masters who expect you to be better than anyone else.

Tread carefully

The next generation will inevitably bring a fresh viewpoint to the business, and indeed one of their main contributions may be to question the effectiveness of its operational procedures and systems. They may feel that it resembles an historical monolith and that there is a real need for professionalisation – but 'proceed carefully' is good advice. The next generation's objectivity, unencumbered by the weight of tradition, may play an important role in helping to position the company for future growth. But both the senior generation and the employees are likely to be wary about altering systems that work, and there is bound to be resistance to the bright newcomer who wants to change everything. Listen and learn, and try not to make the issue into a crusade. Instead, be patient, build up credibility and take a step-by-step approach.

Beware sibling rivalry

Where family members have brothers or sisters also working in the business, it is important to remember that some rivalry is normal and bound to occur, but to try to prevent these feelings developing into a destructive force. This requires a determination to manage sibling rivalry rather than being managed by it (see Chapter 2) and a willingness sometimes to subordinate personal issues to the best interests of the business. A good idea is to agree on a code of behaviour that recognises that the welfare of the business is paramount, and that establishes procedures for the resolution of differences.

Work at establishing personal identity

Everyone working in and doing business with the firm will know that the new arrival is the managing director's son or daughter, so they will have to make special efforts to establish themselves as an independent personality, prepared to succeed or fail on their own merits. It is a good idea to discuss the problem with senior-generation family members so they understand the possible difficulties and the need (conspicuously) to treat family newcomers like any other employee. Extra favours or privileges mark out an individual and serve as a constant reminder to everyone of their special position.

A well-conceived career and personal development programme should help next-generation family members develop their own leadership style as they progressively take on additional management responsibility.

Relationship with the senior generation

The problems and conflicts that can arise in relationships between the senior generation (especially family business founders) and their offspring working in the business should not be overemphasised. Often, both parties enjoy time spent together, and, if temperament, motivation and expectations are in harmony, it is possible for them to benefit from an outstandingly close and productive business life together. But at the other extreme, an incompatible outlook and excessive conflict can turn working together into a nightmare for both sides.

If conflict is an issue, most entrepreneurial parents seem unable to resolve the problems that arise on their own. Apart from the age difference, they can be rigid in outlook and find it difficult to understand that when faced with an alternative, equally valid point of view, it is possible to accept it without appearing to be weak. A lot of the responsibility for finding solutions will therefore fall on the next generation's shoulders, and a mature and patient approach will be required to manage the potential for conflict arising from contrasting perspectives on life in general and the business in particular. It is also important to remember that the psychological issues that arise as the time to step down approaches may be experienced by parents as a loss of authority, status and self-esteem.

Appreciating the existence and scope of these different perspectives should help the next generation understand when and how they are likely to lead to friction. It should also encourage the development of strategies based on patience and diplomacy that minimise the potential for conflict.

The next generation's role in the challenging process of management succession centres on being thoroughly prepared, as well as doing everything possible to ensure that the transition takes place smoothly. The ideal scenario is for successors to gradually take on more and more responsibility so that assuming leadership, when the time comes, represents a natural and trouble-free progression, not an abrupt change. (Some other next-generation perspectives on succession are examined in Chapter 8.)

5

Getting help

Making the most of outside resources

As a company becomes larger and more complex, the foundations have to be laid for a more structured, less centralised organisation. The task is significantly more difficult for family than for non-family businesses because there is a strong temptation in many family firms to depend on internal experience and judgements.

This tendency to introversion can be countered by the effective use of outside talent, discussed in this chapter under three headings: non-family managers; non-executive directors; and advisers and consultants. The decision to appoint outsiders from any of these groups may be a difficult one, marking a cultural shift. But it is often an important step in making the company more open to external influence and can help secure its future. In a 2005 survey of representatives from leading family businesses, when asked what measures had been helpful for them in building unity and teamwork within their businesses, 67 per cent felt that involvement by external parties (non-executive directors or professional advisers) was the most important factor.[1] By being outward-looking and willing to take advantage of external skills, family businesses are better able to grow and respond successfully to change.

Non-family managers

Non-family managers often find that working in a family business – particularly at more senior levels – is difficult and demanding. As was touched on in Chapter 2, there are many instances of talented managers who have resigned because they have run out of opportunities, or because the politics and emotional cross-currents in family-owned companies have become too much of an interference in their work. But managers who are able to cope with such factors are often very good indeed.

Relationships with the family

Family companies often face a recruitment problem when seeking talented outsiders willing to work for them, and, once found, they encounter difficulties in retaining and motivating them. For family businesses in which there is no clearly stated family vision and set of values supported by policies defining the family's relationship with the business, these problems can be serious. There are various issues that may prevent non-family managers integrating effectively and being given a fair chance. 'Is the firm being run effectively by the family – and if it is, why are they bringing in an outsider?' is often the first question. Next, worries centre on whether the salary and overall compensation will be commensurate with non-family firms, the chances of acquiring an ownership stake (or even a leadership role) and the likelihood that decisions may be overruled by family members.

Once recruited, the autocratic management style of an owner can inhibit the development of competent non-family managers. Many start to worry about the effect of family tensions on the business and on their ability to get on with their job unhindered. They are also frequently unsure of their job security in circumstances where the owner is not planning management succession, his or her children may not be qualified to run the business and the most likely outcome is that the company will have to be sold.

One of the difficulties often encountered by non-family managers is a form of triangulation, whereby they become – against their wishes and better judgement – a dumping ground for the problems certain family members have with other family working in the business. For example, the chairman's son is the marketing director, and is annoyed with his father because he promised to retire two years ago but still shows no signs of stepping down. Rather than taking up the issue with his father in an open and direct way, the son continually expresses his annoyance and frustration to the non-family finance director, in the belief that he will pass on his concerns to the chairman. Worse still, the chairman responds, also using the finance director as a messenger and go-between, with predictably adverse consequences for the latter's work and confidence. This all uses up valuable management time and acts as a serious distraction for the non-family director.

Another source of insecurity can arise if family members are suspicious about the loyalty of non-family employees, who, as a result, can

Talented outsiders can bring valuable skills to family companies, helping them to grow and respond successfully to change

find themselves excluded from key planning or operational information. Unlike family members who cannot leave, the freedom of employees to do so, taking specialist knowledge with them, becomes a major worry for some owners.

On a more positive note, managers in family businesses can enjoy some significant advantages, such as the informality of working in a close-knit team, the personal relationship with the owner and a feeling of confidence knowing they are not simply part of a faceless institution. Also, the role of a loyal, trusted manager within the organisation is sometimes cleverly institutionalised by the family. A respected senior manager can become a counsellor and mentor to the next generation or, if there is no obvious successor in the family to lead the business, may be asked to run the company.

A case in point concerned a specialist manufacturing company, formed in the late 1940s, which was founded and run by an autocratic genius who carried all the management procedures and operating data around in his head. The company prospered under his control, although it remained something of a one-man business. In the late 1970s the founder was killed when his light aircraft lost power and crashed into the North Sea. He had two sons involved in the business and two daughters who were not. The sons represented the eldest and the youngest of his four children, but neither was prepared to take over as the new managing director. The founder had made no preparations for succession, and there was no 'drop-dead plan' in place covering what would happen in the event of his sudden death. A new managing director was appointed from within the company – the general manager, who had been with the firm since it began, and who effectively acted as a 'bridge' between the two generations of the founding family. Both sons continued to work in the business, and eventually the point was reached at which the family felt able to resume management control. It happened at a convenient time with the bridge deciding to retire, allowing the younger son to take over as managing director and the elder son to become chairman.

Introducing external executives

So reliance can come to be placed on non-family managers for structural reasons. There may be no genuine family successor, or interim leadership may be required. Furthermore, as a family business matures, particularly by the time it reaches the third generation, it tends to acquire its own identity, distinct from that of the founder. At the same time, management by consensus may have ceased to be viable because there are so many family members, all of whom have a stake in the business. This combination of factors generally leads to greater dependence on external senior executives as the best means of maintaining the continuity of the business.

Bringing in non-family members as senior executives can cause cultural and integration problems, however. Many family businesses have a strong defining culture that may be difficult to absorb and difficult to change. It helps if outside executives have previous experience working in a family company – they will have to believe in family business and carry out their role with sensitivity to the family's emotional involvement.

For example, a family's third-generation leisure business was run by two brothers with complementary skills. The younger was an ebullient, entrepreneurial networker and the elder brother's talents lay in organisation and administration. As a result, they worked well together and the business expanded rapidly. The younger brother died suddenly and his sibling, left in sole charge, realised immediately that although he could keep the business ticking over, he was not the right person to get the most out of the firm's leisure asset portfolio. He therefore recruited a tough, business-focused outsider as joint managing director, providing a top salary and large-scale performance-related bonuses based on the value of the business. In the surviving brother's words at the time:

> I'm happy to give you this incentive package, and I want you to succeed. Come to me for advice and structural things, but otherwise just get on with it, and I'll back you up.

The newcomer made the business hugely successful, but his aggressive, go-getting attitude alienated the family shareholders. He, however, paid them little attention and was not much interested in what they thought – he was there to do a job, and the only family representative he cared about was the surviving brother who gave him the job. There was a family shareholder revolt (although involving only some 35 per cent of the share capital), fuelled as well by the perceived high-risk strategy of the two managing directors as they leveraged the asset base. In the end, these dissenting shareholders were bought out, and the business strategy went from strength to strength. So in this case both the personality and the risk appetite of the incoming non-family executive succeeded in upsetting a sizeable group of family shareholders. More communication, early on, about what shareholders wanted from their family business would have helped a lot.

Some family businesses have discovered that formulating their family's values and vision (often committed to writing in a publicly available mission statement) has been helpful in attracting and retaining top outside talent. Patrick Peyton, the non-family chairman and chief executive officer of Minnesota-based Despatch Industries, has seen this happening a lot in the USA, with its recent history of public company problems:[2]

> I see the pendulum swinging back. Before, employees wanted the public stock and the options. What is happening now is that values are coming back. There is this feeling that you're privately held, you're owned by a family, so there is a sense of security with that value statement. That's bringing some people back from the public companies into the private world.

Once recruited, the aim must be to create a conflict-free environment in which family and non-family can work together and capitalise on the talents of everyone involved. The existing leadership team need to feel comfortable that they understand the competencies and behaviours required from non-family executives, while those senior executives will need reassurance concerning remuneration, decision-making and career development. On remuneration, non-family executives will want to know that their efforts and achievements in growing the value of the family business will be recognised in the level of rewards they receive, in salary terms and possibly via an equity or quasi-equity stake (see below). On decision-making, they will need to know that they can make decisions that have an impact on business strategy without unnecessary family interference. On career development, policies should be in place underpinning a performance culture that ensures promotion on merit regardless of whether individuals are family or non-family.

Another critical aspect of appointing outside executives is how the move is presented to family members – both those already working in the family business and those hoping to join it. Some may leave disappointed, but others (probably the more able family members) will see such appointments as a positive commitment to professionalisation, an outside perspective and growth.

Motivation and rewards

Motivation of non-family managers is an important issue in the development of family businesses. There must be clear evidence of a career path for such employees and of comparability of reward for responsibility and expertise between family and non-family members.

As we have seen, non-family managers have fears about how effective they will be in the job and whether they will be given a fair chance. If the company is professionally managed and there are clear policies defining the family's role in the business, most of these problems disappear, or at least are minimised. The benefits that flow from such a separation were highlighted in Chapter 4, such as key positions ceasing to be the exclusive preserve of relatives, and remuneration and assessment being more objective. Indeed, the overall result can often make the family business an attractive career path for capable non-family managers. New recruits can expect quicker exposure to a wide variety of decision-making situations, and managers find it easier to influence policy and get things done than in, for example, a large, publicly quoted company. Also, they often enjoy a more personal and satisfying working environment, and have greater opportunities to interact with the owners and other decision-makers.

Key non-family managers are sometimes unwilling to remain with the company unless they are given financial incentives, possibly including shares or share options. Where there is an atmosphere of family friction, and there are family members who may have acquired their positions as a result of favour rather than competence, there is a tendency for non-family managers to feel that they are the only people doing any real work and, in the circumstances, they ought to have a stake in any success arising from their efforts.

As share ownership is generally jealously guarded by the family, this often results in an impasse. One possibility is for the company to issue non-voting shares to the employee, or shares with restricted transferability. Another possibility is creating a long-term bonus scheme that does not involve real shares, but nevertheless enables the employee to participate in any future appreciation in the value of the company. These and other devices are examined below.

The common denominators of family businesses that enjoy the benefits of dedicated and highly motivated non-family managers are as follows:

✳ Family and non-family members are recruited and evaluated according to merit – identical, objective standards apply.

✳ Acceptable career development opportunities are provided for non-family managers, and remuneration is related to fair market principles.

✳ If there are any diverging views or conflicts between family members, these are not allowed to affect the business.

✳ A management succession plan has been put in place by the owner, and has been explained to non-family managers.

✳ At a cultural level, the valuable role played by non-family managers and all employees in fostering the success of the business is openly acknowledged and rewarded.

Incentive design and delivery

There are many strategies and plans that can help create and support the vital ingredient of motivation in family businesses. To help select the most appropriate incentive strategy, it is essential to have a clear set of objectives: that is, a careful definition of what it is that you wish your plan to achieve. Selecting who is to participate in the scheme and choosing performance measures that match scheme objectives are also important stages in the design process.

This is not the place for a comprehensive review of incentive theory and scheme design, but, in general, when deciding on a strategy, consideration must be given to the form in which any such incentive arrangement will be paid. Cash and non-cash incentives (such as employee share schemes or other types of equity arrangement) could be used. Some owners offer cash in the form of a pot to non-family executives who stay with the company for a designated period – for example (and obviously dependent on results), £3 million after ten years.

Incentive strategies for senior management in family businesses should be aligned with the goals and values of the owners. In particular, family businesses operate with long time horizons, whereas many executives look at shorter ones – the average tenure for a CEO in the UK listed-company sector is around four years, compared with around 15 years in family businesses. Incentive strategies must be linked to business strategies, so a reward package in a risk-averse family business managed for long-term, steady growth will be different from the appropriate package in a business seeking to grow aggressively in the short to medium term. For example, in a business with an aggressive growth strategy the package will favour leverage in the form of a lower base salary and a larger component linked to growth performance. However, in family businesses more interested in strong but steady growth over the long term, a higher fixed salary component and lower performance-based variable remuneration would be more appropriate. Choosing the right performance measures helps focus executives on demonstrating the right behaviours to support the family's business values and strategy and increases the likelihood that their incentive package will pay out.

The question of whether incentives should be delivered in cash or in shares is a contentious one. Some family businesses have no problem in extending share ownership to outsiders as a way of attracting high-quality talent, but most prefer to limit ownership to family members. A good example of the first model is provided by Ireland's Musgrave Group – a fifth-generation, €4.4 billion turnover food and grocery distributor – which has been extremely successful at integrating and incentivising non-family management. Founded in Cork in 1876, the company has operations throughout Ireland, the UK and Spain, and its core strategy in supporting independent retailers is to be the number one or two player in those markets. The family explicitly acknowledge in their new constitution that, to incentivise staff and executive directors, shares may be issued under the group's long-term incentive plan and profit-sharing scheme. Indeed, the target for family share ownership is to maintain it at 75 per cent, with the balance already owned by employee trusts and former employees. The family has long accepted allocating some of its equity to draw in and motivate outside talent as a key ingredient of its long-term growth strategy. As a result, the family has learned to allow professionals to manage the business without interference and to share in its success. An indicator of the strength of this thinking is that there are now no full-time Musgrave family employees, and the group board is dominated numerically by executive non-family directors.

There are, however, various possibilities that can provide some room for manoeuvre in situations where the family is keen to avoid diluting its stake in the business, but where key managers may be pressing to receive a piece of the action. Some business owners offer senior non-family executives equity in another of the family's investments, such as a side venture or property (although this breaks the rule that incentives should be linked to a performance measure over which the beneficiary has direct control). Others offer long-term bonuses directly linked to the performance of the family business in the form of phantom share options and restricted shares.

Phantom share options

A phantom share option scheme is a bonus plan that feels like a share scheme. The executive is granted an option to buy phantom shares at the current value, and can exercise the option during a set period of time specified in the scheme rules. In some cases the exercise of the option is made conditional on the achievement of predetermined performance criteria. He or she is treated as having sold the shares at the business valuation ruling at the date of exercise, thus making a profit of the difference in value between the grant date and the exercise date. This profit is paid to the employee in the form of a cash bonus.

At one family company, a key non-family manager headed up one of the group's subsidiaries, although it was planned that she should move on to another subsidiary within the not too distant future. A scheme had been set up linking the growth in value of her phantom shares to any subsidiary she happened to be working for. To achieve this with real shares would have presented huge technical problems.

Restricted shares

The second possibility is to issue executives with real shares, but ones that carry voting or transfer restrictions. If, for example, the family is not particularly concerned about the effect of issuing shares from the point of view of diluting the value of its holding, but is worried about loss of control, it can offer non-family managers non-voting or limited voting shares. These are identical to all other shares except they carry no rights (or restricted rights) to vote at general meetings. In most cases, the company may feel it appropriate to enfranchise these shares in the event of a public flotation, although professional advice should always be taken on the taxation implications of varying the rights of employee-held shares.

A variation on this is to issue shares that are required to be offered back to an employee share ownership trust (ESOT), or to the family shareholders, or even to the company itself when the employee leaves (or before they can be sold). This does, however, give the employee all the rights of a minority shareholder, and sometimes families are reluctant to subject the business to this exposure. The level of exposure can be minimised with a well-drafted shareholder agreement. This would normally include features such as a clause ensuring that a majority decision (for example, regarding a sale) is binding on all shareholders.

More broad-based share plans

Some family firms have concluded that if they are to attract professional managers, they must be prepared to release, in an unrestricted form, at least a small proportion of the equity in their company. Employee share plans and ESOTs can achieve this objective.

There are many types of employee share plan. Readers interested in investigating this area in more detail should, for example, find out about three particular schemes: the Enterprise Management Incentive (EMI); company share option plans (CSOPs); and all employee share plans – that is, save as you earn (SAYE) and share incentive plans (SIPs).

ESOTs involve the transfer of shares to the management and workforce via a purpose-built discretionary trust, and they provide an excellent mechanism for ensuring that a significant, long-term employee stake is created and protected. However, the possible uses of ESOTs extend beyond simply helping to motivate non-family managers. For instance, an ESOT can be used as a 'friendly purchaser' of sensitive shareholdings – such as for acquisitions from an outgoing family shareholder. Some family businesses have used ESOTs as an exercise in family swapping. In other words, the ESOT swaps non-committed family shareholders for highly committed employee shareholders, and the work family thus replaces the blood family.

There are, however, some drawbacks to ESOTs. Establishing one is complex because it involves such a wide range of tax and other considerations, so, once again, professional advice is essential.

Non-executive directors

Non-executive directors can bring a new dimension of experience and independent objectivity that is not often found among family members or employees.

Typical non-executive directors are individuals who have made their careers in large enterprises (often a quoted public limited company) at relatively senior levels – for example, divisional director upwards. They do not want to take on full-time commitments, but the idea of attending board meetings 6–12 times a year and using their store of knowledge and experience to help a smaller company is often appealing.

Another resource pool for non-executive directors comprises people who have run their own business at some stage and then sold it. They often make excellent non-executive directors, bringing with them an entrepreneurial get-up-and-go spirit.

Non-executive directors can make an enormous contribution (at modest cost) in a family firm. Particular benefits include objective and seasoned guidance on business strategy from successful business people; an unbiased sounding-board for family-owned business challenges, such as succession; and mediation (not decision-making), helping the family to resolve any disagreements and reduce emotional stresses. More generally, non-executives can often provide specialised expertise that may not be available internally, along with a network of contacts that can be mobilised on behalf of the firm. This covers areas such as potential sources of new business, capital, connections in industry and government, as well as international contacts.

Less tangibly, a good non-executive director can also act as a catalyst, pushing for significant shifts in corporate strategy or objectives that may be beyond the scope and imagination of the internal directors (for example, acquisitions, revamping the senior personnel structure, going public, and so on). Other roles include status provider (bringing standing, credibility and reputation to the board), a window on the world (the source of external information to help inform board discussions), providing a bridge between family shareholders and management, and acting as a confidant for the chairman and other directors.

A professional non-executive director, interviewed during research for this book, had retired early from a senior position with a PLC and joined the boards of six companies, two of which are medium-sized family businesses. He explained how he saw his role:

> The way I approach the job is to always try to take a step back from things and to ask simple, basic questions like, 'Why are we doing this?', 'What are we seeking to achieve?' and 'Should we perhaps be doing this another way?' In the early days I was amazed to find that some family members felt these questions revealed a rude and hyper-critical attitude on my part! The trouble was that the family had tended to follow developments and say 'That's all right with us' and 'The board's doing an excellent job', but it was clear to me that this was sometimes the wrong atmosphere in which to be taking vital decisions about the company's future. So I believe in occasionally trying to give my colleagues a bit of a jolt. There is no magic in it, and it is almost always just common sense. But the point is that things easily get a bit claustrophobic at family firms and a few basic questions usually work wonders in clearing the air, sparking off discussion and helping us move towards the right decisions.

Selecting the right candidate

It is crucial to form a clear idea of the sort of blend of personality, talent and experience that will be of most benefit to the company. In general, the ideal will be for non-executive directors to be bright, logical, analytical, honest and well respected. They should be prepared to stand up for their opinions and be a ready source of constructive advice. Personal chemistry is important – there must be mutual respect and rapport. There will be no benefit if either the managing director or the other owner-directors take umbrage in the face of criticism from the outside director. Give and take is essential on both sides if the board is to perform effectively.

Another important consideration is that the skills, experience and temperament of a non-executive director must complement those already in the company. It may be inappropriate to take on someone whose main background is in the same business as the family firm, because experience of other sectors could bring a fresh dimension to the company. For instance, if the aim is to strengthen the firm's financial expertise, consider candidates with experience in raising external finance from banks, private equity capital or other sources. If marketing has proved a persistent weakness, the most benefit may come from taking on someone with a strong track record in building brands. Seek a balance that will introduce some new and valuable skills to the business.

Some boards shy away from recruiting retired people as non-executive directors. Although they may have the time and experience to make a valuable contribution, if they have been away from business life for a while it can be easy to lose touch. If the candidate's principal concern is to top up their pension with directors' fees, they may not display the sort of detached, objective perspective that is required. Similarly, employing professional advisers such as accountants or solicitors as non-executive directors is likely to be questionable on the grounds of objectivity.

Once a written profile has been drawn up of the type of director needed, the next step is to find him or her, and this is not always easy. The legal responsibilities (and potential liabilities) of directors are significant, and the ideal candidates are often busy, successful people who are unlikely to be strongly motivated by the relatively nominal fees offered. However, many highly qualified people are seeking non-executive directorships and find they provide a rewarding experience. Becoming an important influence in shaping the destiny of a growing, successful firm can be a stimulating challenge.

A number of organisations keep registers of people who are willing to take on non-executive directorships. Recruitment consultants offer a fully fledged candidate search and appointments service; the major banks, venture capital groups, accountants and professional bodies such as the Institute of Directors also keep lists. Personal contacts are another source of candidates, but avoid choosing close friends or, indeed, someone closely aligned with a particular branch or generation of the family. Sometimes there is a serious misconception among non-active shareholders in mature family businesses that, because their family branch is not otherwise represented, they should have their own non-executive director to look after their interests. But non-executive directors (like any other company directors) have a duty to represent the interests of all shareholders, not a particular group or family branch.

Also to be avoided when recruiting a non-executive director are people who do business with the company, because they may not have the required objectivity and independence. But do not underestimate how useful an understanding of family business dynamics might be – it is a rare but potentially valuable quality in a non-executive director. Deciding on the best candidate can be difficult and this is an area where it is generally recommended to seek outside advice before making an appointment.

Lastly, remember that the first selection may be particularly important, because their calibre and experience will set the standard as far as later candidates are concerned.

Board practices

When appointing a non-executive director, it is a good idea to have written guidelines in place setting out how the board should function (see Chapter 6). They will obviously be subject to change as the board evolves, but guidelines serve to clarify expectations as well as to provide evidence of seriousness of purpose, thus helping in the recruitment of board candidates. The role and operational rules of the board should be defined in the guidelines, and information about directors' terms of office and fees should also be included. Once recruited, non-executive directors should have a contract of employment specifying their role, responsibilities and duties and the information they are entitled to receive, and setting out clear lines of reporting and communication. Their contribution should be reviewed on a regular basis as part of a board evaluation process that looks in a broad sense at how effectively the board works.

Consistent with the motivation behind non-executive directors' agreement to serve, their fees should represent a fair return for the number of days they are expected to contribute rather than performance-based remuneration. Fees payable will depend on factors such as the size of the company, the nature of its operations and the frequency of board meetings.

Some concluding thoughts on selecting and appointing non-executive directors would be to aim high. Do not underestimate who will agree to serve your company; make the appointment for a two- or three-year term, renewable; give non-executive directors time to settle in; and involve them in sensitive areas such as appraisal and remuneration of family members. Do not have a non-executive director forced upon you by venture capitalists; do not let them become so involved that they cease to be outsiders;

and avoid having hidden agendas your non-executive director does not know about.

Professional advisers and consultants

Chosen wisely, outside professional advisers and consultants offer an extra dimension of competence, experience and objectivity to issues affecting both the business and the family. They can also contribute significantly to the professionalisation and growth potential of the family business.

Are your advisers keeping pace with your needs?

What generally happens is that family businesses start off with local professional advisers (lawyers, accountants and bankers) – often small firms, chosen with cost as a primary consideration – and quite soon outgrow them.

This team usually works well until the business begins to grow and requires some additional specialist services as well as a more sophisticated general service. For instance, taxation advice may be needed in relation to a complex transaction, or the company may want to establish foreign bank accounts, obtain legal advice on a business contract or plan to acquire another company. The time arrives when the original advisers can no longer cope – the business they are advising has outgrown them. Families are loyal and want to support people who have supported them in the early years, and there may be a reluctance to contemplate a change in the interests of acquiring the services of the most appropriate adviser available.

It is important periodically to evaluate relationships with outside professional advisers. Visiting them regularly is a good idea, even if there are no immediate problems. Keep them in touch with what is going on and with planning. Review their impartiality occasionally – are they perhaps acting more for the senior generation who first employed them ten years ago, rather than impartially for the company in the broadest sense? Challenge them to come up with creative ideas – if advisers can help only on the routine aspects of their field and never make thought-provoking suggestions about your business, this is a clear sign that it is time for a change.

Consultants

When there is no relevant expertise within the company for a specific task, it often makes sense to engage a consultant to help. They are not added to the payroll, and once their job is completed and they leave, if they have been effective the business enjoys a long-term benefit that would not otherwise have been possible.

So selecting a quality consultant is the critical first step. Before engaging them, check their professional credentials and talk to others who have used their services. Insist that the scope of the engagement and the fee arrangement are spelled out clearly in writing in advance. As with most things, but particularly with consultants, you get what you pay for. The general rule is to seek the best your company can afford. There is a range of government grants available that can help defray the costs of consultants for smaller companies, and it is important that companies take advantage of the various government support, advice and information services in this field. Good professional consultants are to be found specialising in virtually every facet of commercial activity.

Family business consultants

A group of professional advisers met with a family business that had succession problems. The business owner had left his wife, with whom he had had one son, and married his secretary, with whom he had had another son. The meeting was chaired by the company's lawyer, who was head of the family department at a large practice of solicitors (that is, he worked with families who own businesses). The lawyer presented the firm's solution, which involved working with the owner of the business to find a strong technical solution based on setting up trusts to deal with the future ownership of the business. But a family business consultant would not approach the case in that way. He or she would see that the facts potentially indicate an emotional minefield and, as a first step, would recommend that all family members become involved in the process of finding, and signing up to, a solution. The company might technically be the client, but a family business consultant would recommend that everyone in the family and key players in the business had a voice in the process. This case demonstrates why family business consultancy requires a unique perspective.

When selecting a family business consultant, as well as checking track record, references, and so on, as recommended earlier for all consultancy appointments, extra consideration should be given to whether candidates possess the special qualities and competencies needed to excel in the field. Perhaps the three most important skills are communication, ability to build trust and facilitation. On communication, discussing family strengths and weaknesses is sensitive and potentially distressing, and it is vital to have communication skills that enable the consultant to pick up on the undercurrents of what is being said – to be a developed listener. Ability to build trust leads on from this. The consultant must build trust with the family quickly – the family must come to understand at an early stage that the consultant is acting on behalf of the business and the family as a whole, not for one particular individual or group at the expense of others. The final skill – facilitation – deserves a short section to itself.

Facilitation

Family business consultants must be able to probe the difficult issues and develop discussion of a family's problem areas in a subtle and sensitive way that minimises the possibility of friction and confrontation. Serious listening underlies the skills of the best family business facilitators – listening to what is being said and (often more importantly) what is not being said, and developing the ability to pick up the signals of what is truly being communicated.

The importance of a family strategic plan that establishes clear ground rules governing the family's relationship with the business and defines the responsibilities of family members was noted in Chapter 3. An experienced family business consultant can often play an important facilitation role at this stage of the planning process, especially when the family council meets to discuss the issues raised by its strategic plan.

An excellent starting point for a family council is a one- or two-day residential retreat, with relatives gathering somewhere quiet, away from the everyday surroundings of job and home. A non-confrontational atmosphere will help family members discuss their future in a constructive way, and all the strategic plan issues should be on the agenda. At the retreat the facilitator would normally be responsible for setting the agenda, chairing or moderating meetings, and ensuring an atmosphere in which everyone feels free to express their concerns. The facilitator will usually interview all family members in advance of the meeting to identify the sensitive issues – the emotional hot spots – that must be faced up to. If possible, interviews should also take place with outsiders such as the company's accountant, banker or lawyer – ideally people who have had dealings with the family and the business over a number of years and who are able to express well-founded, impartial opinions about both.

An important aim of preliminary meetings with family members (held on a one-to-one basis) is to begin to establish an atmosphere in which people feel they can talk honestly and openly about the important issues – and, in particular, the taboo (or elephant-in-the-room) issues, which, unaddressed, can cause so much trouble. The meetings also help to ensure that discussion at the family retreat is tailored to the particular difficulties and needs of the family and their company. The facilitator is not there to solve the family's problems – indeed, it should not be assumed that he or she knows all the answers. Rather, the goals of an impartial facilitator will be to help the family discuss the issues in an informed and logical way; to guide family members as they seek a consensus; and to help them draw together their decisions and codify the results (often in the form of a written family action plan or constitution).

Other family business consultancy roles

Leadership development and executive coaching specifically designed for family members is a growth area in family business consulting. Specialist mediators can also help resolve rivalry and conflict situations within families – for example, by assisting in the establishment of objective family member evaluation procedures, family wealth allocation and fair remuneration principles. Similarly, questions of share ownership and estate planning are complex and often fraught with emotion, and specialist advice can minimise both tax liabilities and the potential for family disagreements.

Lastly, the family can call in an expert to help with succession or changes to the organisational structure to ensure continuity in the future. As discussed in Chapter 8, succession represents a major hurdle for family businesses, and it cannot be assumed that the problems surrounding the issue will resolve themselves, or that they will be easy to handle.

Beware conflicts of interest

When appointing advisers to a family company, it is crucial that both sides are aware of the potential for conflicts of interest. A careful definition should be agreed at the outset detailing for whom the adviser is acting, on which matters, the nature and extent of the adviser's responsibilities, and towards whom the adviser owes a duty of care.

But the problem is not confined to new appointments. Over time, it is easy for the boundaries between formal and advisory roles to become blurred, leading to conflicts of interest. Tax consultants at one family business had acted for the firm for many years and, quite naturally, had developed a close relationship with individuals at the company. The consultants were asked by the majority shareholder to provide personal tax advice. In such a situation, the formal boundaries around professional relationships and duties can become obscured, and conflicts of interest (in this case in relation to minority shareholders whose interests might well have been affected by the tax advice) arise all too easily.

Conflicts of interest affecting advisers are particularly troublesome in that they are rarely obvious, black and white situations that exist from day one. Rather, they come in various shades of grey, and either materialise quietly and progressively over a number of years or are triggered suddenly by an unforeseen event or set of circumstances. Advisers facing such a dilemma should maintain independence, integrity and distance so that they are able to retain objectivity; and family business clients should try not to ask advisers questions on subjects that fall outside their predefined brief. Both these guidelines fit snugly into the much easier said than done category.

Further conflict of interest issues arise when an adviser is appointed as trustee of a settlement involving a family business client. As discussed in Chapter 9, trusts crop up a lot because they can provide flexible solutions to a variety of family business-related problems. A minority stake may often be gifted, to be held for the benefit of, say, three or four young children. The interests of such beneficiaries may well differ from the interests of the company directors for whom the adviser is acting on a day-to-day basis. In such situations, conflict problems all too readily arise because advisers find themselves acting for just one generation or one side of the family.

Relationships underpinning an advisory role

As we have seen, often a firm's relationship with a particular family business adviser develops from particularly close ties between the adviser and just one company director or owner. The adviser gets to know and works with other directors or owners and officials in the company, but the original link remains strongest and effectively underpins the adviser's relationship with the firm as a whole.

In this situation, as well as possible conflicts of interest, the adviser could be seen by others at the company to be allied with and sympathetic to the views and outlook of that particular owner or director. It helps if family business clients are on their guard to try to avoid such undercurrents, but, more to the point, family business advisers must take a strict and uncompromising stance in these circumstances. If there is any possibility that their neutrality might be seen to be compromised, advisers should step aside from the particular advisory role they are being asked to play and arrange to be replaced by a colleague who has no historic links with the firm. Family business issues are generally complex and always emotionally sensitive, and – put simply – if family business advisers are regarded by a particular branch or generation of the family as perhaps not wholeheartedly neutral, their effectiveness in promoting successful resolution of the issues facing that business is almost certain to be flawed.

6

Professionalising the boardroom

The role of a balanced board of directors

The role of boards in the governance structure of a family-controlled company is critically important, and establishing a board of directors that includes independent outsiders is probably crucial for the vast majority of family businesses if they are to achieve long-term success. Such a board brings objectivity and experience to operational and policy deliberations, and imposes important disciplines. When a family introduces board diversity, it sends a positive and motivating message to customers, shareholders and employees. In larger, more mature family companies there is a balance to be struck between the interests of the family as owners of the business and the managers entrusted to run it. No single model works for all, and instead a solid set of principles and processes must be drawn up and applied in the unique circumstances of each company.

The rubber-stamp board

Acceptance of the proposition that outside assistance from a talented, balanced board of directors can contribute significantly to the potential of the family business does not always come easily to family business founders or owner managing directors. The founder's or family chairman's or managing director's character is often incompatible with bringing in outsiders: indeed, many attribute their success to pursuing their own objectives, in their own way, paying scant attention to what others have to say. It should come as no surprise, therefore, that introducing outside directors and thus moving towards a more accountable system of corporate governance is often seen as an unpalatable option, and one that may threaten the family's culture.

Research confirms that the boards of private, family-owned companies normally consist of family members.[1] The board's activities are often confined to the minimum necessary to fulfil statutory obligations. These boards operate as a rubber stamp and exercise few, if any, of the serious management functions or the authority that can be vested in a board.

In effect, the boardroom is seen as a family preserve, and to suggest outside directors might add any value is often regarded as implying that the family is not competent to run its affairs. In such family firms the managing director's view of independent directors is, 'I created and built this company on my own, I'm the controlling shareholder, and I make all the decisions: what would the involvement of outsiders bring to my company, and why would I want them?' The last point is often the crux of the matter, with managing directors taking a negative view about establishing a properly structured board of directors to which they would be accountable. They worry that their decisions will be challenged and that they risk losing control.

There is also sometimes a problem at longer-established family businesses that appear to have made the move and introduced independent outsiders to strengthen their board of directors. Frequently, the decision is taken to introduce the same number of outsiders as there are family members on the board, so the family chairman will always have a casting vote in favour of the family if needed.

There is a misconception among some families that only big, public companies should have broadly based boards with a significant complement of independent outsiders. Owners of family businesses, who often operate in an atmosphere of informality and privacy, can be less than comfortable with the thought of sharing confidential business information and airing difficult family issues. But the privacy point is often overstated because directors are, of course, bound by a fiduciary duty to protect confidential information and, in any case, the screening process should mean that family members select only trustworthy candidates. Nevertheless, there is admittedly a trade-off if the benefits of a well-balanced board are to be obtained. Generally, the issue for family business managing directors is not that this price is too high, but that they may not fully appreciate how valuable such a board of directors can be.

Making the transition

Long-term family business success probably depends on developing an ethos of accountability and building a board that includes talented outsiders, but not all firms would obtain enough benefits from the process

If the boardroom is seen as an exclusively family preserve, the wrong messages can go out to customers, shareholders and employees

to justify the effort and cost involved. In deciding if such justification exists, a number of questions should be considered:

✷ Are the managing director and controlling shareholders committed to making the idea work?

✷ Is it a growing, maturing company rather than a one-man business?

✷ Is the business substantial enough so that shareholder and operational issues can be easily distinguished from one another?

✷ Does the business have sufficient resources to implement and take advantage of the decisions and recommendations of a well-constituted and rigorous board of directors?

The first of these questions is the most important. The board can be effective only when the managing director or controlling owner have the confidence to accept a degree of reduction in their power and control over the business, and are willing to subject their stewardship to examination by outsiders. There will be less scope for the aura of operational secrecy practised by many family businesses and greater transparency to allow for informed decision-making.

The relationship between the family managing director and the board is subtle and delicate. Unless the managing director believes in the concept and is willing to submit to board recommendations, the board cannot succeed in helping to develop the business. This does not mean that the managing director must relinquish all control, and there may be times when he or she may find it necessary to exercise the prerogative of a major shareholder and make decisions contrary to the board. Board members will generally accept this, but they must believe that their opinions are valued and that their viewpoints have an impact on the business. A board should probe, challenge and offer recommendations, and it should do this in an atmosphere of mutual respect that is supportive rather than adversarial. This balancing act can exist only among mature people who are willing to subordinate their sensitivities and egos to the good of the company. The board members have a final weapon – resignation – if they believe that the managing director is too intransigent.

So enlisting independent outside directors does not necessarily limit the managing director's flexibility or ultimate authority as owner. And although a properly constructed board may require more formal management procedures, these often represent needed disciplines rather than bureaucracy. Family members, active in the day-to-day running of the business, are unlikely to spend precious time preparing detailed reports and analyses when they themselves will be the only readers.

Establishing a well-balanced board

Family business people are often pleasantly surprised at the kind of talent they can attract to their board. But questions like 'Who should I ask?' or 'Who might I ask?' are not very helpful because they limit the options. A better starting point is 'What am I looking for?', after which the search begins to find people who fit the bill. Establishing a selection committee to define an ideal independent director profile is often a good idea, after which the committee can move on to drawing up a list of candidates or delegate this task to an outside firm specialising in the recruitment of directors.

Board composition

A lot of research has taken place into the ideal size and composition of a board of directors. On numbers, the experts broadly agree that there is a limit to the number of people who can work productively together in a group, and that the ideal size for a family company board is around seven.[2] The consensus favours having at least three independents, with family business professor John Ward, for example, believing that three is much more valuable than two:[3]

This is because two have to deal with each other, whereas three bring much more creativity, challenge and courage, and much less politeness – in other words, three contribute the most in terms of boardroom dynamics. So with three or four independents, plus a managing director, plus (especially in the United Kingdom) a separate chairman of the board, numbers quickly push up to the optimal six or seven.

It is becoming more common for larger family companies to have a majority of independent directors.

On family/non-family balance, the more family members on the board the less effective that board will be because the more meetings will become family meetings rather than board meetings. Like non-family directors, family members should of course be chosen for the quality of experience and judgement they can bring to board discussions. Musgrave Group, Ireland's largest food and grocery distributor (see Chapter 5, page 98), has recently agreed and implemented wide-ranging family governance processes and structures, and in the new constitution the family make it clear that up to three family non-executive directors should normally be appointed to the board, and that they 'recognise that management skill and business acumen must be taken into account as priorities when selecting directors'. Each family branch (as a result of share inheritance, the family share-holders today divide broadly into three distinct family branches) decides by consensus which individuals should be put forward for approval by the board and, once identified, candidates are assessed by the board selection committee. The committee decides on the best candidates based on the role description and qualitative attributes defined and listed in the constitution. These procedures introduced significant robustness and transparency into the selection process which all the family felt was important.

Ivan Lansberg believes that an 'ideal profile' should be drawn up for family directors, listing qualifications that will help to ensure that they fully understand the board's duties and can add value to the board's work:[4]

> The insistence on director quality, however, is not meant to exclude talented family members who may lack some of the specific qualifications. For those who wish to serve, the family should offer educational opportunities and training programs to help them fill gaps in their knowledge.

Individuals who should be invited to join the board as independent directors include people with a strong track record of business achieve-ments in areas useful to the family company, and people with skills that complement and broaden those of existing board members. Individuals from a commercial background that enables them to understand the problem areas for family businesses, such as introversion, family dynamics and succession management, often make especially good directors. For example, business owners whose companies have been through succession can bring valuable insights and significant added value to the board of a company where a similar process is in prospect. Seek out people who are able to identify with the risks, responsibilities, rewards and goals of owner-managers, and who are supportive of the values, principles and vision of the family.

Individuals who should not be invited to join the board include long-term professional advisers, such as the company's lawyer or accountant (their expertise is available anyway, and putting them on the board often needlessly creates conflicts of interest) and key managers – including family managers – because boards supervise management, and managers should report to the board rather than become members. In particular, it is generally advisable to avoid putting on the board family-member employees who are working their way up the organisation. At a packaging business visited while researching this book, a 25-year-old next-generation family member – accepted by everyone as being groomed for an eventual leadership role – was three years into a detailed career plan whereby he was gaining experience working in different divisions within this large group of companies. The career plan was progressing smoothly until, as well as being appointed as a manager in the next division listed in the career plan, the young family member was also appointed to the main board. This latter appointment caused significant problems for the individual concerned, and it made things hard for the people around him. Suddenly, he had access to confidential information, had become privileged and his progress was hampered. His supervisors complained that it was not clear whether he reported to them or vice versa. A lot depends on the personalities involved and the circumstances at each particular company, but, as a general rule, putting family employees on the board is probably best avoided until they are in very senior positions or are close to assuming the leadership role.

Similarly, spouses and relatives with little to contribute to professionally oriented business meetings should not be on the board (minority investors are best served by seeing that their company has the best possible board). Appointing retired employees and friends should also be avoided because the focus of board discussions should be on tomorrow, not yesterday, and few friends are able to provide objective input. Finally, having customers, suppliers and agents on the board will – sooner rather than later – lead to serious conflicts of interest.

Organising the board

Having written guidelines in place setting out how the board should function is a good idea (see Chapter 5, page 103). These will obviously be subject to change as the board evolves, but guidelines serve to clarify expectations and to provide evidence of seriousness of purpose, thus helping in the recruitment of board candidates.

Most importantly, the guidelines should define the role of the board: what it is that the board should be trying to accomplish. Items that might be in a board charter or job description include reviewing the company's mission statement and philosophy, remuneration and evaluation policies, its succession plan, and its strategy process and direction.

The guidelines should include information about directors' terms of office and fees. They should also set out the board's operational rules, such as the frequency of meetings (too frequent and the board risks becoming too heavily involved in the micro-management of operations); principles for agenda setting (for example, difficult questions at the top); how meetings can be organised to ensure directors make a full contribution; comprehensive and precise minute taking; procedures whereby the contribution of directors is reviewed regularly as part of a board evaluation process.[5]

Effective, working boards

In summary, the main duties of the board of directors are as follows:

✳ To protect the interests of shareholders. Good boards strike a balance between their commitments to the company and their commitments to the needs of shareholders. For example, the board of directors should not always authorise large dividends or help promote other family goals such as family leadership of the business if it believes such actions would weaken the company and ultimately reduce long-term shareholder value.[6]

✳ To make big-ticket decisions. These include changes to the scope or nature of the company's operations; overall strategic planning; approving individual strategies in areas such as marketing, production, investment and financial management; changes to the company's organisational structure; and major corporate decisions, such as selling the business or a significant portion of its assets, along with mergers, acquisitions and large investments.

✳ To oversee management performance. Duties in this area include monitoring the effectiveness of management in implementing corporate strategies; ensuring objective decisions and fair, honest processes; planning for management succession; and setting management remuneration levels.

✳ To monitor and mediate the family's involvement in the business. Clearly, a number of corporate policy and management responsibilities can involve sensitive family questions that many family members are reluctant to face up to – in particular, succession, organisational structure, job definitions and remuneration of family members. These are, of course, precisely the sort of elephant-in-the-room issues on which the unemotional and objective viewpoint of independent directors can be especially helpful.

The following account illustrates well how independent directors can bring their influence to bear with family members, thereby helping to clarify the future direction of the business. This director's story began just after joining the company board:[7]

> The president told me that his twin thirty-year-old sons were extremely able, chips off the old block, and dedicated to continuing the heritage and tradition of the family's leadership of an enterprise. … During the next few years, I became a good friend of the two sons and an admirer of their imagination and intellect. But as I came to know them better and share their interests and aspirations, it became clearer and clearer that what they wanted to do more than anything else in the world was to get out of the business. One wanted to return to his prep school as a teacher of English and drama. The other wanted to travel, write poetry, and paint. Their father was completely unaware of these carefully disguised and concealed feelings. At a board meeting I asked the sons, 'Do you really want to run this company for the next five years and for the rest of your lives?' The sons hesitated and then almost in unison said, 'No.' … The father was startled, shocked, amazed, incredulous. This was the first disclosure by the sons that the father's dream of continued leadership by family members would not be fulfilled. Over the next several months the chairman became reconciled to his sons' position, and … decided that the best solution would be to sell the enterprise.

Beyond fiduciary duties in overseeing operations, boards of family companies also have special responsibilities to understand the family's values, vision and objectives for the business, and they help to ensure that the family's reasonable long-term goals – with the board defining reasonable – are met. If, for instance, the family wishes the management of their business to be guided by social, ethical, religious or environmental principles (as defined and communicated by, in most cases, the family council), the board is responsible for ensuring that management adheres to such principles. In short, in family businesses board members are effectively custodians of the family's core values, which ultimately shape corporate culture.

Relationship with the family

In non-family companies every board member has equal rights and standing, but owner members on private family company boards cannot realistically be regarded as equal to non-family board members. Of course, this does not mean that views expressed by outside board members are devalued, but it does mean that that the owners have the final say, and everyone needs to understand this. In principle, this is the same situation that applies in any publicly quoted company, but because of fragmented ownership it is usually impossible for owners to express a common will.[8]

In view of this special situation, and the fact that the board will be involved in helping the family resolve issues in the family company, it is important that independent directors establish a good working relationship with the family. Lansberg explains well some of the delicate consequences of this apparently straightforward statement:[9]

> The board's obligation to look after the best interests of shareholders requires the members to raise questions about how family and ownership matters may affect not just the economic efficiency of the business but its long-term viability as a family enterprise. For directors to fulfil this obligation, they must negotiate the kinds of relationships with key stakeholders that will allow them to enter into discussions about ownership and family concerns without feeling they are inappropriately meddling in the family's private affairs. The responsible management of succession and continuity issues requires boards to adopt a proactive stance toward them. It is impossible for directors to examine the long-term continuity of the enterprise without taking into account what the owners have (or have not) done with regards to estate planning. Likewise, responsible boards of family businesses cannot ignore the process by which family candidates for leadership are developed, evaluated, and selected.

The board's role should not be seen as institutionalised arbitration when family views are divided, but if the board has the family's confidence and respect it can be valuable in helping to defuse potentially dangerous situations and proposing alternative strategies. A vivid illustration of this is provided in cases where the managing director has suddenly died or become disabled. Rather than the unprepared family being saddled with responsibility for the business, the board can take over, if necessary hiring a professional manager. The business can then continue to operate in an orderly way with the support of the family until, if appropriate, a member of the next generation is ready to assume leadership.

When the board of directors is not functioning effectively, serious tensions can surface, with independent directors believing the owners 'don't respect us' and the owners feeling the independent directors 'don't understand us' or 'don't understand how family businesses work'. Many researchers have concluded that the family managing director/CEO is the key to success, or lack of success, of a family business board, in that it is generally the managing director's philosophy of management that most profoundly influences a board's ability to function optimally.[10] When boards work well, board members individually and collectively respect the managing director as a leader, while the managing director sees the board as a partner and a source of learning, and seeks ways to help the whole management team take advantage of the board's ideas and contribution. It is also been noted that managing directors who have worked for public companies before starting their business have more successful boards than other founding managing directors, because they come to the job having already absorbed public company disciplines and are more able to interact with the board in a collaborative way. Another factor is that second and subsequent generation managing directors seem more able to work effectively with boards, perhaps because their psychological need for control is not as pronounced as that of the founding generation.[11]

In some family companies, the board works more effectively because the roles of managing director and chairman are separate, allowing the chairman to focus more on the processes and practices of board meetings. Where these roles are combined, however, there may be less managing director accountability because the individual concerned may avoid direct, critical feedback on their performance. Ward believes that if there is a choice between a managing director family member and a chairman family member, choosing a chairman family member is preferable. This is because the chairman of the board is the ambassador of the owners' values – the ambassador to all the company's stakeholders – and it is more important to have a family member in the supreme ownership role of chairman than it is to have one in the supreme management role of managing director. There may be exceptions to this principle where, for instance, a family business may be contemplating a public flotation, in which case the aim will be to make the board look good for outside investors, or where a non-family chairman of the board might create added prestige in the company's marketplace. But such exceptions should never lead to an abdication of the power and responsibility of ownership.[12]

Indeed, ownership is the central dynamic governing the board's relationship with the family. All directors serve at the discretion of the majority shareholders. If an independent director behaves inappropriately and loses the confidence of the family, a shareholders' meeting can be called and that individual removed. For their part, outside directors understand that the shareholders are the ultimate authority; they accept that the family created the business and have everything at stake in it, and that if the family want to go one way and the independent directors another, the independent directors must resign.

A good idea is for families to formalise the terms of their relationship with the board of directors in a written statement (which can be included within the family constitution).

Two-tier boards

Some larger family businesses split their board into two separate structures: a 'top co' board (sometimes also called a holdings board), responsible for strategy and vision; and below this an operations (or trading) board, responsible for business operations.

The role of the operations board is to run the business, while the holdings board concentrates on shareholder issues such as asset allocation, risk parameters for the business, family values and succession. A good way of visualising the division is that the operations board runs the business within the culture as defined by the holdings board. The holdings board is often composed of senior family members, perhaps serving alongside non-family directors, who may be either executive or non-executive. Family input at holdings board level is designed to keep management goals aligned with shareholder values.

There should be clear, documented guidelines about the distinction between the functions and responsibilities of the separate boards. There should also be constant dialogue between key individuals (for instance, the chairman of the holdings board and the managing director of the operations board) to ensure that family strategy is being communicated effectively and that the value of the two-tier structure as a buffer between the family and executive management is being maximised.

It is important to remember that a two-tier structure can serve to underpin family influence as regards strategy and vision, but it does not replace having a family council or family meetings. The holdings board is a statutory body and should not be confused with the family council or equivalent.[13]

No single model of family and corporate governance works for all family businesses. What successful multigenerational companies have achieved is to arrive at a solid set of principles and processes that work in the unique circumstances of their company.

7

Cousin companies

Family governance in multigenerational family firms

B y the time a family business reaches the third generation there may be dozens of family members who have some sort of stake in it. Ownership is generally in the hands of many cousins from different sibling branches of the family, with no single branch having a controlling shareholding. Some of these owners will work in the business, but probably most will not. The potential for friction and dysfunctional behaviour if the large-scale complexity arising with these family and shareholder groups is not controlled and managed is significant. Governance architecture must be tailored to meet the unique needs and circumstances of particular families.

Introduction

In Chapter 2 we saw that because many family business challenges hinge on the inherent conflicts that can arise between emotion-based family values and task-based business values, looking at family businesses in the context of overlapping, and often competing, systems of values and goals provides an excellent starting point to gaining an understanding of their complicated dynamics. We discussed how, in non-family businesses these two almost incompatible systems operate independently, but in the family business they not only overlap, they are also interdependent. Their differing purposes and priorities produce special tensions in family firms, creating at the point of overlap operational friction and value conflicts for owners and other family members.

We went on to discover that, rather than just family versus business, a more subtle model is needed to portray what is going on in the full range of family enterprises (especially the older, third-generation-and-beyond, more complex family businesses that are the main focus of this chapter). As well as family and business factors, a further distinction – that between owners and managers – throws some useful light on dynamics, leading to the three-circle model (see Figure 2.2 on page 42) in which the independent but overlapping systems comprise the family, ownership and the business. With everyone involved in a family business falling within one (and only one) of the seven sectors defined by the three circles, this model helps identify and clarify the different perspectives and motivation of family business people, as well as the potential sources for interpersonal conflict and role confusion.

What distinguishes successful families is that they learn to communicate and share their thinking about the critical issues the family must face up to. They devise strategies and set up governance structures that help them to keep the overlaps under control, minimise the friction the overlaps can cause, maximise clarity and transparency, and minimise the scope for misunderstandings. In short, they formulate and adopt policies that strike an appropriate balance between the best interests of the business on the one hand and the well-being of the family on the other.

But families do not learn these things all at once. Randel S. Carlock, a family business professor, proposes a step-by-step model to help visualise the process. He explains:[1]

> As the business family and the business simultaneously grow and mature, the family enterprise is constantly challenged by new tasks and issues. The growing family business needs to become a 'learning organisation'.

Carlock's learning family model (see Figure 7.1) helps families apply the tools of learning organisations to the special challenges of the family enterprise, supporting the family through nine steps, from building an awareness of family business challenges through to practising stewardship.

The model illustrates that there are no quick fixes; for example, families cannot transfer ownership and control (step 8) before creating governance mechanisms (step 7). In more detail, the nine steps comprise the following:

1   Becoming aware of family business challenges. The family learns about the unique challenges created when a family owns a business, and how the goals of family harmony and success of the business can generate conflict.

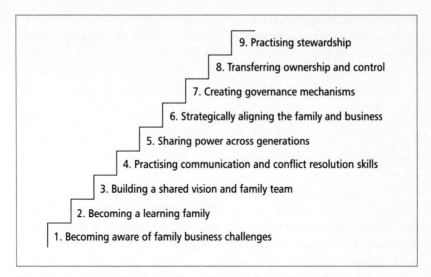

Figure 7.1 Critical steps to becoming an effective family enterprise

Source: Randel S. Carlock (1999) *Becoming a Learning Family: Tools for Growth and Development of Effective Business Families*. Minneapolis, MN: University of St Thomas College of Business Center for Family Enterprise.

2   Becoming a learning family. The family commits to a model that focuses on developing its organisational skills. The goal is to improve the family's effectiveness in addressing business and personal issues.

3   Building a shared vision and family team. Families learn to build this vision by aligning individual and family values and goals. The vision becomes a guide for planning, decision-making and action.

4   Practising communication and conflict resolution skills. Family members practise dialogue instead of discussion. They gain insight and explore sensitive issues, build trust and take risks.

5   Sharing power across generations. This is the first concrete step that demonstrates commitment to a planned transition and therefore represents an important point in the family's development. It requires the senior and successive generations to be committed to transferring authority for managing the family firm.

6   Strategically aligning the family and the business. The family starts to share power and crafts a strategic plan that reflects its shared future vision. Learning family tools and models help the family address the continuous changes in its enterprise.

7   Creating governance mechanisms. Families develop family and business governance structures. Shareholders and management agree to review performance and strategy regularly.

8   Transferring ownership and control. Ownership and control are transferred between generations, completing the family succession process.

9   Practising stewardship. Stewardship, encouraging a balanced and long-term perspective on plans and decisions, is a core value reflected in the company's policies, practices and strategies. It can take many forms and will be shaped by the family's experiences, traditions and vision for the future.

The step 1 starting point could well be learning to recognise and manage the complexity implied by the three-circle model, but it is important to remember that this model, although helpful, is static – it is a snapshot in time. Family businesses, however, are constantly changing and evolving across all three dimensions of the model. Here we concentrate on an area that has a particularly severe impact on multigenerational family enterprises: the way that ownership dynamics develop over time.

Evolution of family business ownership

Understanding the ownership structure in a family business is often fundamental to understanding the forces at work within it. In Chapter 2 (see page 44) we noted that ownership of family businesses usually progresses through a three-stage sequence, reflecting ageing and expansion of the owning family: owner-managed business; sibling partnership; and cousin consortium. By the cousin consortium stage, the third generation is in place, there is a well-established business and there may be several dozen or more family members who have some sort of stake in it.

Ownership is generally in the hands of many cousins from different sibling branches of the family, often with no single branch having a controlling shareholding. Some of these owners will work in the business and many will not. It is not hard to imagine the potential for friction and dysfunctional behaviour if the large-scale complexity arising with these family groups is not controlled and managed. There are many real-life dramas that illustrate the point. See, for example, the case note on the footwear retailer C & J Clark (page 46), where tumbling profits in the early 1990s resulted in drastic dividend cuts, angering many shareholders who, with no day-to-day involvement in management, had come to rely on the family company for a steady income.

Unlike siblings brought up in the same family, cousins (especially the more remote cousins who proliferate once a business has reached the

By the cousin company stage, special governance systems are needed to manage the diversity of family interests and demands

fourth generation and beyond) often have little in common, and some may never have met. The powerful family connection that worked for the business in the first two ownership stages may now be significantly weakened. Even more than with sibling partnerships, therefore, there is a fundamental need for cousins to ask basic questions like 'What's our business for' and 'What are we trying to achieve?' and to develop a shared vision about the future of the business that provides vitality as well as a sense of purpose and direction.

Special governance systems and mechanisms are needed to manage the diversity of interests and demands, and to let everyone have their say. In building a common and workable vision together, it is often useful at this point to allow those family members who do not buy into or believe in that vision to exit as shareholders. There are no one-size-fits-all solutions, and the importance of tailoring governance architecture to meet the unique needs and circumstances of particular families is a central theme of this chapter.

Culture shock

A final point to remember from the Chapter 2 discussion of family business life cycles is that whether the transition is from a single owner to a sibling partnership, or from a sibling partnership to a cousin company, it amounts to much more than just changing the people – it means changing the system and the ways in which things are done. In short, the transition involves introducing a different type of business structure with a different culture, different decision-making, different procedures and different ground rules.

The need to recognise that it is the system that is changing, not just the personnel, applies particularly in transitions to the third generation when a sibling partnership is passing to cousins. Siblings cannot assume that what worked for them in growing the business will also work for the cousins. Nor can they assume that the cousins will behave as they have done. Siblings generally forget how little the cousins will have in common and that they will operate within a different system that has different values, rules and methods. In sibling-to-cousin transitions, siblings may also overlook the added complexity with which cousins will have to cope, and fail to appreciate the extra structure, formality and governance systems that the cousins will need to help manage this extra complexity.

Complexity in cousin companies

The cousin consortium is the most complex of the family business ownership structures.[2] By this stage – the third generation and beyond – ownership will have been significantly diluted and generally will be in the hands of many minority family shareholders. Each of them will have a different view about their investment, depending on whether or not they work in the business and the extent to which they feel connected with and committed to the business.

To help visualise the large-scale family governance challenges that face these multigenerational, cousin-owned companies, some fundamental assumptions about the nature of family need to change. Ivan Lansberg illustrates the point well: instead of looking at a family business pyramid structure with seniors at the top, siblings below and descendants forming the base, he suggests that the focus needs to change to a circular structure where a network of sub-families, each with its own little pyramid hierarchy, revolves around, and interacts with, the family enterprise at the centre of the circle.[3] Each sub-family connects with the family enterprise at the centre in ways. For example, some may be employed by it, some may not; they may have different core values; they will have different levels of psychological commitment to the business; some may be geographically close to the business, others may be on a different continent; some may want to be involved at least to a limited extent in the enterprise, others will just want to collect their dividends.

The complexity of businesses that have reached the cousin consortium stage is reflected in the two family business dimensions highlighted in this chapter: the increasing complexity of the family as it grows naturally through marriages and childbirth; and the complexity of ownership as shares pass down the generations, creating a variety of shareholder situations.

Family complexity

One of the most clear-cut aspects of family complexity is sheer numbers. By the third generation it is quite possible for the founder to have 15 or more grandchildren, and, in total, there can be 30 or more members of the family with some sort of stake in the business. With cousin companies in the fourth generation and beyond, it is not unheard of for there to be hundreds of cousins participating in ownership.

Another issue is branch dominance. By the third generation, management control of the business has often been assumed by one particular branch of the now multibranch founding family. It may be reassuring to some relatives that the wealth and commercial prestige of the family is being taken forward by this branch, but any skills shortages of the branch and how its members exercise their authority can generate tensions and resentment (for example, if they show branch favouritism in recruitment or remuneration).

In some families, emotion-based rivalries (like father–son and sibling rivalries) that may have featured in earlier generations of the business have often been toned down by the cousin consortium stage, but they may well have been replaced by a preoccupation with satisfying personal and branch objectives. In other families, however, the passing of time has no such soothing effect on the cousin generation, and old grievances can loom large, magnified by the weight of history and constant retelling. Indeed, members of the senior generation sometimes go to extraordinary lengths to keep alive old grudges and complaints that serve little purpose other than to perpetuate family divisions and undermine trust and confidence in succeeding generations.

Ownership complexity

Ownership complexity in the cousin consortium stage manifests itself in a variety of ways. In particular, as family businesses evolve and their owning families become more complex, a migration takes place towards ownership by family members who are increasingly remote from the operations of the business. In the early days the business is typically operated by its owners, but as time passes the connection weakens until, by the cousin company stage, many family owners are pure investors in the remote sense that applies to purchasing a holding in an FTSE 100 company.

Another aspect of this concerns divergent interests. In cousin companies, the needs, expectations and ambitions of owners running the business can be very different from those who are not employed by the firm. The latter, for example, relying on dividend income to maintain lifestyle expectations formed in earlier, smaller generations, may oppose any reduction in dividends, even if that money is to be reinvested for future growth of the business. In contrast, the spouses of share-owning relatives working in the business may feel that their partners are being under-rewarded and their careers undermined by the regular payout of dividends to shareholders not involved in day-to-day operations.

As well as the sheer numbers of individual family shareholders, ownership will usually have become further confused as a result of the use of trusts, holding companies and so forth, introduced over the years to meet estate planning and other objectives.

With shareholdings normally passed down within branches of the family, by the cousin company stage issues arise because some branches may have one child, while others may have six or eight, producing obvious imbalances (real and imagined) when it comes to individual ownership interests in the business. A good example is provided in the history of the Warburg banking family. In the late 19th century there were two equal Warburg family branches, each traditionally represented by one bank directorship. But one branch had five sons and accounted for much of the family wealth before the devastation of the second world war. (These were the famous Five Brothers: Max, a prominent banker, and confidant to the Kaiser; Fritz, a social reformer; Felix, a playboy and philanthropist; Paul, who moved to the USA and helped create the Federal Reserve; and Aby, an eccentric collector and founder of a cultural institute.)[4] Their cousin, Siegmund, was raised believing that his branch of the family had not received fair treatment or representation, and, as he rose to prominence in the post-war era, he both fought and co-operated with his cousins for control of the scattered Warburg enterprises.[5]

Also, as touched on earlier, by the third generation management control of the business has often been assumed by one family branch. Although generally accepted, this is unlikely to have been greeted with universal family acclaim. Often another branch (generally not itself involved in management and possibly motivated by some historical grievance, real or imagined) will take on the role of critic and challenger of ruling branch policies, campaigning and seeking support for its opposition from elsewhere in the family.

Another facet of ownership complexity at the cousin consortium stage concerns information flows. Most shareholders in cousin companies are not employed in the family business, and, over time, they come to feel they are receiving less and less direct information about it. Whereas once they used to have regular reports from involved parents, spouses or children that served to keep them in touch with events and able to feel protective of the interests of their branch of the family, they are now subject to the company's shareholder communication policies, if there are any, and otherwise ad hoc information from those who are involved. Often there are issues concerning the consistency and reliability of information, with different branches hearing different things. The company's task in distributing information is made more difficult by the differing attitudes between some family branches and the branch that runs the business, the likely geographical dispersion of family shareholders, and the different skills, knowledge, income levels and so forth of family shareholders.

Lastly, quite often by the cousin consortium stage the business will have been professionalised and be led by non-family senior executives. This will generate issues about how family control can be retained, and how non-family senior personnel are to be motivated if share ownership is not a realistic prospect.

Responding to growing complexity

The challenge at the cousin company stage becomes, therefore, how to cope with an expanding network of sub-families, with different degrees of involvement in and commitment to the family business, which generates the large-scale imbalances and complexities discussed above. There are really only two choices available. The first is to reduce complexity by buying out cousins and consolidating ownership of the business in far fewer hands – but usually with these mature businesses this is too expensive and often is achievable only by selling the company. The second is to retain the complexity, in which case it must be carefully managed to prevent it running out of control.

Managing complexity requires introducing structure in the form of rules, policies and procedures that help the family develop a cohesive approach to its involvement in the business. In short, what is needed is effective governance, which means creating organised accountability and alignment among the different interests of the owners, the family and the business. In Chapter 3 we examined the policies to be defined in the critical area of family–business relationships (see Table 3.1 on page 62). Here the focus shifts to the main issues likely to require the particular attention of older, multigenerational family businesses: ownership, business and family.

Ownership policies

Values are what a family and its business stand for; vision is a shared sense of where each is heading. Together, values and vision provide a major source of strength and resilience for the family firm. Questions about values and ownership centre on how the business is to be run and what is important to the family: what binds them and keeps them in business together? Vision and ownership involves clarifying how the family shareholders see the future: do they regard themselves as owners of an asset that they seek to maximise, or as stewards and custodians of the shares for future generations? If, for example, the shareholders see themselves as stewards and custodians, is everyone aware of this and is the company geared up to provide income and pension rights in place of capital asset status for the shares? What will happen to share ownership in the next generation?

Policies are needed on who can own shares (bloodline, in-laws, non-family, and so on), share valuation and transfer, the expected return on investment and protecting the interests of minority family shareholders. Policies on in-laws and ownership deserve special mention because choices will certainly need to be made about how to manage the role and influence of family members' spouses in relation to the family business. They will have an influence – to pretend that they do not hold strong opinions about subjects that affect their children's assets and futures is a fantasy. Approaches to the issue vary. At one extreme (common in some Mediterranean countries and in Latin America), in-laws are fully accepted and effectively enjoy family member status in relation to the business. At the other extreme, in-laws are excluded, not just from share ownership (via rules laid down in the articles of association and in prenuptial and other compulsory legal agreements) but also from any involvement in the business or its family governance architecture.

Ringtons Holdings' rigorous stance on family governance was discussed in Chapter 3 (see page 68). The firm's family constitution lays down that, on marriage, all family members must enter into a prenuptial agreement with the aim of preserving family ownership of the company. Anyone in breach is liable to penalties in the form of restricted involvement in the business and shares being passed down by way of trust rather than direct ownership. In-laws who have been married to a family member for at least five years may work for the company. Once working in the business they may qualify for share ownership, but if they divorce the shares must be sold back.[6]

Whatever viewpoint is adopted concerning in-laws, achieving a family consensus on rules is likely to be a delicate exercise. But it is not an issue that can be left to chance. The role and voice of in-laws need to be actively managed through the mechanisms of family governance, with the aims of building trust, ensuring clarity and managing stakeholder expectations.

For interesting historical reasons, a compromise was struck on this issue at T. & E. Neville, a fifth-generation construction, funeral directing and property development group based in Bedfordshire. During a corporate reorganisation, a family member argued the case for including a new clause in the articles stating that only bloodline members of the family should be shareholders. While recognising the force of the argument, other family members had reservations because of the firm's history. Early in the 20th century the founder's daughter married a senior non-family employee of the firm. There were succession problems and direct bloodline members of the family were not available to take over, so if the company had had this provision in its articles at that time there would have been serious problems. It was the non-family employee who took a controlling hand and helped secure the firm's future. So at that particular time, the lack of restrictions on transferability was a strength and may have helped ensure that T. & E. Neville survived as a family business. A compromise was reached on the new bloodline-only proposal. The articles of association allow the transfer of shares to people who are not bloodline members of the family, but only after they have first been offered to family members.[7]

In cousin companies, questions concerning branch ownership need to be addressed. What rules, if any, should apply to interbranch decision-making, and how should differences (and possible deadlock) be dealt with? Should there be branch representation on the board of directors?

Lastly, policies will be needed on exiting. If shares in the family business are viewed as a realisable capital investment, is everyone aware of this and are exit procedures in place for owners who want to cash in? By the cousin consortium stage the shareholders are likely to be a mixture of disparate and disconnected first cousins, aunts and uncles, second cousins and more distant relatives who will have inherited rather than purchased their shares. Creating a workable internal capital market so that those who want (or financially need) to sell can withdraw from ownership is a wise precaution.

A mechanism for sale of shares within the family can be one of the topics covered by a shareholders' agreement. These agreements, signed by all family shareholders, spell out the rules on share transfers, ensuring, for example, that shares are sold back to the company (if legal requirements are met) or that they are offered on a first refusal basis to other family shareholders. With later-generation family businesses, the shareholders' agreement may require sellers to offer shares to members of their own family branch first, before offering them to other branches, so that sales by cousins do not alter the balance of power among family branches. Alternatively, when a cousin from one branch sells shares to a purchaser from another branch, a compulsory follow-up transaction may be triggered that will restore the previous ratios of shares held by the two branches.[8]

Whatever mechanism is adopted, shareholders must be bought out for fair value at prices that are calculated according to a transparent and objective process. Getting everyone to agree on how this process will work in advance often avoids conflicts over valuation issues such as minority discounts. Because the valuation process has potentially serious tax and legal ramifications, outside professional advice is essential.

Business policies

Business issues likely to require attention include the following:

✳ Management philosophy. How is the balance struck between the best interests of the family and the best interests of the business?

✳ Corporate culture. How can a corporate culture be created that reflects the family's values?

✳ Board composition. What is the right mix of executive and non-executive directors, and family owners or their representatives?

✳ Board responsibilities. What is the best way to achieve clarity regarding the relationship of the board with family owners and with other stakeholders (see Chapter 6)?

✳ Strategic input. How are core strategic issues on the development and goals of the business (on which family owners should have a decisive input) distinguished from day-to-day decision-making that is the sole responsibility of management?

✳ Executive remuneration. How should the level and nature of rewards and long-term incentives be defined? In particular, should equity-based incentives be available to senior executives?

✳ Management succession. What should be the criteria for selecting the next leader (or leaders)? Who decides? How will they be appraised?

✳ External relationships. For example, what role should the business play in the community?

Family policies

Once again, there are crucial questions to be addressed on core family values and the family's vision. Why is our business better because the family owns it? Why do we as a family want to stay in business together and what rewards are we seeking? Do we want to work for the business or the business to work for us?

Creating governance bodies becomes critical by the cousin company stage. Forums like a family assembly and a family council allow communication and the needs and interests of the wider family to be addressed without disturbing the business. Such bodies help draw up rules and policies on how conflicts (such as interbranch friction) are to be resolved without damaging the business; the family's relationship with the board; the conditions under which family members enter, work within and exit the business, including remuneration, incentives, appraisal and reporting lines; how family perks are to be monitored and controlled; and how the family's philanthropic objectives are to be organised.

Education and development of family members will be the focus of another important policy debate. Preparing the next generation for both ownership and leadership will involve programmes on, for instance, leadership development, mentoring and career planning. If families are to take their vision forward, they need educated shareholders who can get to grips with the complexity of a multigenerational business. When people inherit shares they do not inherit understanding – education holds the key.

Lastly, devising ways to ensure more time is spent together is important, because owning a multigenerational family business is not made any easier when relatives do not know each other very well. The family assembly (discussed later in this chapter) should provide a good starting point, but special efforts may be needed to get to know one another in formal and informal settings, helping to build a stronger and more cohesive unit.

Setting up a family governance process

Themes and ideas that should inform the establishment of a family governance process include fairness, inclusiveness, transparency and clarity of procedures, accountability and ensuring a collective buy-in to the process. Many families who have been through the experience stress the importance of having a driver or champion – somebody trusted from within the family who leads the work and motivates and involves family members in support of the plan.

When setting up a family governance process, which family members to involve (and which not) and when to involve them (or not) can be contentious. Opinion is often divided. Some may feel that collective buy-in to the process is best achieved by involving everyone from the start; others may hold the view that it is better to confine planning meetings and discussions to just the key people at the beginning, and then progressively widen the process to bring in more shareholders, trustees, shareholders' spouses or partners, and so on. It is hard to generalise, but if in doubt the presumption should probably favour inclusiveness as a way to promote collective family buy-in to the governance framework that is under construction. Ultimately, the end-product of the building process may not be as important as ensuring that everyone feels they have participated in a fair and open process.

Recording decisions: the family constitution

The family's agreed conclusions about their values and the relationship they want to have with the business should be formally written down and recorded in a family constitution.

Content

Sometimes also called a creed or charter, a family constitution is a written statement (gained by consensus) of the family's shared values and policies in relation to ownership and operation of the business.

The central aim of this document is to set out guidelines that will help management, the board and the family work together, with each constituency clear about its roles and responsibilities and where the boundaries lie. A family constitution should address the basic points of principle and practice set out in Table 3.1 (see page 62) and, in the current context, should also cover the issues affecting more mature cousin companies highlighted in the previous section. In particular, policies should be included on how the managing director, chairman of the board and leader of the family council are to communicate with each other and with other stakeholders.

Formulating a family constitution is a significant and time-consuming undertaking, and if the process is to be successful, a major commitment is necessary from everyone involved. Sometimes work on a family constitution can be brought to a halt because the process has opened up a Pandora's box of surprise issues that need to be dealt with in advance of finalising the constitution. It is also an all-or-nothing process because all its main headings are, to a significant extent, interlinked and inter-dependent – it is not generally possible to formulate policies on some of them and ignore others.

Legal status

Family members generally expect the finished document to be a confidential family statement of intent rather than an enforceable legal agreement. But as detailed provisions start to come under the microscope, the view sometimes develops that legal enforceability may be desirable for certain aspects. Typically, this is brought home by clauses that are intended to protect the business but that may place potentially onerous burdens on individual family members.

A common example concerns exit procedures for shareholders who want to leave the business (a crucial issue once the family business has reached the cousin consortium stage). The family constitution makes clear their freedom to leave but states that the consideration for their shares is payable over, say, a period of 3–5 years. The delay is designed to protect the company against a large-scale and unexpected withdrawal of cash, but it may represent a serious burden as far as exiting shareholders are concerned. Clearly it is preferable that such important matters are not left to chance and, therefore, family constitution provisions can be made legally enforceable (although more usually such provisions form the basis of a separate legally enforceable shareholders' agreement or an amendment to the company's articles of association).

Another area where legal enforceability is desirable concerns share valuations on exit. Principally, this should cover whether minority share-holdings are valued at full value or whether a discount will apply, and if there is to be a discount, how it is to be calculated.

Monitor, review and amendment

The constitution should be regarded as a living document and provision should be made for it to be formally reviewed every four or five years. In the meantime, there should be mechanisms for family members to record any constitutional concerns or worries before the next formal review.

Structuring family governance

This chapter has highlighted concepts, co-ordinating structures and committees designed to help families create organised accountability

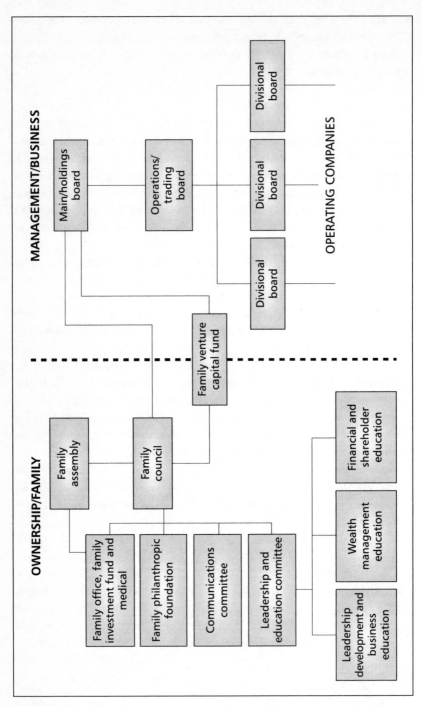

Figure 7.2 Governance structure overview for a multigenerational family business

Source: The author

among the different interests and priorities of ownership, the family and the business. Figure 7.2 provides an overview of some of the principal structural components of family governance. These enable families to separate family and business issues and help them manage complexity in multigenerational, cousin-owned companies.

The first point to note is that this does not mean that all the best-run family firms must have all the governance entities shown in Figure 7.2 or discussed in this section. Figure 7.2 is designed to illustrate some of the available options. It conveys the idea that multigenerational family businesses are often diversified into a number of separate business units or divisions (often managed by a mix of cousins and non-family professional managers), which are controlled by an operations board (sometimes called a trading board). An elaborate governance structure supervises the operations board, including via a main board (sometimes called a holdings or supervisory board) with representatives from family branches and outside directors (see page 119 for information about two-tier boards), along with a family council and family assembly. But there are no templates – family governance architecture and its linking communication channels must be custom-designed to match a family's unique requirements and stage of development.

Family council

The family council, introduced in Chapter 3, is the main forum through which the distinctive interests and concerns of family members and shareholders can be articulated.

At the risk of being too dogmatic (because everything depends on individual circumstances), at its best a family council in a multigenerational business probably has around ten elected members representing all family members, generations and branches. It is a working group serving as an executive committee of the family assembly (an open forum for all family shareholders or all family members). The family council will often be responsible for drafting and finalising the family constitution. However, its longer-term role is to operate as a bridge between the board of directors (or the operations/trading board in companies with a two-tier structure) and the family shareholders.

As noted in Chapter 6, in family businesses the board of directors has an extra area of responsibility beyond those of non-family enterprises (which centre on maximising shareholder value). Board members must understand the family's relationship with the company, mediate its influence on the firm and help ensure that the family's reasonable long-term objectives for the business are met. The principal family council task is to clarify the family's values and vision and help family members unite behind a common goal. Another central function is to send clear signals to the board of directors on strategic, long-term issues: for example, business risk and reward parameters that are acceptable to the family; the return on investment sought by family shareholders; and the family's attitude to ethical and moral issues that may arise in connection with business operations. Another important role is to debate and recommend policies on the rights and responsibilities of individual family members, and to draw up guidelines on relationships between family members and the company, including preparing the next generation. However, as the family expands, the family council often switches its focus to communication, social, educational and charitable issues, leaving these strategic policy decisions to an executive family team.

The council, which may include family managers as well as family owners, should operate on a consensus basis, not by majority vote or in accordance with shareholding. (Indeed, it is a general rule for all these family governance structures that voting is to be avoided, except as a last resort.) The council has no formal authority, but it aims to create the family glue, enabling the family to speak with one voice to the board. Family shareholders can be seen as having just one role – to back the board of directors. If they are unable to provide this backing, they have the ultimate power to remove the board.

In smaller families, the council might comprise all the family shareholders. But, as mentioned earlier, in complex cousin-owned businesses that have large numbers of family shareholders, traditionally each branch of the family has nominated someone for election to the family council. Recent trends, however, suggest that families are trying to move away from this notion of branch representation, often seen as outdated and potentially divisive. In some mature UK family businesses, for example, the new generation has been adopting fresh guidelines that replace branch representation in governance structures with policies and procedures designed to emphasise and foster a more unified family approach to the business. This is clearly a development that places a high premium on establishing and maintaining good intra-family communication.

Recent developments at footwear retailer C & J Clark provide an example of a family council helping to save a multigenerational business. Currently in its sixth generation, Clarks Shoes is one of the UK's oldest family-owned businesses and a household name. Some 80 per cent of the shares are owned by around 200 individual family shareholders, none of whom owns more than 2 per cent, and the balance is owned by employees and institutions. Troubled times in Clarks' history were discussed earlier (see Chapter 2, page 46). In the early 1990s years of family feuding came to a head against a backdrop of bad trading results and dividend cuts. In May 1993, the shareholders only narrowly rejected a proposal to resolve the situation by selling the company.

The business that emerged from these crises, although family owned, is managed by non-family professionals, and the family council, set up in 1993 to help handle the relationship between the family and the board, is regarded as the pivotal governance structure. Features of the council include the following:

✻ It represents virtually all the family and has its own secretariat paid for by the company.

✻ There are 17 council members drawn from family shareholders and, to be eligible, they require the backing of at least 4.5 per cent of the share capital.

✻ It meets with senior management and the company chairman a fixed four times a year. (To a large extent, the effectiveness of the family council is seen as dependent on the sponsorship of the chairman and the openness of the executive directors.)

✻ It also feeds into the board via two family members nominated to the board by the council.

✻ Its main role is to inform and educate shareholders and to allow for consultation on issues that require shareholder consent.

In the period since its establishment, both inside and outside observers have commented that the family council at Clarks Shoes has worked effectively in securing clarity as well as a closer understanding and alignment between ownership and management. Its main challenge for the future is to bring the next generation into the family council.[9]

Other governance entities

A variety of other entities may also be built into a mature family firm's governance architecture. The family council, as we have seen, often serves as an executive committee of the family assembly, which is an open forum for all family shareholders or all family members to learn about the family business and ask questions about its activities. Assembly meetings should be scheduled to maximise attendance and are often combined with social activities. They provide an opportunity for accountability, with family leaders who work in the family governance process able to report back to the wider family. Families need to decide at what age children should attend these meetings. Whatever the age limit – if there is one – families should organise group activities so that the next generation can learn about the business and develop relationships with their siblings and cousins.

This is a good place to re-emphasise that there are no hard-and-fast rules about the detailed roles of governance bodies in family businesses. The family concerned must feel comfortable with the governance process it has constructed, and a flexible approach to deciding who does what often helps achieve this goal. For example, GMR Group, a family business based in Bangalore, has recently put together a broad-based governance system (see case note on page 69). The family council is composed of eight family members: Grandhi Mallikarjuna Rao, his wife, their two sons and daughters-in-law, and daughter and son-in-law. Its core purpose is to assist the family to connect to the business and to ensure effective communication between family members. However, distinct from the family council and feeding into it through the governance hierarchy, GMR has created two extra bodies: a family business forum and a non-business family forum.

The family business forum consists of all family members working in the group. Its role is to act as a bridge between business and family, to make decisions on big-ticket business-related matters – such as setting the family's required risk exposure limits and approving large acquisitions or disposals – and to represent family interests and values. The rationale for the forum is to make sure the family are meeting to discuss shareholder issues so that they speak with one voice to the top entity in the business structure. In parallel is GMR's other unusual body, the non-business family forum, which is composed of spouses of the working family members. Broadly, this is an educational forum with regular facilitated discussions that aim to ensure effective communication, develop interpersonal relationships among family members, foster personal development and parenting, and provide information about the business to the wider family.[10]

A similarly flexible approach to governance architecture – with the family aiming to build structures that work for them – has been taken at Musgrave Group (see Chapter 5, page 98, and Chapter 6, page 113). It has a shareholder committee – also bridging the ownership management divide and linking the family council to the operations board – which is formally a subcommittee of the board, but does not have corporate decision-making power. The shareholder committee consists of the group chairman and chief executive officer, all family non-executive directors (representing the three family branches) and all non-family non-executive directors. It exists primarily as a forum for the board to obtain shareholder views and opinions on items of particular interest to shareholders (especially big-ticket items) and to support board proposals unless the committee members believe that the actions are prejudicial to the interests of the shareholders generally. The shareholder committee meets for half a day before every board meeting, or more often if required.[11]

So, as at GMR, Musgrave sees it as critical to have the family speaking with a single, clear voice to management to avoid the risk of mixed messages from a large shareholder group. As these examples show, however, family companies can approach the issue in a variety of ways. In Chapter 6, for instance, we saw that for some the preferred solution is a legally constituted, two-tier board configuration, whereas for GMR and Musgrave, establishing more informal (although no less rigorously defined and tasked) structures was the favoured route. The objective remains the same – to provide a means for the family to talk with one voice to the board of directors so that its mandate is unequivocally clear – but families can engineer this in flexible ways that fit comfortably with their particular needs and family circumstances.

An interesting cultural contrast is seen in the Middle East, where, as well as family councils and assemblies, the family governance architecture in many family businesses includes an extra body – a council of elders or seniors. Because of the deep-seated respect for the senior generation that underpins many aspects of Middle Eastern life and culture, this entity will be at the top of the family governance hierarchy, with the family council acting as its executive committee.

Returning to the Western model, family wealth management activities may be co-ordinated by a family office. This is an investment, liquidity management and administrative centre that supports the family governance structure. It can also oversee family estate and tax planning and co-ordinate insurance, banking and accounting. Allied to this may be a family foundation – a philanthropic body that serves governance functions by working with the broader family to implement shared values. (Family offices and family philanthropic activities are discussed in Chapter 10.)

A leadership and education committee will be responsible for nurturing the family's human capital by promoting leadership development, business and financial education, and skill-acquisition opportunities for family members. This would also be open to family members who are not employed by the business.

A venture capital fund, operating like a professionally managed fund, may be set up to manage resources that are set aside to stimulate and facilitate entrepreneurship among family members wishing to pursue a career outside the business while still maintaining a connection with it. A large family in Spain has gone one step further, creating a junior board

of family members to oversee new family ventures and provide opportunities for leadership and development of the next generation. The group
will eventually succeed on the board of larger family ventures.[12]

For a large business, a communications committee may take on an
important role, controlling the quantity and quality of information
disseminated by the family business to its shareholders. By the cousin
company stage, most family shareholders (sometimes in their hundreds)
have become detached from traditional, often informal sources of news
and information concerning the family business. Management control of
the business will often have been assumed by one particular branch of the
family, meaning that non-employed family members in other branches
will be out of touch or – just as potentially damaging – will feel out of
touch with what is happening in the business. Keeping these shareholders
informed requires thoughtful and well-planned communications management. This can be a particularly difficult challenge if family business leaders
have acted on the presumption (to an extent justifiable) that only those
active in the business have rights to a free flow of information about it.

At a basic level, it is clearly important to plan for and manage the
announcement of sensitive information, such as the company's dividend
policy. If there is to be a significant change in the policy, especially if this
means reduced dividend payouts, communicating the change needs to
be carefully managed and the ground needs to be prepared so that family
shareholders are not taken by surprise. More generally, money and effort
need to be invested in assessing what types of information should be
compiled, so that everyone is receiving appropriately timed information,
in the right quantity and in a clear format that they can understand and
will find useful. There is also often a case for appointing a shareholder
relationship manager, usually a non-family member whose main role is
to manage the company's communications and relationships with shareholders. The effectiveness of this sort of initiative is supported by putting
together an accompanying education programme for shareholders, aiming
to teach them how to be responsible shareholders.

Communication issues were felt to be at the heart of recent problems
surrounding enfranchisement of the next generation at William Jackson
& Son, a Hull-based food manufacturer and winner of the JPMorgan
2004 Family Governance Award.[13] At that time, the fifth generation were
running the business, but generation six comprised 19 individuals, of
whom nine were then over 18 years old. A few of those 19 attended the
formal family meetings, but mostly communication with them was routed
via their parents, and there was a concern that they were not sufficiently
connected with the business, thus jeopardising a successful generational
transition.

The fifth generation recognised it needed to take a lead, and agreed to review the William Jackson family constitution with a view to bringing the sixth generation on board. They employed experienced facilitators who sent questionnaires to three generations. These were followed by interviews – mostly individual but some of the sixth generation took part in small groups – and a family retreat was organised. The outcome was the establishment of a family steering group, operating as a workhorse between the family and the board of directors. It comprised four members of generation five and three representatives of generation six. As company chairman Christopher Oughtred explained: 'It is up to generation six to talk to each other because they have to select the three representatives amongst themselves.' The steering group's tasks include liaison between the family and the board, educating family members on business issues, discussing dividend policy with the board and the family, and giving advice on taxation, pensions and other matters.

Lastly in this review of governance entities, a family social committee may be set up to organise regular events designed to foster family relationships and unity.

Roles and membership

The assigned role of each of these governance bodies, how they communicate with each other, and who should serve on them, for how long and with what authority, are matters that should be laid down clearly in the family constitution. Selection and staffing in particular raise difficult issues.

When family businesses reach the cousin company stage they are forced – by numbers and diversity – into a representative system under which some family members are empowered to make decisions on behalf of others. How representatives are chosen, for how long they serve, and the scope and extent of their authority are all hard questions that need to be resolved.

Staffing options include open election, volunteers only, outgoing seniors picking their replacements, family branches choosing personnel and nominating committees making selections. The problem is that each of these options comes with its own set of advantages and disadvantages, where, for instance, competency has to be set off against transparency of the process, impartiality against the danger of favouritism, and a rigorous system against one that fosters competition among committees. A good guiding principle when negotiating this difficult balancing act is that recognising the need for a good fit between tasks to be accomplished and the talent available is critical for good governance.[14]

Getting the structure working

The most carefully designed family governance structures will not work unless there is effective collaboration and communication between family members.

The problem is that even at the best of times families can find communication difficult, and more so with the onset of the cousin company stage as the family grows and fragments. Meeting agendas and early discussions with family members often give company advisers the erroneous impression that full and frank communication is taking place within a family business. But when they probe a little deeper, it often becomes clear that family members are not communicating at all about the things that really matter. There is often a forbidden agenda covering a variety of potentially sensitive family issues deemed to be risky and too likely to generate conflict.

Even where there is a desire to talk about important matters openly, it can still be difficult to discuss big issues that go to the root of family members' relationships with each other and the family's interaction with the business. A family business adviser and facilitator can play an important role (see Chapter 5), providing a safe environment in which to talk about the forbidden agenda, coaching individuals to improve their communication skills, helping them develop the capacity to empathise with others' needs and facilitating effective group meetings. In the context of cousin companies, valuable family business facilitation skills include being able to communicate with people who have varying levels of understanding and to connect with different generations and genders within the family. It is important that the whole family buys into the process and that family members enjoy working with their facilitator – the chemistry must be right.

Some golden rules for family members at meetings include listening to each other; trying to understand each other's viewpoints; listening for what is not being said; showing respect; being prepared to explain their reasoning; and being honest while avoiding personal attacks.

A final point is that communication between family members is often inhibited by fear of conflict. But it is important to distinguish between constructive conflict – where different perspectives are accepted and appreciated, and where debate can lead to positive, creative outcomes – and destructive conflict – which generally centres on disputes about personal identity and relationships, and where debate leads nowhere.[15] The most effective families focus on ways of managing differences rather than dealing with conflict.

Conclusions

Multigenerational cousin-owned enterprises need the right family govern-ance structure to suit their particular business and family situations. There is no one-size-fits-all solution. These large families are diverse, and the leadership skills required to forge a common agenda and resolve differ-ences among family members should not be underestimated.

Effective family governance requires introducing points of contact between the family and the enterprise – family assembly, family council, committees, and so on – that enable discussion and resolution of the complicated and often emotional family, ownership and business issues that confront mature family businesses. But governance structures, however well-designed, are only part of the answer and only the start of the journey. Families entering this process need high levels of motivation, and they must be prepared for discomfort, and sometimes trauma, as they learn to talk to one another frankly and grapple with taboo issues. The other required ingredient is a shared passion for making the governance system work, which means educated shareholders, strong leadership and a family-wide commitment to effective communication.

8

Managing succession
The leadership challenge

The willingness of family company owners to plan for their succession is often a decisive factor determining whether the business survives or fails. The mortality statistics make bleak reading. Worldwide, only about one-third of businesses successfully make the transition from each generation to the next, and some studies suggest that only around 5 per cent of family firms are still creating shareholder value beyond the third generation.[1]

Some family business observers believe that family firms should never be put in the hands of the next generation, arguing that successors are rarely as talented as their predecessors. Also, the more successful the predecessor, the larger the company and the less likely that the next generation will be capable of running it. But more than 76 per cent of UK private companies are family owned,[2] the desire to leave a legacy is a powerful motivation for many business owners, and there are many examples of highly profitable and well-run family firms (both private and public) that have remained in family ownership for generations. A key element of their success is that those leading the business have been able to manage the complex and emotionally charged issue of succession to the next generation.

This chapter explains why preparation and planning for succession are so difficult and important, analyses the options, and aims to provide practical guidelines on ensuring that transitions are accomplished as smoothly and as advantageously as possible. Family business succession is a two-stage process involving the transfer of both management and ownership, but they tend not to pass at the same time, with parents often willing to hand over the burden of management before they are willing to let go of the reins of control.

Initially, we concentrate on succession from the first-generation business founder's perspective. Many first-generation succession issues are equally applicable to transitions between later generations. However, transitions from the second generation onwards are recognised as involving some distinct issues, so later in the chapter the focus shifts to considering succession within these older family businesses. In all cases, an important conclusion is that it is a dangerous mistake to regard succession as simply a question of transferring a tried and tested way of running the business from one generation to the next: as well as a change of personnel, the transition will involve a fundamental change of system and culture.

The words 'retire' and 'retirement' crop up throughout this chapter. The problem with the ingrained negative connotations attaching to these words was discussed in some detail in the Preface, and a quick check of any current dictionary throws up a series of unhelpful and downbeat concepts – such as withdrawal from work or business, retreat, becoming a recluse – that comprehensively fail to define and explain retirement as it is understood today. The challenge for family business leaders has less to do with deciding how to leave their business than working out how to reshape their connection and attachment to it. Unfortunately, however, we are saddled with particular words even when their meaning and the concepts they convey are in the process of transformation, and qualifying or rephrasing all references to retire and retirement would soon become irritating rather than illuminating. So these words are retained, but readers are asked to view and understand them in the constructive and positive sense described.

The succession paradox

Doing nothing about succession is often disastrous for family companies. Yet many business owners, reluctant to give up control and preferring to live with ambiguity, decide that avoiding the issue is the best course.

Transferring family businesses to the next generation creates difficult and emotion-laden problems. Planning for the transition cannot start too early, and the whole process needs to be carefully managed. But many entrepreneurs are reluctant to face up to the thought of giving up control, and succession is one of the main causes of divisions and tensions that can damage family life and undermine business performance.

Succession in terms of business leadership confronts the founder of a family business with a complex set of options, which can be summarised under six headings:

✳ appoint a family member;

✳ appoint a caretaker manager;

✳ appoint a professional manager;

✳ exit via sale of the business, in whole or in part;

✳ exit via liquidating the business;

✳ do nothing.

Each option is distinctive and carries its own set of advantages, disadvantages, opportunities and threats. The scope and impact of the options will vary from one family business to another depending on, for example, the ability to attract family and non-family successors who are willing and have the skills to carry on the business, and the financial needs of the family (for instance, whether cash needs to be extracted from the business to provide for the retirement of the senior generation). The personal and corporate taxation consequences of the options will also be relevant, as will the health and size of the business, and the external commercial and business environment at the time of succession.

If there is a commitment to retain direct control over the business (this is the focus of this chapter), the first option of appointing a family member to succeed is seen as particularly attractive by many founders. It gives their personal ideas and values a greater chance of survival, and they can feel their life's work is in good hands. Also, they do not lose contact with the business and may even retain some influence over it.

The appointment of a non-family successor, either to a permanent position or as a caretaker (the second and third options), may become the strategy by default if no family successors are available, motivated or have the necessary skills for the task. Genetics do not guarantee that families can produce entrepreneurial business leaders generation after generation.

In terms of exit routes, some form of sale as a going concern (the fourth option) is likely to recover most value from the business. Alternatives within this option include a trade sale (an outright sale of the whole business for cash), which may be particularly appealing where no suitable successors can be found, or a stock market flotation, if external capital to finance growth is a priority. Similarly, a management buy-out financed by private equity funding (a sale by the founder to the existing management team, which may include family members) can offer a compromise between transferring the shares to the family and an outright trade sale.

Liquidation (the fifth option) entails selling off all the company's assets, paying its outstanding debts and dismissing the workforce. It also involves substantial expenses and is unlikely to result in the best price being obtained.

Owners' reluctance to cede control and plan for succession is common, and it is often disastrous for family businesses

Lastly, the founder may simply avoid planning for succession by adopting the do-nothing approach (the sixth option in the list), and here lies the central paradox. Despite founders professing that a family solution is their preferred course, in practice the dynastic dream is rarely achieved. Doing nothing is the least logical, the most costly and the most destructive of all the options, yet it is by far the most popular.

Resistance to succession planning

Complex forces are at work in family companies, favouring doing nothing about succession. These forces operate within the founder, the family and the business, and understanding them is the essential first step in successfully managing the transition process.

We are all mortal, so to safeguard the continuity and vitality of the business, owners should regard planning for succession and making sure that it takes place as smoothly and efficiently as possible as one of their principal responsibilities. It is strange, therefore, that despite the logic of this apparently natural transition (as well as the compelling business and family reasons for planning succession) the do-nothing option is the one founders most frequently adopt.

An example (one of many cases) concerned a business that was started by a university professor who took early retirement. He was in his late 40s and had a brilliant idea, based on technologies he had studied, so he decided to go into business to exploit it. He built a prototype in his garage and then set up a manufacturing plant, selling the product at high margins to military and commercial end-users around the world. The professor was a genius and a perfectionist, and the business enjoyed spectacular profitability and growth. His two sons and a daughter worked with him, but he never took them into his confidence, their careers were not planned and they were never trained or allowed to take on serious responsibilities. Nevertheless, the professor loved the idea of passing the company on to them, and spoke about this often, but made no plans for the transition. In his mid-60s, and still very much in control, he fell ill unexpectedly and died. The next generation felt totally unprepared to take over – despite working at the firm for a decade they had no experience of managing the company at that level, nor did they have a clear picture of how the business worked. The firm was sold.

In general, the alternatives are stark. Succession may be an organised and gradual process, in which case a trained successor grows into the role under the owner's supervision and guidance; or it takes place abruptly and unexpectedly when the owner becomes ill or dies, in which case an unprepared family member can suddenly find the job forced upon them.

Jeffrey Sonnenfeld of Yale University has categorised the departure styles of family business founders into groups he labels 'monarchs', 'generals', 'ambassadors' and 'governors'.[3] Monarchs do not leave office until they are decisively forced out through death or an internal 'palace revolt'. Generals are also forced out of office, but plot their return, and quickly come back out of retirement to save the business. Ambassadors leave office gracefully and frequently serve as post-retirement mentors. (Tom Watson Jr of IBM, for example, after a heart attack at 57, instituted a retirement age of 60 throughout the company, and served as a mentor to the board until his death – unlike his father, the founder of the business, who refused to pass on the reins until he was 82.[4]) Governors, the last category, rule for a limited term of office, retire and then switch to other vocational outlets. Describing these four exit styles provides a helpful framework for understanding the psychological factors that make the succession issue so difficult to confront.

Sonnenfeld concluded his study by comparing the average annual company growth achieved while in charge, analysed by departure style. Monarchs were far and away the best performers, followed by ambassadors, generals and governors. But he also looked at performance during the last two years of their periods in office and found a completely different picture; the governors now came top, and the autocratic monarchs, by this time clinging on to power, had slumped to being the worst performers, reinforcing the idea that they had passed their sell-by date.

Why is it that monarchs and generals so often provide the template for the exit styles of choice? Failure to address succession is often put down to a combination of the entrepreneur's instinctive desire to keep control of his creation and a natural aversion to planning. But the reasons are normally much more subtle, and in many cases are rationalisations designed to avoid deep-rooted anxieties and fears. A great many factors conspire to reduce the likelihood of planning for succession. Ivan Lansberg has categorised the range of deterrents into those connected with the founder, the family, the employees and the general environment in which the firm operates.[5]

The founder

First under this heading is fear of death. Few people find it easy to come to terms with their own mortality, and this is often a particular problem for entrepreneurs, whose success is usually driven by a powerful ego and the conviction that they control their own destinies. Reluctance to let go of control and power also plays a part. Many owners become entrepreneurs precisely because of a strong need to acquire and exercise power over others. It is not surprising, therefore, that surrendering authority can be seen as a huge sacrifice.

Owners often identify strongly with the business, seeing it as a personal achievement that defines their place in the world. Letting go can therefore feel like a loss of personal effectiveness and can reawaken old identity issues that may be hard to cope with at this late stage in the owner's life. There is also often a bias against planning. Successful management transitions are generally the result of a major planning exercise that begins many years before succession takes place. But owners are generally doers rather than planners, and they often perceive formal planning as bureaucratic and restrictive.

Inability to choose among children often works against succession planning. We saw in Chapter 2 that, under business principles, the choice of a successor should be based on competence, whereas family values dictate that children should not be the subject of a selection process but should be loved and treated equally. Family values generally prevail in this conflict, with founders unwilling even to contemplate what they see as preferential treatment of one child at the expense of the others.

Fear of retirement is also a powerful factor. Owners of family firms are often in love with their businesses, and the thought of moving out of day-to-day work into what they sometimes see as the vacuum of retirement can be regarded as little short of a life-threatening event. The founder will probably have few outside interests that could be developed in retirement, and will therefore focus on negative considerations such as the expected loss of self-esteem and the risks of entrusting the business to an unproven successor. 'Nobody can run this business as well as me' is symptomatic of the view many owners struggling with succession develop about their own importance, encapsulating the feelings of rivalry and jealousy they can feel towards potential successors waiting to take over control of their beloved organisation. When founders and potential successors are fathers and mothers and sons and daughters, this can become even more serious, introducing an extra psychological dimension of fear and hostility. There was a case of a father who had promised to hand over the business to his son. The son worked for his father for 15 years, only to be told that he had to buy the company. The two have not spoken since.

The family

Forces operating against succession planning are not confined to those involving the founder. The family provides another source of pressure that favours avoiding the issue. The founder's spouse is frequently reluctant to welcome and encourage a partner's move into retirement (even in the more positive sense that this word is coming to be understood). He or she, too, may not relish the prospect of giving up many key roles played in and around the family firm. As well as direct involvement in the business, the company will probably have become a centre of activity and a significant component of the spouse's social identity.

Family taboos also play a role. The cultural norms that govern family behaviour discourage discussion between parents and the next generation about the family's future after the parents die. This is particularly so in relation to financial matters. Succession planning, of course, involves open discussion of precisely these topics and is thus usually avoided, even in the most well-adjusted families.

Finally, there is fear of parental death. The next generation typically have deep-rooted psychological worries about abandonment and separation, and such feelings can be too painful to permit participation in discussions about succession.

Employee and environmental factors

Employees can present obstacles to succession, even though the prosperity and continuity of the business are in their best interests. For many employees (especially senior managers) their close personal relationship with the founder constitutes the most important advantage of working for the family firm. Replacement of the founder with a newcomer, viewed as inexperienced and likely to make sweeping changes, is seen by employees as a threat to their job satisfaction and security.

External worries about change also play a role. Outside the firm, important customers are likely to prove resistant to change, reluctant to trust a new face. Similarly, the unwillingness of other entrepreneurs – the owner's peer group – to deal with their own succession reinforces the founder's bias against planned management transition.

So owners have to face up to a range of complex and interrelated processes – psychological, emotional, individual, organisational and external – that are all operating against any kind of planned effort to manage succession. It is hardly surprising, therefore, that so few family business founders are willing and able to organise effective succession planning, concentrating instead on coming up with one delaying tactic after another designed to put off the day when they will have to grapple with the issue.

Leading the transition

Alan Crosbie, an Irish businessman who lectures on family businesses, draws a nice analogy between running a family company and flying a plane:[6]

> There is not much danger to anybody when the plane is in the third hour of a transatlantic journey, but at take-off and landing the craft is much more vulnerable to an accident. The point of succession is very much like landing and taking off again. It presents a radically greater threat of danger than is posed by any of the other periods in the history of the company.

Strong leadership is required to guide the business through such transitions. Succession planning – done well – takes a long time, and the most successful transitions result from establishing a partnership between the generations based on mutual responsibility, respect and commitment. They also result, however, from a willingness, early on, to address fundamental questions, such as does the business need to remain family owned and, if so, why? Then there are the all-important drop-dead questions: 'What would happen if the family business leader dropped dead tomorrow, who would take over, and what would be the impact on the business?' There is no room for vagueness, assumptions or guesswork. Orderliness is a key component of succession planning, which requires a framework of mutual understanding, as well as clear leadership and direction.

Once it is decided that the long-term objective is to keep the business in the family, guidelines for managing the succession process (which are discussed below) are to:

✳ start planning early;

✳ encourage intergenerational teamwork;

✳ develop a written succession plan;

✳ involve the family and colleagues;

✳ take advantage of outside help;

✳ establish a training process;

✳ plan for retirement;

✳ make retirement timely and unequivocal.

But succession should also be seen as an opportunity to refresh the family's values (what a family and its business stand for) and vision (the shared sense of where each is heading). We saw in Chapter 3 that values and vision provide a major source of strength and resilience for the family firm. It was also noted that if values and attitudes remain static and entrenched in the past, the family risks creating a vacuum in which – with no relevant vision to unite the family – disconnection, communication failures and conflict are likely to flourish.[7] Renewal of a coherent ownership vision is required with each generational transition of the family business, and the instability and flux of the transition process itself provides an opportune time for the family to collectively engage in this task, before policies and positions take root.

Start planning early

As discussed previously, in business one of the main routes to success and huge profits derives from being able to solve tomorrow's predictable problems today. Entrepreneurs come to a view about what the future holds and deliver commercial solutions that take advantage of their foresight, and that is how fortunes are made. This, of course, is difficult to achieve, but a distinctive feature of family businesses is that it is always possible to solve a range of tomorrow's predictable problems simply because, for the most part, they can be identified in advance.

Succession provides a classic example. Rather than waiting till the reading of the will to resolve questions like 'Who gets the shares?' or 'Who is best suited to take on managerial leadership?', in a family business there is the opportunity to address such issues ahead of time, in a calm atmosphere, under an agreed process, thus reducing the potentially damaging impact of unexpected yet predictable events. But despite this, often the first real thoughts about succession are prompted by the death or ill health of the chairman or managing director. As well as the potential for serious damage to the business, this will be a time when the family is least able to give the matter proper consideration.

Insufficient planning for the death of the majority shareholder may expose the family to major cash flow problems in the form of tax liabilities but no liquid assets with which to settle them. In other cases, the succession proceeds in an atmosphere of mutual acrimony and guilt as family members, unable to understand or control the process they are caught up in, search for somewhere to place the blame.

The succession process should be carefully planned and take place over time. Ideally, the owner's reduced involvement is so gradual as to be almost imperceptible. Rather than being abruptly ousted from the top job, the founder gradually separates his or her identity from that of the business and becomes accustomed to a new role. At the same time, successors should grow into their roles, earning the respect and confidence of the founder and other stakeholders.

Developing a full understanding of the transition process and its effect upon family members is critical, and this also takes a long time. The various options need to be assessed; the family must be given adequate opportunity to reflect on the implications of decisions; and a gradual succession timetable needs to be structured and agreed.

Encourage intergenerational teamwork

It is important to establish and foster intergenerational teamwork if the build-up to the transition, the transition itself and what happens afterwards are to be as trouble-free as possible.

There is no substitute for leadership by the senior generation. If possible, the elder generation should become coach and mentor to the next, leading to a staged shift of power and control over time. Father–son and other family rivalries often inhibit the development of such a scenario, but such intergenerational partnerships, when they work, are powerful and effective. Judge Thomas Mellon (1813–1908), an Irish immigrant to the USA and founder of a banking empire, saw his primary mission as the preparation of his five sons for leadership. He spent time with each of them, helping them learn from their mistakes and imbuing values of trust and collaboration. On 5 January 1882 Thomas fulfilled the plan he had when he founded his bank by stepping down and giving it to his son, Andrew W. Mellon, who had worked with him for nine years (and had been given a one-fifth interest at the outset). Shortly afterwards Andrew gave half of the bank to his brother Richard B. Mellon, thus beginning an era of co-operation and banking success which grew to worldwide status. Judge Mellon, at the age of 75, rather than trying to get back into the business or act as a sideline adviser, simply departed the scene and went away to start a new business.[8]

Unfortunately, the reality often falls short of this ideal scenario. With succeeding generations, the intensity of emotional factors that surround the family's involvement in the business can increase, and bits of emotional baggage – unresolved issues left over from the previous generation – can develop a life of their own. For example, if one brother feels he has been done down by another brother and this grievance is not settled before the siblings die, when the next generation succeeds the grudge may well live on and fester. Establishing intergenerational teamwork implies the generations recognising these sorts of problems, talking about them and trying to find solutions. Assuming such issues will just be forgotten about over time can be a fundamental mistake; the problems generally resurface later on and become more complicated and more difficult to resolve.

Financial independence between generations is important and, if necessary, provision should be made for it in the succession plan. One way of achieving financial (and a measure of psychological) independence between generations is through an intergenerational loan. To buy out the departing generation and ensure that it ceases to have any financial claims on the company, the new generation takes out a loan, secured on the assets of the business. This will usually involve the purchase of shares, so advice must be obtained to make sure that the transaction does not fall foul of legal prohibitions on companies giving financial assistance (including security) for the purchase of their own shares.

Establishing financial independence is illustrated by a case involving a son buying shares from the family. In his mid-30s, the son was experiencing enormous frustration trying to run the family business in the face of interference from his parents, who had spent many years building up the company. The son had ambitions to expand the firm but was worried that he was not able to function effectively within the business because he did not have a clear mandate from his parents. The parents, for their part, were reluctant to empower the son because the business represented the bulk of their personal wealth and they were worried that any deterioration in profits would adversely affect their retirement.

The first step in resolving this impasse involved establishing with the parents how much money they would need to provide for their retirement – in short, how much money they wanted in the bank, after tax, so that they would no longer care. The figure was calculated to be equivalent to around 40 per cent of the value of the business, so a plan was devised under which the son formed a new company (in which he owned all the shares) and the parents gave him 60 per cent of their equity in the family business. Following this, the new company took a bank loan (secured mainly on the underlying business assets) to enable it to purchase the parents' remaining 40 per cent interest. Subsequently, a share exchange took place and the new company was left owning 100 per cent of the family business. The net result was that the son acquired complete control of the business and his parents received sufficient cash, after tax, to provide financial security for their retirement. The case illustrates (as in previous examples) that once agreed objectives are established, designing suitable structures and mechanisms to achieve those objectives is the easy bit.

Develop a written plan

Chapter 3 stressed the importance for families of establishing formal mechanisms, rules and procedures as a way of helping them avoid (or at least manage) tensions and divisions which, if left unchecked, would interfere with the effective functioning of the business. It was shown that setting up a family council and drawing up a written family constitution (recording the family's agreed policies on the business and other issues) will provide a structural framework that helps family members focus on the important issues, progress through problems and find ways of working with each other.

For the same reasons, developing a written succession plan that incorporates a step-by-step approach to dealing with the practical and psychological aspects of the transition process will prove invaluable. The thought required to formulate and write down the stages of the process will be useful in itself, and the existence of a formal document that everybody is aware of, and has been consulted about, will significantly reduce the potential for doubts and misunderstandings.

The plan should cover a leadership and skills development programme for potential successors. This would include outside work experience and a preliminary outline of a planned career path within the business. The process for choosing a successor should also be made crystal clear: the timing of the decision; the business criteria to be employed; whether the decision is delegated to the board or a committee of family members; how the decision is to be confirmed and communicated to the family, the company and outside stakeholders (such as creditors and key customers). It is important to have a detailed timetable that plots each phase of the owner's reduced participation in the business, while mapping out the chosen successor's expanding role and responsibilities. The plan for organisational succession, covering the structure and functioning of the management team after the transition, should also be included, with details, for instance, of new career paths for key managers and future family participation.

When the written succession plan is complete, communicate it (or at least its principal conclusions) to the family, the employees and outsiders who have an interest in the continuity and success of the business, such as the bank manager, customers and suppliers. Tangible evidence of a serious approach to the problems of succession will impress and reassure them and, at the same time, will give everyone the opportunity to plan for a smooth transition.

Involve everyone and obtain outside help

It is a good idea to appoint a succession working party, consisting of the owner, selected family members, non-executive directors and trusted employees. This group is responsible for developing the succession plan and monitoring its implementation. The latter is important in ensuring that the plan is accomplishing the desired organisational results, including generating individual psychological responses that will be required to sustain the transition.

It is the business owner's responsibility to initiate and lead the succession planning process, but the working party gives everyone most directly concerned an opportunity to discuss their thoughts and fears openly. By providing a forum for debate, it should help to reduce negative emotional reaction within the family.

Input from the family and employees about their concerns, interests and priorities is important, but only the founder fully understands the complex emotional and managerial issues associated with succession planning. Because of this, founders should try to involve as many people as possible in the process – absolutely anyone, in fact, who may be able to offer useful advice and support during this critical phase. For example, a strong, balanced board of directors that includes outsiders is an invaluable source of expertise and objectivity during succession planning, as are family business consultants and other professional advisers who have a good understanding of the firm and are skilled in dealing with these issues. Peer groups – business colleagues who are themselves facing, or who have already been through the succession transition – will almost certainly be helpful. Sharing and comparing experiences can serve as a much-needed source of ideas, strategies and support.

Establish a training process

Many owners assume that their children will want to enter the family business, or they put pressure on them to do so. Inadequate preparation and training, or undue pressure, condemns many next-generation members to unhappy careers that are neither satisfying for them nor productive for the business. Preparing successors for leadership is discussed on page 161.

Plan for retirement

It is important that owners prepare themselves emotionally and financially for a new phase of their lives that does not revolve exclusively around the family business. They need to take advice on financial preparations. At the emotional level, experts are more or less unanimous that this phase is most likely to be successfully negotiated if business owners are retiring to a new life of interesting activities, rather than from their old one, which implies that their useful and productive days are over. It is neither desirable nor possible for founders to sever their connection with the family business – after all, it is part of the fabric of the family. Founders must think, therefore, about how best to reshape their attachment to the business and to plan their future work activities.

Founders remain a vital resource to the family firm, even though they have passed on day-to-day operational responsibility to their successors. Many founders, as part of their succession plan, assume new roles in the company, taking on, for example, new product development or special projects. They can also play a role in fostering management continuity, connecting the new managers with individuals and organisations that may be important to the future success and prosperity of the company.

Decide when to retire and stick to it

As noted in Chapter 4, clear and explicit management criteria need to be drawn up relating to human resource management issues and family members, but even family businesses that do have formal policies often encounter difficulties when family executives simply refuse to adhere to the retirement guidelines. The problem is particularly troublesome in the case of founders who are reluctant to step down from day-to-day operational control of the business because, among other things, they believe they are indispensable to the enterprise. Thus they resist pressures to retire that come from potential successors, their spouses or other family members in the business. The difficulties are highlighted in a great many reported cases in which the sequence of events runs roughly as follows. The managing director's retirement date is fixed; succession arrangements are in place; the company's people, family and non-family, gather on the appointed Friday evening to mark the event with champagne and speeches; the managing director explains all the wonderful plans designed to ensure a busy and enjoyable retirement; the following Monday, to every-one's astonishment (and the appointed successor's horror), the managing director turns up as usual, explaining: 'There are one or two things I still need to sort out.'

Succession is much more likely to proceed smoothly if founders step down at a time when they are still in full command of their abilities and can provide guidance to senior managers when they seek it. Life-cycle analysts have highlighted the difficulties that can occur when founders hold on too long and become out of synch with their successors. Psycho-logist Frederic Hudson, for example, has defined the developmental chal-lenges for people in their 50s and 60s as securing self-renewal and creating new beginnings; in contrast, developmental work for those in their 70s and beyond focuses on reflection, creating a legacy and mentoring.[9] It is clear how family business seniors who are unable to start planning the renewal of their lives in their 50s and 60s can end up seriously out of phase during their 70s and beyond. This in turn affects the lives of next-generation successors, themselves in mid-life and probably impatient for independence, recognition and opportunities for leadership. As society ages, these pressures and imbalances are likely to increase. At a personal level, it is not hard to visualise how staying put may seem the easiest option for family business seniors as they get older and face the prospect of trying to disentangle the complicated mix of emotional, commercial, financial and legal arrangements that have ruled their lives for decades.[10]

Vagueness and imprecision about how long a family chief executive or managing director will run the company belongs to the past. There is a strong argument for including provisions in the family constitution and/ or the written succession plan specifying how long the managing director should be allowed to hold the top job. This does not mean that seniors must cease to play any role in the business, but it does mean that their new role has been well defined and does not encompass participation in day-to-day operations. Successors sometimes report having to devote significant amounts of time to seniors who were previously in charge, and whose need to share and know has not diminished. However, the requirement for regular briefing chats usually diminishes over time, and, rather than being resented by the next generation, is generally seen as a legitimate but costly payback.[11]

Selecting the right successor

In evaluating candidates, important questions to consider include the following:

✳ Are they committed to the company's mission?

✳ Do they have the ability to move the business forward?

✳ Can they think independently and exercise good judgement?

✳ Do they have the leadership talents required to take hard decisions and motivate others?

But who is the right person to be asking these questions and making the choice? A number of experts have concluded that senior family members working in the business should not be responsible for the selection of their own successors. Harry Levinson has summarised the argument well:[12]

> Each of us in his own unconscious way seeks omnipotence and immortality. To varying degrees, each wants his achievements to stand as an enduring monument to himself; each wants to demonstrate that he was necessary to his organisation, that it cannot do without him. This pressure is particularly strong for entrepreneurs and those who hold their positions for long periods of time. As a result, although executives consciously seek to perpetuate their organisations through the wise choice of successors, unconsciously they also seek to demonstrate that no one can succeed them.

To avoid these dangers, the advice and assistance of a strong board of directors is invaluable, both in assessing the capabilities of family members in the business and any non-family candidates and in making the final decision. In particular, an experienced and independent non-executive director may be able to offer a perspective free of the dynamics in which the chairman, managing director and other members of the firm and family are caught up. Outside professional human resource management consultants will provide an extra source of objectivity.

An interesting alternative approach to the 'Who should do the choosing?' question has been built into the family constitution of GMR Group (see Chapter 3, page 69, and Chapter 7, page 140). It will be remembered that the founder, Grandhi Mallikarjuna Rao, has been joined in the business by his two sons and his son-in-law, all of whom are group directors. Rao, now aged 57, has set 70 as his retirement age, at which point he plans to devote his full attention to the GMR Foundation's charitable activities. Five years before this, however, a process will begin to select and appoint a successor, and the constitution provides that it will be the next generation who do the choosing – that is, Rao's sons and son-in-law will come together to act as a selection committee. The selection committee is required to come to a unanimous decision, and a process is in place, if needed, to resolve deadlock (as well as a clause governing what happens in the event of Rao's permanent absence or incapacitation).[13]

Who to choose?

Consideration of succession candidates from within the family can raise difficult issues. Before the process starts, however, it is important for the family to reflect upon its values, vision and goals, using these as a guide for decision-making. If, for example, a risk-averse, wealth-preservation and stewardship approach is one of the family's core strategies for the business, a successor likely to follow high-geared, high-risk tactics aiming for spectacular growth should not rank near the top of the candidate list. Also remember that, while the senior generation may have provided individuals with excellent managerial, leadership and entrepreneurial skills, it may be necessary to accept that these combined talents are not available in the next generation gene pool, which possibly stretches only to providing a good manager. In this case, a different approach to – and structure for – succession will be needed. Similarly, if there is somebody who is not a good manager but who has brilliant leadership qualities, it may be more appropriate to focus on a structure that puts outside management talent in place below him while he becomes, say, family chairperson as opposed to family managing director.

Sometimes the choice of successor seems straightforward. There can be a single successor – regarded by the family as the logical choice – who is both capable and committed and who, during the succession planning process, grows naturally into the role. But some families define logical to mean that the eldest son is automatically the first choice. Although this eliminates uncertainty and reduces the likelihood of rivalry among the children, such a rule may result in the appointment of a leader who is less qualified than other candidates. A recent McKinsey study concluded that family businesses run by eldest sons tend to be managed relatively poorly, and that the prevalence of such companies in France and the UK seems to account for much of the gap in effectiveness – and perhaps in performance – observed relative to family businesses in Germany and the USA.[14]

To an extent, searching for a single successor reflects a bias that exists in favour of the single-leadership model for family companies. Thinking about succession in terms of choosing one, and only one, leader to be the successor can be misleading. There may be compelling reasons for family firms to combine two or more people in leadership, such as parental refusal to face up to the decision of choosing a successor from among their children, or it being too early to undertake a complete handover between generations.[15] So second-generation family firms run by the sibling offspring of the founder sometimes contravene the single-leader model by taking one of two other forms: first among equals partnerships, where one sibling in the partnership has perhaps a marginal edge on the others, who are willing to accept the individual as the respected leader of the company and its figurehead; or true partnerships (two or more siblings operating as a team of equals), where leadership is shared and the siblings manage the business on the basis of consensus.

Both types of partnership depend on there being some sort of shared vision, clarity of roles and responsibilities, appreciation of diversity in personalities, and a strong sibling bond that fosters collaboration and helps create and maintain successful teamwork. It also helps if co-leaders have relatively equal abilities, as well as a willingness to compromise and accept consensus decision-making. Even then, mechanisms should be in place for resolving deadlock.

At one business visited while researching this book, the division of leadership responsibilities between two second-generation brothers was helped by the business itself being divided into two fairly distinct geographical operations of more or less equal size, each overseen by one brother. The leaders described their role as a true, balanced partnership, which they regarded as a huge source of strength. One reason it worked for them appeared to be that they had completely different personalities, with strengths and backgrounds that complemented each other. However, a shared vision and a strong bond also existed between the brothers, as one of them explained:

> I think it only works because I grew up with him and know him very well. I trust him completely, don't interfere, and allow him to get on with his area of responsibility, and he does the same with me. Also, we both are very clear about who does what because we've written it down so that everyone in the company knows the position.

A survey of the children of owner-managers of UK family businesses found that gender factors seem to be involved in decisions by the next generation not to join the family business. Of the children surveyed, 75 per cent of sons worked in the business, compared with only 35 per cent of daughters – and daughters accounted for 77 per cent of those whose main reason for not joining was a lack of interest in a business career.[16] More daughters seeking a career in the family firm might make a difference, because the absence of the potentially troublesome father–son relationship can smooth the succession process.

Similarly, in-laws should not be overlooked. The involvement of committed sons-in-law or daughters-in-law can provide an additional pool of potential next-generation leaders and bring new strengths to the family business. Remember though that the increasing incidence of divorce can have a severe impact when it involves an in-law who is in a key management position. (The statistic was quoted earlier, but it bears repetition: females born after 1965 in the USA will have more husbands than children.) Following separation, some families are able to draw a distinction between family and business considerations, and the in-law continues to work in the business. Others find this untenable and the in-law has to leave. Families can anticipate such problems through agreements providing for an immediate buy-back of the firm's shares held by the in-law in the event of divorce (see also the discussion on prenuptial agreements in Chapter 2, page 27). Ultimately, the risks of a potential marriage breakdown have to be weighed against the benefits an in-law can bring to the business.

Succession from the second generation onwards (discussed later in this chapter) generally involves more than one family unit. Usually, the number of potential successors is larger and the choice becomes more difficult. As participation in the business grows, so does the potential for conflict, particularly when share ownership is equal between the family units.

Hiring professional managers to run the business provides a clear solution to the co-ownership problem. But if the families want to remain actively involved in the business, the owners need to develop strict policies to govern its future management. The creation of a voting trust is one possibility. Even though shares in the company are spread among the various family units, voting control is centralised in the hands of those responsible for the management of the business.

What if no one fits the bill?

Although family business owners may have a huge amount of emotional capital invested in it, and wish to see it continued by their children, it may be self-defeating to force a family management transition if the right circumstances do not exist. Perhaps none of the children has the ability needed to run the business, or maybe rivalry between them is so extreme that none would accept one of the others as leader. If, after an honest assessment, the conclusion is that there is little chance of a successful management transition to the next generation, owners should begin to look for some alternatives.

Dividing the business

If sibling rivalry effectively precludes the next generation from proceeding together, it may be worth considering a division of the company. Assuming the business can be structured to allow a demerger, the next generation can take over different parts, which then develop independently. But companies should not take this route purely for family reasons – it must also make good business sense.

Selling the company

When a transition within the family is not achievable, an owner may be better off selling the business rather than forcing the succession issue. The decision to sell is likely to be traumatic and, compared with a transfer of the firm to the next generation, may carry some adverse tax consequences.

It is important to try to disentangle the emotional considerations from the financial ones. A useful idea for business owners who have ruled out the possibility of a sale is to imagine they receive an approach from a possible buyer, who says: 'If I gave you a cheque this afternoon for £20 million representing the value of your business, would you put the money into a building society, or property, or the stock market – or would you buy a business like yours?' The response to the last possibility is likely to be 'No'. The question is rarely posed in such stark terms, but it should be. A sale may be the best option to preserve both the owner's financial security and harmony in the family.

Appointing non-family managers

Many families decide to hire outside professional managers if it is not feasible for a family member to take over. The central issue is one of trust – will the family's principal store of wealth be safe in the hands of an outsider? However, family members in the business, aware of the problems they would have in filling the role, often prefer reporting to a respected professional manager.

The appointment of outside managers becomes particularly relevant once the family business reaches the third generation and beyond. By this stage there can be dozens of family members with a stake in the firm, and introducing professional management often represents the only realistic solution to the succession issue.

Sometimes families try to avoid having to resort to outside managers by appointing as managing director someone who has worked for the family for years, and who is seen as part of it. This can be a high-risk strategy. Such a manager will have had little opportunity to develop the required leadership skills and is frequently under considerable pressure from the family to adopt a stewardship role. In these circumstances, the business can start to drift in the absence of a strong leader capable of driving it forward.

Employing a bridge

If the obstacles to family succession are temporary (for example, if the successors have not yet acquired the experience to take over), a caretaker managing director can be appointed to run the firm until the transition within the family takes place. Referred to as a bridge, the individual is usually a talented professional manager who will expect to be well paid to compensate for the short-term and essential nature of his or her task.

It is not uncommon for such a caretaker also to act as a mentor to the succeeding generation. Such individuals may find it easier to take advice from this professional manager than from a parent, and the bridge takes on the role of overseeing their career development plan to prepare them for a future position of leadership in the business. (See Chapter 5, page 93, for a case note illustrating the appointment of a non-family employee to act as a bridge.)

Some conclusions on selecting a successor

In the last analysis, family company owners must be honest in assessing the capacity of the next generation to become business leaders. If a son or daughter lacks that capacity, the owner must face up to this because, like so many other family business problems, brushing it under the carpet will only make it worse.

Overpromoting successors does them (and the firm) no favours. As well as damaging the business, putting any family member into a job that is beyond his or her capabilities risks causing alienation among family members and destabilising the career, and possibly even the life, of the individual concerned. Consider the possibility of bringing in an outsider to run the company – family members who still want to be involved may well fill other roles.

Judging whether someone has the capacity for the job can be risky. It is possible that although they may not be up to the job at the moment, they could grow into it in the future. Thus a balance should be struck between, on the one hand, cutting the family member off from opportunity, and, on the other, giving them a chance to make the grade.

Third-party advice can play an important role for both successors, in helping sort out priorities and objectives for their future career, and owners, in objectively assessing the business acumen of the next generation. The third party could be a non-executive director, or one of the company's professional advisers, or a trusted non-family manager. The crucial thing is that the chosen individual knows about the business, is respected by both generations, and is able to combine the roles of mentor for the family member and provider of candid advice and performance assessment for both the owner and the successor.

Sometimes it becomes clear that a family member will grow into the top job in time. In this case, a useful solution is to employ a caretaker managing director until a transition within the family can take place.

Preparing next-generation managers and leaders

Succession should involve a well-planned partnership with the next generation. Parents must take responsibility particularly for ensuring that their children receive a sound, broadly based education; that they are well nurtured and develop self-esteem; that they learn about money, business and investment; that they have extended outside work experience before joining the family business; and that if they do join, there is a training programme for them that is both relevant and worthwhile.

As noted in Chapter 4, many owners assume that their children will want to enter the family business, or they put pressure on them to do so. While the children are growing up, it is important to try to keep an open mind about this possibility, and to remember that their perception of the business is being formed mainly on the basis of what the senior generation tells them about it. If they regularly hear complaints about the problems of running the firm, it is likely they will shy away from the prospect of joining and choose other careers. Similarly, if the children are conditioned from birth to believe that the business represents a golden inheritance and that perpetuating it is their destiny, they will view joining the firm either as an easy option or as a weighty obligation, rather than as an opportunity. Entirely insulating the children from the business is probably not achievable because this may convey an unintended message that there will never be the possibility of pursuing a career in the family firm.

Senior-generation members should try to find a balance that enables their successors to share their dream, making sure they do not put excessive pressure on them so they feel they have no choice but to be part of it. Telling them about the exciting and challenging aspects of running the business as well as the negative ones can help. Letting them get first-hand experience of the firm, perhaps working in it during school and university holidays, may also assist. But always balance any enthusiasm for their entry to the firm by making it clear that the family will understand and support them should they choose other careers.

Ultimately, their decision to join should be freely made and based on a thorough understanding of the privileges and responsibilities that come with the job, and an acceptance of the hard work and commitment required. Inadequate preparation and training, or undue pressure, risk condemning the next generation to unfulfilling careers, and the business too may suffer.

In-house training and development

The typical route to the top for the heir apparent in many traditional family firms involves a series of positions within the firm, sometimes beginning at the lowest level. Learning every job on the way up can have a value in particular businesses, but the development of managerial talent is a long process and care should be taken not to waste time on direct experience of menial tasks simply for its own sake. Overall, the important point is to make sure that all training is worthwhile and appropriate in relation to the career development strategy set out in the written succession plan.

Be aware that because of the emotional involvement, parents can be poor teachers, so help young family members joining the firm to establish a special relationship with a non-family mentor figure within the organisation. A key manager who has been with the firm for a long time and who knows the business inside out will often be available to take on this dual role of teacher and friend. For a young person joining a family business, a mentor relationship can operate largely free from all the emotional aspects of the family connection, and is almost always valuable.

It is important to define next-generation roles carefully, set objectives and provide feedback. Conflict and uncertainty over their functions in the business can be a major source of tension. Young family members need to know what is expected in their jobs, and they also need regular feedback about their performance, including recognition for achievements and constructive advice on aspects of their work and leadership development that need improving.

The best results are generally achieved by setting up tailor-made, systemic programmes for developing the next generation.[17] Start by looking at the individual and deciding on their capabilities, strengths and development needs. For most individuals, the focus will usually have been on what it takes to join the firm, not what it takes to own it or lead it. Knowledge transfer to the next generation should be accompanied by behavioural learning, action learning and hands-on experience learning. It is important to build confidence among young individuals that they can take over and be good at the job. Next is team development – combining individual assessments to uncover team dynamics. Team member learning is fostered in areas such as influencing skills – how to work within an organisation so as to make an impact – and the ability to communicate effectively and manage conflict constructively. Then there are the inter-generational and executive interfaces – deciding on the extent to involve other generations and non-family executives in developing the next generation for responsible ownership.

Joachim Schwass, a family business professor at IMD, has drawn together some conclusions on effective successor development strategies. Growing in the role of business leader can best be facilitated, he believes, if it is understood as a managed process:[18]

> Three important lessons have been culled from the experience of leading family businesses. First, successors must submit themselves to a career development plan. Second, the successors must systematically develop their own vision for the future of the family and business relationship. Third, the leadership transition from the outgoing generation to the successors should be staged as a formal celebration … A growth-based initiative by the next generation recognizes succession as a phased process that begins with personal development and discipline. It is this humility, coupled with a transparent development process, which has the potential to obtain the support of family and others as the successor qualifies for the leadership position.

The next generation's perspective

The next generation in a family business have a unique opportunity to build a challenging and enriching career for themselves. The advantages of their situation are obvious: the business is already up and running; it offers job security and possibly an attractive remuneration package; working in a family business can be extremely rewarding; from a personal standpoint, family members enjoy a special status both inside and outside the firm, and there is a distinct possibility that one day they may become leaders and owners of the business.

Nevertheless, there is a price to be paid for these advantages. Family businesses are generally not diversified enterprises that can easily withstand downturns in some of their markets. There may be doubts about whether the business will survive in the long term, and if the family members are looking for career security, the family business may not be right for them. If they join for the wrong reasons (searching for a safe haven, for example, or because they have not thought through the emotional complexities of family business life and the commitment they must be prepared to make), it is possibly a decision they will live to regret.

Before joining the family business, the next generation should discuss the prospect as well as other career possibilities with the founder and/or other senior family members and directors. If they do join, it should be because they are committed, not because it is expected of them or an easy option. They should also obtain outside career experience first (as discussed in Chapter 4). Once a decision to join has been taken, they should establish a long-term planned training programme, work hard and provide an extra dimension of commitment, earn the respect of employees through behaviour and dedication, and reject special privileges.

The next generation often have a valuable role to play in the seniors' retirement process. If relations with seniors have centred mainly on the business, trying to cultivate more personal ties is a good starting point. Make an effort to understand what retirement means for them (encourage discussion of their hopes and fears), acknowledge the importance of their achievements, and help them draw up and implement a detailed succession plan along the lines discussed earlier. If they are worried that their usefulness will end when they step down, look at ways in which they might continue to have an input and maintain some involvement with the business after retirement. A coherent strategy like this, based on communication and a shared understanding of the issues, provides the common ground on which to preserve a constructive relationship with the senior generation, as well as helping them to overcome the main emotional difficulties of the succession process.

Succession in older family businesses

As we have seen, the approach to succession from first to second generation is dictated largely by the character of the business founder, with all the issues made more complicated by the founder's dual role as parent and employer, and probably ambivalent attitude to relinquishing control and coming to terms with the realities of age and mortality. Later-generation transitions, in contrast, are much more likely to be governed by the size and nature of the company, and by market conditions.

Second to third generation

The transition from second to third generation is often easier for the family to cope with. They will already have successfully come through the cross-over from first to second generation, almost certainly learning a lot from the experience.

Furthermore, members of the second generation have a number of factors working in their favour: the business they have inherited is up and running; the second generation will probably have received a better education than the first; they may well be more skilful when it comes to business management; and they should represent a source of fresh enthusiasm and vigour that can take the business into a new phase of expansion and growth.

Some successors, however, having grown up in a protected atmosphere of comfort and financial security, may not share their parents' dedication to the family business. They may have joined under a feeling of obligation, and their lack of motivation and commitment can lead to the firm's demise, often accompanied by a deterioration in family relationships.

Second-generation members face particular problems in relation to ownership of the business. Whereas the founder probably enjoyed both day-to-day control and 100 per cent ownership, his or her successors find themselves operating with a new leader, who they may or may not wholeheartedly support, and as co-owners, perhaps even with only a minority stake. When they come to consider succession, they must face similar problems to those that the founder had to grapple with, but on a much larger scale. There will usually be more succession candidates when the second generation comes to decide which of their children should take over the business (a situation often exacerbated by equal second-generation voting power and a history of unresolved conflicts). Cousin relationships will have become an issue. Cousins will have, as one of their parents, an in-law who grew up outside the family, and he or she may hold radically different values as a result. As noted in Chapter 7, this diversity means that in the transition from the second to the third generation, an important challenge involves developing effective communication, leadership and difference-management skills among cousins.

Third to fourth generation and beyond

By the time the third generation is in place, there is a well-established business and a widening circle of family members. As we have seen, an important characteristic of the third generation is its diversity. A range of in-laws is likely to have become involved as brothers and sisters have married people with widely differing values and perspectives, and they themselves have had children. The diversity can be such that it is difficult to believe that all the children come from the same family. Some will grow up loving the family business because they were taught to by their parents; others will hate it because they feel trapped in it. At this stage it is crucial to have some sort of escape mechanism in place enabling those who want to exit from the family business to do so.

Strategic issues in the transition from the third to the fourth generation, over and above those that affect every generation, frequently centre on a loss of direction and purpose. The drive, ambitions and objectives of the founder may have become no more than an interesting piece of family history, or the original goals may have been overtaken by events in a changing world. Family members can feel hemmed in by a conflict between a desire to be rid of an historical relic that they are now perpetuating from loyalty rather than choice, and not daring to dispose of the business for fear that they will be cast as the traitor who sold out 100 years of family tradition.

At this point, either the company is sold or the vision must be recreated by members of the third and fourth generations, who need to revitalise the business by engaging the family's enthusiasm and commitment to its future.

New generation, new system, new culture

John Ward's analysis, based on the idea that understanding the ownership structure in a family business is often fundamental to understanding the real forces at work within it, was introduced in Chapter 2. He was the first to draw attention to the fact that, in broad terms, ownership of a family business progresses through a sequence, reflecting ageing and expansion of the owning family: owner-managed business, followed by sibling partnership and then cousin consortium.[19] The important point in the context of the succession process is that whether the transition is from a single owner to sibling partnership, or from a sibling partnership to a cousin company, it is not just a question of changing the personnel, it is changing the system. In short, ownership succession amounts to introducing a different type of business structure with a different culture, different procedures and with the requirement for a different set of ground rules.

In the first generation, the culture celebrates the heroic achievements of a founder who has built a substantial business from nothing, and who continues to guide it through adversity. In contrast, the culture of a sibling partnership celebrates the achievements of the team working together, and no individuals are seen as heroes. So what works in the owner-manager structure does not always work (and can indeed be a recipe for disaster) with sibling partnerships. If siblings look to what their father or mother did in achieving success at the owner-managed stage and try to emulate it in the sibling partnership phase, they usually fail.

An added complication is that these changes in system and culture do not take place overnight. In most successions there is a transitional period (illustrated in Figure 2.3 on page 49) during which the business is effectively between systems. Depending on the spread of ages within generations, these periods of overlap can last up to 20 years. So in owner-manager to sibling partnership successions, as the transition progresses the business loses some of its owner-managed characteristics (heroic culture, centralised decision-making, and so on) and gains more sibling partnership characteristics (shared vision, effective teamwork, and so on). During the transition there is in effect a hybrid system, and this can be confusing for everybody.

One reason for the confusion is that behaviour, strategies and methods that used to work effectively in the outgoing system no longer work in the incoming system. This creates a dual need: to forget or unlearn what used to work, but no longer does; and to define and then master what used not to work in the old scenario, but now does in the new. Not surprisingly, it is challenging for people involved in succession to understand and get to grips with these counter-intuitive ideas. So, for example, around the mid-point in the succession transition from owner-manager to sibling partnership, there will typically be a group of siblings trying to become a team but working under the owner-manager, who not only finds it hard to understand teamwork but may well see it as a sign of weakness (it is slower, it is cumbersome, no one is really the boss, it confuses the employees and so on).

The need to understand that it is the system, not just the personnel, that is changing applies equally in transitions to the third generation, when a sibling partnership is passing to cousins. The siblings are looking at the incoming cousins and trying to work out how, as family diversity increases, unity of purpose will be maintained. But siblings cannot assume that what worked for them in growing the business will also work for the cousins. Neither can they assume that the cousins will behave as they have done; siblings generally overlook how little the cousins will have in common and that they will operate within a different system that has different values, rules and methods. They also overlook the added complexity with which cousins will have to cope, and fail to appreciate the extra structure, formality and governance systems that the cousins will need to introduce to help them manage this extra complexity (see Chapter 7).

There is a helpful sporting analogy here. Think of owner-managers as tennis players who are brilliant at the game but can only play singles – they are no good at doubles because they cannot do teamwork. The sibling partnership can be represented as a basketball team, where having individual stars is helpful but no single star alone would ever win the game. The cousin company equates to a 15-player rugby side, where teamwork is overwhelmingly important and the side has no hope of success unless the players operate effectively as a team. Personality types and strategies that succeed brilliantly in the context of one game may well prove a recipe for disaster in another.

The different ingredients that make for success in the three types of family business – for example, the heroic entrepreneur in owner-managed businesses, the shared vision in sibling partnerships and effective governance systems in cousin companies – emphasise the point that feasibility is a critical question to consider in the succession process. Take, for example, the case of families with flourishing owner-managed businesses who do not possess enough of the necessary ingredients for the establishment of a successful sibling partnership in the second generation, but who nevertheless press forward towards this unsuitable and potentially damaging objective.

In any succession, families need to question whether the conditions surrounding the business today are right to allow it to make a successful transition to the form to which it aspires in the next generation. When there is an element of uncertainty and doubt, it is necessary to try to foster and consolidate the right conditions and weigh up the case carefully, looking at the business needs and the capabilities of the family. If the answer is clearly 'No', family members need to face up to the fact that what they are planning is neither feasible nor sensible, at which point other solutions should be evaluated, including an exit.

Finally, a particularly valuable aspect of Ward's analysis of succession is that it helps to focus attention on the issue of intergenerational teamwork. Both generations on either side of the particular succession transition can work on the task at hand, and having such a pretext for collaboration is precisely the sort of intergenerational rallying point that often helps families negotiate transitions successfully.

9

Building financial security and relinquishing control

F inancial security is important for the family business owner's retirement (a word that should be construed throughout this chapter in the positive sense proposed in the Preface). This may be stating the obvious, but many owners neglect their personal finances. Even basic personal financial planning involves an array of increasingly sophisticated products and strategies. For business owners the choices are especially complex, and few are willing or able to devote enough time to planning their financial future properly. Also, people who own successful enterprises often believe that the business itself represents their personal nest egg – that it will, in some unspecified way, guarantee them financial security when the time comes for them to step down. This may well turn out to be true, but it involves a number of assumptions that cannot always be taken for granted.

Sometimes the way ahead is clear and uncomplicated. If owners have enough money invested outside the business to provide for a secure retirement, and they have planned for management succession, they may want to pass on their shares in the family firm to the next generation. The best ways to accomplish this are discussed later in this chapter, where we see that when passing the family company on to the next generation, continuity of the business, liquidity and family needs are the cornerstones of estate planning. Ensuring ownership ends up in the right hands in the next generation may require treating heirs differently, depending on whether or not they are active in the business, and passing on voting control to selected heirs. The uses of trusts are also explored.

Some owners, however, have no suitable successor, or they may feel that family relationships are likely to improve if the business is taken out of the equation. Perhaps they have simply had enough of the business and would like to take on a new challenge. The answer in such circumstances may be to sell the company. One owner, after refereeing the latest in a long series of squabbles between his children, said; 'I've moved on from the sell the company idea. I'm now seeking offers for the family!'

In the first part of this chapter, therefore, the aim is to explore ways of providing for the owner's financial security during retirement, as well as how to sell the business if that is what is decided. Taxation is a critical consideration affecting both areas and, while it is possible to give a few indications of the tax consequences of different courses of action, it is not practical to present a detailed analysis. Tax laws, regulations and interpretations are complex and constantly changing, and competent tax advice must be obtained before pursuing any of the options highlighted.

Insurance and share purchase agreements, enabling the buy-out of family shareholders, are also discussed. Such mechanisms can be crucial in resolving the complications of multiple family ownership that arise when family firms reach the third generation and beyond.

Building financial security

Family business owners will often have become accustomed to a substantial salary, along with a package of valuable benefits such as a company car, private medical insurance, and so on. But if they continue to own the business after retirement, this financial situation is likely to alter abruptly. The amount of money they can draw from the business will be limited by its capacity to pay a salary to both the outgoing and incoming generations, and by rules that limit tax deductibility.

If most of the outgoing generation's assets are tied up in the company (as is the case for many family business owners), their retirement income will be dependent on the ability of the next generation to manage the business successfully. This may not be a problem, but some owners are forced out of retirement to take over from incompetent next-generation members in order to protect their own financial security. This scenario can also lead to emotional blackmail in cases where the outgoing generation retains an advisory role but there are fears that advice is loaded in ways designed to protect their income from the business. The same sort of worry can arise in the (increasingly common) situation where seniors gift the next generation, say, 60 per cent of the business on condition that they buy the remaining 40 per cent (often with the help of a loan secured on the assets of the business). Here, senior-generation advice might be coloured in ways designed to maximise (or at least not to jeopardise) the value of the share purchase balance due.

Successful family business owners often believe the business itself will guarantee their financial security; it may do, but this involves assumptions that cannot always be taken for granted

Money into or out of the business?

Financial peace of mind is an important ingredient in a successful retirement, but there are two schools of thought on the best way for business owners to engineer this security. Broadly, they can either operate a policy of continuously taking money out of the business during their period of tenure, or they can leave the money in the balance sheet so that it builds up to the point when, on retirement, a restructuring is arranged to transfer personal wealth to the departing owner.

A programme of cash withdrawal from the business (to finance pension plans, life insurance policies, savings schemes, and so forth) may, in the long term, represent a significant drain on the firm's resources. On occasions it can seriously weaken company finances. Building up the balance sheet instead, however, exposes owners to the risk that if the business suffers a financial downturn at some stage in the future, the effects will spill over into their personal financial affairs.

There are no obvious right or wrong solutions. Much will depend on individual circumstances – in particular the cash flow and general resilience of the business concerned. From the owner's point of view, if the business can accommodate it, a long-term cash withdrawal programme certainly offers important advantages: it protects owners' personal wealth against business failure; it enables owners to spread their assets, freeing money for investment in a balanced and diversified portfolio; and owners can maximise investment returns by switching between markets when opportunities arise.

Strategies are available that represent a middle course between the extremes of continuous cash withdrawal and building the balance sheet. A popular example concerns business property, where the owner takes out a personal loan to finance the purchase of a property needed by the business, and then leases it to the business at a rental that hopefully is sufficient to repay the loan interest. The loan is secured on the owner's pension fund so that the capital will be repaid on retirement. A lot of owners set up their own property companies to enter into leasing agreements with the business. In the early stages, the arrangements are unlikely to be particularly profitable as the rental income is applied against interest payments. But after, say, five years and an upward rent review, the revenue position is likely to move into surplus and the capital value of the project becomes apparent. This capital value is being built up in favour of the owner, not the business.

Many other techniques can be used to extract wealth from the family business to provide financial security for the owner before he or she relinquishes control, including the company buying in some of the owner's shares, partial liquidations and the sale of shares to children working in the business (see case note in Chapter 8, page 156, where a son bought shares from the family). There are so many options – all of which need to be tailored to individual and business circumstances – that it is not practical to undertake a detailed analysis here. Similarly, this is not the place for a broadly based discussion of personal financial planning for family business owners. These two areas are fraught with complexity and specialised assistance should be sought before making any decisions. Tax professionals, business consultants and personal financial planning experts can help owners design a programme and approach that is right for them, their family and their business.

Selling the business

Where an owner has no heirs willing (or able) to take over the family firm, or perhaps has insufficient funds independent of the business to provide for retirement, or if he or she has simply decided the time has come to start a new venture, selling the business may be the best solution.

A hard decision

Although there may be good reasons for selling, there may be equally good reasons for not selling. Pro-selling factors might include insufficient personal liquidity; the need to finance retirement; industry consolidation; receiving an excellent offer; no suitable successor; or a poor prognosis for family relationships. Anti-selling factors might include feeling that the business is part of the family; an important legacy; the best long-term investment available; an opportunity for the next generation; a better inheritance for the children than a pile of cash; or important for the employees. A detached and logical weighing up of the financial and business-related considerations (which, interestingly, predominate in the reasons-for-selling list) will be essential, but the process is also likely to raise some emotional dilemmas (mainly in the reasons-for-not-selling list).

Some entrepreneurs are able to start businesses, build them up, sell and start all over again, taking a dispassionate view of the nature and results of their endeavours. For most owners, however, it is not that easy. Along with the investment of money, time and energy over the years in establishing the business, there is also an emotional investment, the true extent of which may become apparent only when considering selling. Family businesses have unique characteristics that will be under threat following a sale, and many of the employees may be close friends, generating feelings of betrayal for the owner if the company is sold (especially if it is sold to a competitor). Moreover, issues may arise if the purchaser decides to reorganise the company – introduce a new corporate philosophy, for example, or shift its focus to different market sectors.

Sometimes it will be part of the deal that, once the business is sold, the vendor and perhaps some other managers will continue to work for the acquiring company. It is tempting to believe that this will help reduce the impact of some of these problems, but sellers should not set their hopes too high. During negotiations, as purchaser courts vendor, many vague promises are likely to be made about the wonderful prospects and how the vendor will effectively stay in control, but ultimately the buyer may view the seller's employment contract as merely an extra to be added to the purchase price. Also, once the sale goes through, the bureaucratic culture of many large businesses is so alien to that of smaller family enterprises that owners generally find the transition extremely difficult and, not infrequently, impossible.

Sale mechanics

Finding a buyer, valuing the business and negotiating the sale are huge topics in their own right and beyond the scope of this book. However, a few points to note and some broad guidelines are included in this section. As regards finding a buyer, in a recent UK survey almost 90 per cent of family company respondents indicated that an approach had been received within the past six or seven years.

On valuation, despite some myths to the contrary, there are no completely objective or scientific ways to value a business. The negotiated price will represent a hybrid of many factors including asset value, earnings (both quantity and quality), the growth rate and period, rate of return, comparison with other companies, tax considerations, and the market supply and demand of companies for sale. Negotiations are often best handled by someone other than the owner, and they should be planned for and not treated casually. Tax implications will also have a profound effect on the transaction.

Drag-along rights are useful – they enable a majority shareholder to force a minority shareholder to join in the sale of a company. Many advisers have found themselves in the situation where the sale of a family business has been agreed, all the shareholders have indicated they accept the terms, the contract is about to be signed and the phone rings. It is Uncle Mortimer, who owns a few shares inherited from his mother, saying, 'I don't think the price is enough', effectively holding the sale process to ransom. To avoid this happening, a drag-along clause can be added to the articles of association (via a special resolution passed at a time when a sale is not contemplated) which effectively forces Uncle Mortimer to join in the sale, entitling him to the same price, terms and conditions as any other seller.

Principal exit options

Broadly, there are six ways in which wealth tied up in the business can be realised so that cash can be enjoyed in retirement and, subsequently, by the family:

✳ liquidating the business;

✳ a trade sale;

✳ a sale to institutional acquirers;

✳ a stock market flotation;

✳ a management (or occasionally employee) buy-out;

✳ employee share ownership trusts.

Needless to say, high-level professional advice must be sought before contemplating any of these exit options.

In a members' voluntary liquidation, a liquidator is appointed to sell off the company's assets, pay its debts and the liquidation expenses, and distribute the cash surplus to shareholders. The company is then dissolved. The procedure carries bankruptcy connotations, but it is a perfectly legitimate method of realising cash proceeds from the business. It can be a viable option, especially in cases that do not involve large closure costs and significant redundancies. Generally, however, liquidation is unlikely to generate as much money as selling the business as a going concern.

A trade sale is usually a more attractive proposition as far as most entrepreneurs are concerned. Selling to purchasers within the trade, who understand what the business is all about, will often result in a better price than a sale to outsiders. In many cases, owners will receive a straightforward cash consideration and can effectively wash their hands of the company at the date of sale. Structuring the sale agreement is inevitably complex, and particular attention must be paid to the terms of warranties and indemnities requested by the purchaser.

In recent years, rather than a trade sale, a sale to an institutional acquirer in the form of a private equity provider (or venture capitalist) has become increasingly popular. As with a management buy-out, a sale to a financial institution has attractions where trade secrets or other competition issues preclude a sale to the vendor's competitors.

The owners of some sizeable companies can achieve personal liquidity and raise additional capital for the firm via a public flotation, but it is usually difficult for entrepreneurs to float their firms with a view to retirement. Not surprisingly, the stock market's assessment of public offerings centres on the issuer's prospects and investment potential. Companies coming to the market simply to provide an exit route for retiring founder managers are unlikely to get a rapturous reception, so it is essential to build up a good management team (family or otherwise) so that founding shareholders can sell shares without causing too much concern.

Careful consideration should be given to the decision on whether or not to float. No two companies are the same and there is no right or wrong for every situation. Some family businesses find that going public is highly advantageous and provides an answer to most of the problems they wanted to resolve. Others, however, discover that the adverse aspects of the move – extra accountability and the focus on short-term performance – can be significant, as evidenced by the recent steady trickle of listed companies seeking to return to the private sector.

Another option is a management buy-out. As successful family firms grow, the core team that founded the business is often reinforced by other managers – brought in from outside, family members or promoted employees – so why not consider selling it to them? When family members are part of the management, a management buy-out represents, in some respects, a compromise between transferring the shares to the family and an outright trade sale. A management buy-out can provide solutions to a number of problems. In particular, the business is likely to keep its identity, sparing the owners some of the moral dilemmas involved in a sale to an outside organisation. This type of exit also protects brand equities, critical business data, trade secrets and valuable staff with commercially sensitive knowledge from being transferred to a purchasing rival.[1]

However, there are two important difficulties associated with management buy-outs. First, during the capital-raising exercise to finance the acquisition, managers will devote a lot of their energies to talking to venture capitalists, drafting business plans and preparing institutional presentations, and there is a risk that they will cease to pay proper attention to managing the business. Even if they succeed in raising the finance, it is possible that the company (and what it is worth) will have suffered in the process. Second, if the managers fail to raise the money, everyone ends up back where they started, except they now have a team of managers who have been distracted from their work for months and are suffering disappointment and disgruntlement because their hopes and ambitions have been dashed.

The price owners can expect to receive for their business also has a double-edged aspect. Part of the popularity of management buy-outs is attributed to the fact that a loyal management team, thoroughly conversant with the business, is likely to pay more for the company than a wary, cost-conscious outsider with years of acquisitions experience. Conversely, some management buy-outs fail because the management knows the business too well, and is unwilling to try and come up with anything like the asking price.

The topic of employee share ownership trusts (ESOTs) was introduced briefly in Chapter 5 (see page 99). The discussion centred on the role such trusts can play in creating a long-term employee share stake and in motivating employees. ESOTs, however, have a wide variety of other incidental advantages, including providing a means by which family shareholders can realise cash from the business in a tax-efficient way. Some family businesses have used ESOTs as an exercise in family swapping, whereby the ESOT swaps non-committed family shareholders for highly committed employee shareholders, and the work family thus replaces the blood family.

Passing down the business

So far we have concentrated on methods for owners to dispose of their interest in the business, and to realise cash, during their lifetime. This section centres on ways that the family company can most effectively be gifted or bequeathed to the owner's heirs. Owners of family companies can substantially reduce or delay taxes payable when the business is passed on, but this requires forward planning. As early as possible, owners need to decide on their long-term objectives and use lifetime gifts or trusts to pass on ownership tax-efficiently.

Capturing values for later generations

Before discussing estate planning principles and implementation, however, we will look at the broader issue of the ways in which owners can pass on their family values and their ideas about how the business should be run after their death.

Opinions on this issue can be polarised. Many commentators object to the idea of one generation appearing to try to control another via will provisions that can be seen as attempts to rule from the grave.[2] For example, some seniors within family businesses have definite ideas on how the business should be organised, and this sometimes includes how it should be organised after they have gone. What purports to be a benign and helpful set of testamentary guidelines for their successors is often a restrictive and controlling will, which has potentially damaging conse-quences for the next generation and for the business. For instance, some wills specify that inheritors can sell their shares only to other family members, or that the sale proceeds must be divided equally among the inheritor's brothers and sisters. Leaving shareholdings with a variety of provisos attached may be logical and justifiable at the time the will is drawn up, but 20 years later the restrictions may amount to a straitjacket for the heir who is then trying to run the family business.[3]

Ivan Lansberg has drawn a parallel with family business governance structures being imposed on successors. He explains his opposition:[4]

> Incumbent leaders often feel obliged to define the vision for the family enterprise in the future. In an effort to reveal their own preferences and avoid conflicts with their relatives, they meet with their advisors and make fundamental decisions that shape governance options well beyond their tenure. Such efforts are misguided and this is why so many legal trusts are borne [sic] from family mistrust. Those who will be forced to live with consequences of a predetermined governance model should be the ones to determine it. We are not suggesting that incumbent leaders should abdicate their responsibilities completely, but they must create

conditions for the next generation to explore future governance options and assess their feasibility.

In short, those who are alive and running the business should have the right and the flexibility to make decisions that are appropriate for the business at that time.

As Lansberg says, however, this does not mean that leaders should abdicate their responsibilities, and perhaps a better way forward is for seniors to focus more on the successful transmission of their values and vision to the next generation, rather than promoting favoured governance structures or share-transfer restrictions. It is, after all, shared goals, and the guiding values and principles that help achieve them, that give family businesses such a strong foundation and the scope to achieve long-term competitive advantage and sustainability. So guidance for successors in this area is likely to have real worth, and one approach that is growing in popularity, particularly in the USA, concerns ethical wills.

Rather than passing on material assets, an ethical will is generally a written document designed to codify, preserve and transmit the senior generation's often more prized legacy – its values, beliefs, morals, lessons learned from life and family stories that it hopes to pass down to the next generation.[5] Creating an ethical will has been described as a means of living on in a positive way in the hearts and minds of family and friends after we are gone.

Unlike a last will and testament, ethical wills are not legally binding. They come in a variety of forms, from a short letter to a lengthy autobiographical statement, from a message recorded on DVD to a leather-bound volume. Even though the ethical will is traditionally read after death, many people choose to share their ethical wills during life, usually at an important anniversary or family milestone, such as retirement from the family company or when the children leave for university.

Many families in business are as concerned about preserving their values as about maintaining their performance strategies. Articulating the beliefs and practices that account for the family company's success (through good and bad times) and the satisfaction they bring to the family can be a powerful statement. There should be nothing embarrassing about discussing the family's way of doing business, including such things as honesty, loyalty, bargaining in good faith, being considerate of others' needs, supporting those who count on you, and the other principles and values that underpin many of the best family-owned businesses. Because the fabric of family values is so important in differentiating a family business and keeping it strong and durable, it is important that the family's values and vision, as well as the business and other tangible assets, flow downstream to succeeding generations.

Estate-planning principles

Turning to the techniques and tools of estate planning, there are three guiding principles that must be taken into account: continuity of the business; liquidity; and family needs. Effective management of a family company must provide for continuity. The main eventualities that should be planned for are disability, retirement and death – and of these three only retirement can be planned within a predetermined timeframe. The most critical factor in preserving the family's business assets is to avoid the forced sale of the firm.

As regards liquidity, the departure, for whatever reason, of a key figure in a family business can create sudden demands for cash to pay taxes, provide family support, or provide retirement income. Effective planning requires estimates of the family's future needs and the means to provide for them, including the necessary liquid resources to cover the payment of personal estate taxes.

The third principle concerns family needs, and evaluating the financial needs of the family, as well as their future role in the business, is the most important part of estate planning. The financial well-being of each family member must be kept in mind, including contingencies such as birth, death, marriage and marriage breakdown. In considering the family's future relationship with the business, it will be necessary to address the question: 'What is fair?'

Treating heirs fairly

Our social rules dictate that wealth should, in the absence of powerful reasons to the contrary, be passed on to the next generation under arrangements that can broadly be described as fair. But fairness is a particularly subjective concept. The main cause of trouble is often the assumption that fairness means equality of treatment. (On the dilemma of favouring one child at the expense of another, the prophet Mohammed said: 'I would favour the youngest until he was older; the one who was absent until he was present; and the one who was sick until he was better.') But applying the equality of treatment idea to a family company is generally destructive and dangerous. Alan Crosbie, who has made a study of family businesses, has described the issue graphically:[6]

I am conscious that it sounds unpaternal and very harsh for people running the family business to start looking at their children in a judgemental way. Maybe so, but this approach is a great deal kinder, in the long run, than the attack of sentimentality that strikes the many business people who look at their families and say, 'This is all for you. I did this all for you.' Then they say, 'Equity demands that all four of my children get equal shares' (or however many children they have). They divide up the shares, give jobs to all of their children, and wait for the line that runs, 'And they all lived happily ever after.' In fact, the line is much more likely to read, 'And at this point, all hell broke loose.'

A reluctance to choose between children often leads to the next generation having equal equity stakes in a business in which they have very different roles and to which they have very different relationships. Some of the children will be better able to manage the business than others; the eldest child may not be the best business person; some of the children may be working in the business, while others may not and may have no interest in it. As well as providing ammunition for future disputes between the children, such a policy (unless effective family governance is introduced) can damage the business. Equal shareholdings, for example, can leave a business locked, with nowhere to move if shareholder disputes fall neatly into two halves. Conversely, if one side of the family depends on the executive efforts of the other side of the family, the wealth of the entire family is riding on the successful direction of just a part of it. Even if they have equal shares, they do not have equal influence.[7]

Owners can go a long way to reducing the scope for strife by thinking through the potential problems in advance, and sharing their thinking with their heirs, who are more likely to accept perceived inequalities if they understand the large-scale objectives being pursued. The problem is that owners generally do not have a large enough estate to enable them to leave the business to active, interested offspring, and other assets to the remaining children. Because this ideal solution is not achievable, they may well have to depart from the principle of equality and bequeath shares in the business to selected heirs, thus treating heirs who are active in the business differently from those who are not. Structures are available to help achieve a compromise between short-term fairness and solutions that are in the long-term interests of the business and the family (these are considered later in this chapter).

The following case provides a salutary reminder about the complexities of family business. Even if many of the recommendations in this section are faithfully adopted, it is not possible to assume a problem-free future. At this company (a specialist manufacturer established in the late 1960s) the owner had four children – three girls and a boy. The boy joined the business, was very talented and relished the prospect of taking it forward, while the three girls were not interested in a career in the company. The owner was understandably keen that his son should succeed him in the business and, having consulted with the family and gained their understanding and agreement, during his lifetime bequeathed 51 per cent of the shares to the son and the remaining 49 per cent to the three daughters jointly.

Following his father's death, the son became chairman and chief executive of the company. Six uneventful years passed, but then market conditions began to deteriorate and the son concluded that some high-risk strategies were needed to reposition the firm and help ensure its survival. The seemingly sensible share ownership arrangements under his father's will placed the son under enormous strain as a result of a conflict of interest. His sisters were exposed to a financial gamble concerning his ability to reposition the business. How could he take risks reorganising the business – including large-scale borrowing – when the company was almost half-owned by his sisters? Once again, by mutual agreement, it was decided that the sisters should dispose of their interest in the business. As well as shares in the company, the siblings also owned the freehold of the firm's main premises. A scheme was devised whereby the son purchased the shares from his sisters, thus giving him effective control. At the same time, the firm bought the freehold property. As a result of careful planning neither transaction gave rise to a tax liability, and the scheme resulted in half of the company's distributable reserves being passed, in cash, to the sisters.

Ownership and control considerations

Ordinary shares in a company generally carry three basic entitlements: the right to an equity interest in the business; the right to vote; and the right to receive dividends. As we have seen, if possible the ideal method of passing on the family company is to bequeath the shares to the active members and other assets to the inactive members. If, however, the business represents most of the value in the owner's estate, this may not be practical and it will be necessary to consider other options that at least provide the active members with voting control.

There are various methods of isolating voting and equity ownership rights which will be discussed later. First, however, there are some other courses of action involving life insurance, splitting the company and attaching ownership conditions to shares.

Life insurance

A life insurance policy in favour of named beneficiaries can be used to provide cash for heirs who are not to be active in the business. The amount of money they receive under the policy can be made roughly equivalent to the value of shares bequeathed to the active members.

It may be possible to take out a key-man insurance policy to provide the necessary funds for the company to purchase its own shares. A buy-back arrangement can be put in place whereby the company will buy the shares from the estate of the deceased. The surviving shareholders retain control of the company as the deceased's shares are bought back by the company and cancelled, and the dependants of the deceased shareholder can realise their shares for cash.

Splitting the company

Where a company, in addition to its business, has substantial property assets, the current owner may wish to maintain an interest in the properties and allow the succeeding generation to own only the trading assets. Subject to taxation clearances and a number of technical considerations, it is often possible to place the firm in a members' voluntary liquidation under a scheme whereby two new companies are formed, one trading and one property. If circumstances permit, this procedure can achieve a useful result.

An alternative form of split involves hiving down the trading operations of the business into a new subsidiary, while property assets are retained by the holding company. Provided there are no intercompany guarantees, this will isolate the value of the properties from the risks of the trading company. It is then possible for the succeeding generation to take over the subsidiary as a first step in securing control of the whole.

Conditions attaching to ownership

Another approach to the problem involves bequeathing the shares to both active and inactive members, but imposing ownership conditions via a private share purchase agreement. Such an agreement can stipulate, for example, that inactive members are required to sell their shares to the active members (thus avoiding the sort of conflict that can arise between those who own the business and those who run it, illustrated in the case note on C & J Clark, see page 46). Bargaining and potential disagreements between siblings about the value of shares can be avoided if the agreement includes a clear formula for price calculation.

Share purchase agreements can also provide for the mandatory purchase by the surviving shareholder of another shareholder's interest if the latter dies first. Cross life insurance policies can be used to fund the purchase of a deceased's shareholding. Clearly, it is best to establish share purchase agreements at a time when the participants are healthy and nobody knows who will be the first to die. It is generally in the survivors' best interests to secure ownership of the shares involved, while the deceased's family is usually better off with cash. Family members who are not going to be actively involved in the business generally prefer income-producing assets to a minority interest in a private company that may not pay dividends.

Share purchase agreements can also provide a clear-cut solution to other sensitive family business issues. As we have seen, some companies restrict share ownership to bloodline family members and enforce this through agreements that give the family first refusal before shareholdings may be transferred or sold. Similarly, a family member's involvement in divorce proceedings can be made to trigger a compulsory offer of their shares to the family. Share purchase agreements, therefore, can provide an effective method of limiting both the number and character of owners, and the opportunities for outside, potentially hostile investors to purchase an interest in the company.

Isolating voting control

If it is not practical to pass down all the shares in the family business to the active members, there are a number of options under which they can at least be assured of voting control. Three are highlighted here: restricted voting shares; voting trusts; and freezing an estate.

A company's share capital can be divided into two classes, with only one class carrying full voting rights, while the other is subject to voting restrictions (for example, 100 shares represent one vote) or, indeed, carries no voting rights at all. This division enables owners to bequeath voting shares to heirs whom they wish to control the firm and restricted voting shares to the others.

In the second option, shareholders can agree to the creation of a voting trust, and to relinquish their voting powers (but not their equity ownership) in favour of the appointed trustee, or trustees. The trust has the effect of centralising control of all participating shareholdings, and can be established during the owner's lifetime or come into existence upon death. The benefits of voting trusts increase in step with the number of shareholders. They thus become especially useful by the time a family business reaches the third or fourth generation. For example, the Ford family's 40 per cent interest in the US car giant is held in a voting trust that allows the family to be represented in a unified way. This particular trust also includes mechanisms for generating liquidity by reserving a proportion of the dividends and diverting them into a huge pool of capital so that family members can leave and be bought out without diluting the family's control. As well as a mechanism for allocating control of the business among heirs, a voting trust can be used to help provide continuity and orderly management if the owner falls victim to premature death or disability.

Where there are fewer shareholders (for example, in a second-generation business), an independent outsider may be appointed to the voting trust to act as a deadlock trustee. This is a useful model for resolving situations where votes are tied or a required majority cannot be secured. The deadlock trustee is most helpful where differences arise over strategic decisions for the business, which often throw up complex choices supported by persuasive arguments on both sides. The deadlock trustee, who must be an individual accepted by all parties as fair and impartial, has a balance of votes, and their role is to act as a built-in mediator for the family business. Disagreements that cannot be resolved are quite rare, because the mere existence of the deadlock trustee generally acts as a powerful incentive for resolving differences before a casting vote is required.[8]

A deadlock trustee was the mechanism chosen for resolving any impasse in the novel succession process set up at India's GMR Group (see Chapter 8, page 162). In due course, responsibility for selecting a successor to the group's founder, G.M. Rao, will rest with the next generation – Rao's two sons and his son-in-law – who will come together to act as a selection committee. (This succession mechanism was designed to ensure that G. M. Rao does not himself have to make the choice of who will succeed him, which might have caused family discord.) The selection committee is required to reach a unanimous decision. If they fail to agree, any one of the three members of the committee can call on the deadlock trustee to assist them in resolving the issue. In this case, the rule is that the deadlock trustee will need two people on his or her side to pass a resolution – that is, the deadlock trustee and one other can block a resolution. A structure like this is designed as a deterrent to make sure that the three family members get along, while allowing them certainty in the process of selecting a successor if they are unable to agree.

The third way in which active members can at least be assured of voting control is by freezing an estate. Owners wishing to allocate voting control and the benefits of future growth of the business to particular heirs can achieve this by providing for a recapitalisation of the company on death. If there are accumulated reserves in the profit and loss account, these can be converted to non-redeemable preference shares that are passed down to inactive members and the ordinary shares are bequeathed to active members. This procedure is often called estate freezing because of its uses in situations where the recapitalisation takes place during the owner's lifetime, and he or she retains the preference shares rather than bequeathing them. The value of the preference shares is effectively fixed at issue, thus enabling owners to freeze the value in their estates at then current levels. The heirs receive ordinary shares that can, of course, appreciate with any future growth of the business.

In the present context, however, the recapitalisation may represent a method of satisfying the main needs of different classes of heir. The active members, as ordinary shareholders, assume greater risk but are entitled to participate in the rewards of future growth. The inactive members are entitled to current income from their preference share dividends, as well as preferred status in the event of the firm's liquidation.

Implementing the estate plan

In the absence of adequate planning, inheritance and other tax liabilities on the transfer of shares in the family business can cause costly problems. Gifting shares in the family business may give rise to charges to either capital gains tax or inheritance tax (or, indeed, both or neither) depending on the precise structuring of the transaction and the nature of the business. This range of tax permutations arising from what is essentially the same commercial transaction (the gift of shares) speaks volumes about the need for specialised professional advice before implementing a succession plan. This book is not a tax guide, and because of the complexities and the unique circumstances and needs of each family business, specialised assistance should always be sought before making any decisions.

An important general point, however, is that shareholders need to recognise that their family business strategy should not be determined by tax implications (especially given the essentially political nature of tax legislation). For example, the younger generation may not take kindly to the older generation retaining shareholder control (and hence management influence) for tax reasons at a time when they are (or should be) enjoying their retirement.

Trusts and their uses

Trusts can be a valuable device when dealing with the issues surrounding the transfer of a business and its control after it is transferred. The main technical advantage of a trust is that it allows separation of the control and management of an asset from its ownership, accomplished via the legal arrangements put in place when a trust is set up. A trust is a legal relationship between three parties: settlors, trustees and beneficiaries.

The settlor is the person who sets up the trust and contributes assets to it. The settlor also lays down instructions on how the assets are to be used or managed and who will benefit from the assets. The person or group of people the settlor appoints to control and manage the assets in the trust are the trustees. Lastly, there is the person or group of people who will benefit from the assets owned by the trust, referred to as beneficiaries. The trust agreement will either specifically name the beneficiaries or state that they will come from a certain group such as the children or grandchildren of the settlor. This sort of definition can therefore include individuals as beneficiaries who are not even born at the time the trust is set up.

In summary, a trust is a device that enables property to be given to another person or institution to administer for the benefit of a third party or group. The use of trusts in a family business context is sometimes criticised because of the resulting disconnection between management and ownership. At a time when family business outperformance is being understood more and more as a product of shared values, shared economic interest and a long-term perspective, underpinned by ongoing engagement between concentrated ownership and control of the business, some families are reluctant to follow the trust route because of the emotional feeling they have about ownership. They prefer the idea of taking their chances relating with each other as shareholders rather than beneficiaries, playing their full part in the family legacy and taking responsibility if tough decisions need to be taken. Nevertheless, trusts do enable firms to be passed on to the next generation in a tax-efficient and flexible way and, as such, they remain a popular element in family business estate planning. The terms of a trust can be extremely flexible – in some cases, it is possible for the settlor to be one of the trustees and one of the beneficiaries. Also, the trustees can be allowed to increase the class of beneficiaries and appoint capital back to the settlor.

Trust types

Most trusts can be divided into one of three categories: life interest trusts; discretionary trusts; and accumulation and maintenance trusts.

A life interest trust, also known as an interest in possession trust, is a trust where one or more persons have the right to receive the income from the trust property. This right can be for life or for a fixed period of time. Under a discretionary trust, in contrast, no person has a right to the trust income. It is for the trustees to decide on the distribution of income and capital. The third type – an accumulation and maintenance trust – is a form of discretionary trust set up for the benefit of children. (Following recent changes to the inheritance tax treatment of trusts, it is unlikely that accumulation and maintenance trusts will be set up. Indeed, for all practical tax purposes they no longer exist.)

Gifting shares into trust may provide a solution, for example, if the owner is concerned to retain control over major policy decisions affecting the company. If, for instance, the share capital is divided equally between the donor and her brother, and she gifts one share to, say, her son, voting control could shift to her brother if her son decides to vote with his uncle on an issue affecting the company. If the gift is to a life interest or discretionary trust, however, the donor may be able to pass wealth to the family while effectively retaining voting control in the company. The gift could also ensure that shares in the family business do not have to be sold to pay tax liabilities on death.

Another advantage of trusts is that all the shares can be gifted, as a block, to be held for the benefit of, say, three or four children. The division of shares between them need not take place until much later. This might be appropriate, for example, if the children are very young and it is not clear which of them will join the business. Traditionally, an accumulation and maintenance settlement would probably have offered the best solution in this case. However, under new tax laws it is no longer possible to set these up, and a traditional discretionary trust might therefore be the answer.

For older children, or where there are difficult family situations (such as a pending divorce), a discretionary trust might provide a solution. For instance, to guard against younger family members who have inherited shares being tempted to sell (particularly if they are not employed in the business), or against family members bequeathing shares to non-family members, the older generation could place their shares in trust for subsequent generations. The documentation could authorise the trustees to retain the shares in the business and protect against the beneficiaries breaking up the trust. Trusts can also be drafted to guard against beneficiaries dissipating their share of the assets, or to allow trustees to revoke beneficiaries' interests, or indeed to leave all decisions about income or capital payments entirely to the discretion of the trustees.[9]

An example of shares being placed in a family trust is provided by Samworth Brothers, a privately owned, third-generation family business and an important player in the production of savoury and sweet food products for many of the UK's leading retailers. The group employs 6,000 people and turnover exceeds £450 million. David Samworth, the third-generation leader, has one son (who works in the business) and three daughters (who do not), and in the early 1990s he began exploring how family share ownership going forward could best be aligned with family management of the company. In 1994 the family concluded that the best solution was to place the company's entire share capital in trust, the beneficiaries being David's lineal descendants, both born and unborn. David and a group of non-family financial, business and legal experts are the trustees.

Samworth Brothers has a two-tier board structure (see Chapter 6), and the trustees along with the holdings board are responsible for major policy issues affecting the business. Below this in the hierarchy is the group executive board, which has operational responsibility and includes the non-family group chief executive, David's son, Mark, and three other non-family directors, and at the base of the structure are the boards of the operating subsidiaries. In a few generations' time, when there will be an increasing number of beneficiaries, David expects that more formal structures will need to be introduced designed to maintain dialogue with the family as beneficiaries.

Recently, the tax rules relating to trusts have been completely overhauled and are now more complex than ever. New inheritance tax rules introduced on 22 March 2006 also potentially affect trusts in existence at that date. There is a short period (until 6 April 2008) to restructure, otherwise the trust will fall into the new regime. Broadly speaking, a gift into these now attracts an immediate inheritance tax charge of up to 20 per cent. The trustees are also subject to a tax charge of up to 6 per cent of the value of its assets on every ten-year anniversary of its creation, and also on distributions to beneficiaries. As ever, the rules are complex and expert advice should be sought.

Finally, a point raised in Chapter 5 about trustees is worth repeating here. Conflict of interest issues arise when a family business adviser is appointed as trustee of a settlement involving the family business client. Where, for example, a minority stake is gifted to be held for the benefit of, say, three or four young children, the interests of such beneficiaries may well differ from the interests of the company directors for whom the adviser is acting on a day-to-day basis. In such situations, conflict problems can arise because advisers find themselves acting for just one generation or one side of the family.

Charitable trusts

Sometimes charitable trusts can be used to mitigate the tax consequences of transfer of shares in the family company. Shares can be gifted to a charitable trust that can be formed by the family. The settlor could be a trustee and so effectively control the voting rights of the shares. By using a charitable trust, the value of the shares is moved outside the family as the shares must be held for charitable purposes, but voting control of the company can be retained within the family. This structure may be used if the donor no longer wishes to gift any further assets during his or her lifetime and the family wants to ensure that measures are taken now so that the shares need not be sold on death. The shares would be gifted to the charitable trust during the donor's lifetime, or on death by amending the will.

However, care needs to be taken when gifting unquoted private shares to a charitable trust because disparity of interest can arise between the trustees and the family. If the company underperforms, or something else goes wrong, and the trustees feel they are not getting a good enough return, they have fiduciary responsibilities that could ultimately prompt them to seek a buyer for the shares. Again, this is a complex area and families contemplating using a charitable trust as part of their succession planning must seek professional advice.

The benefits of life insurance

As mentioned earlier, life insurance can be used to finance cash inheritances for heirs who are not active in the business, allowing owners to pass on shares to active heirs, and it can supply a source of ready cash with which to pay tax and other estate debts arising on death. Life insurance may also help resolve a range of other family business issues discussed elsewhere in this book, including providing funding for family share purchase agreements; guaranteeing the financial security of a surviving spouse; and enabling surviving shareholders, via cross-life policies, to finance the purchase of shares in the business from the deceased's estate.

Conclusions on estate planning

It has not been practical here to provide more than a broad overview of the philosophy of estate planning for family business people, the principal considerations that should guide their thinking, and an introduction to the main tools and techniques for implementing an estate plan. Everything rests on the particular circumstances of the individual, the family and the business – and on complex and rapidly changing tax laws.

However, the important message that this brief survey has tried to highlight is that opportunities exist for creating flexible, tax-efficient estate-planning structures. If an estate plan has been carefully thought out, in good time, and has been properly implemented, the death of the owner of a family firm should never require the sale of business assets to meet tax liabilities.

10

Wealth management
Family offices and philanthropy

Once larger family businesses have established the family governance structures and mechanisms they need to manage complexity and the relationship between family and business, they often look for other ways to help foster their family commitment and vision, and to perpetuate their family's legacy. Opportunities to achieve these objectives can be provided by the family office and philanthropic initiatives.

The family office

A family office is an investment, liquidity management and administrative/concierge centre. Because it enables family members to invest as a group, a family office improves the family's buying power and lowers its portfolio management costs.

Despite some well-known US models (such as the Pitcairn family office, established in 1923 to hold the investments of the Pitcairn family, founders of Pittsburgh Plate Glass), this concept of how successful family business people set about organising the management of their other family business – the family's hard-earned assets – is a relatively young one in Europe and the UK. Compared with more than 3,000 family offices (defined in the restricted sense of formal entities professionally managing their investment portfolios) in the USA, it is estimated that the UK has just 20–25 offices, although the trend is upwards.[1]

Roles

The rationale behind the growth of family offices is that the co-ordination of all the various professional disciplines necessary to manage a family's financial affairs results in much more efficient and effective asset management and advisory services for stakeholders. In the past, families generally relied on single financial institutions to meet all their investment needs, but complex specialisation and fragmentation in the financial services industry (particularly in the investment management sector) has created opportunities for independent family offices to capitalise on the huge array of product and provider choices now available. A central value-added service of family office operations should support independence – the provision of unbiased, non-product-motivated advice on asset allocation and diversification. Also, the determination of an appropriate asset allocation and investment management strategy takes place with a comprehensive understanding of the family's financial situation and objectives as far as risks and returns are concerned.

The family office is a separate operation from the business, although some of the same individuals may participate in both. It should have a formal business structure with a management board (which can consist of family members as well as outside advisers), and it should report to the family on investment performance, liquidity and other operating information. Professional managers allocate assets, monitor investment performance, manage risk, develop financial planning, oversee tax compliance, co-ordinate group insurance, banking, accounting and taxation services, and manage implementation of intra-family transactions such as share transfers and estate plans (in which capacity the family office is acting as an administrative centre in support of the family governance structure). Some family offices go further than this, delivering a comprehensive package designed to encompass every aspect of living with wealth as a family, including non-financial services such as consolidated reporting, project management and property management, through to the planning and execution of concierge services.

Listing the services that family offices provide should not be taken to imply that all family offices offer a basic set of services. No two family offices are the same because they have been established and have evolved to serve the individual needs of their families. The services offered by family offices and the systems designed to deliver those services are therefore as varied as the individual families who own them.

Structures

There are two main family office models – the single family office (SFO) and the multifamily office (MFO). The SFO is the traditional model, serving a single family, but SFOs are dying out. Rising costs and the difficulty of retaining top-quality talent are causing fewer families to open individual offices. MFOs, which offer services to more than one family, are often formed by a family deciding to open the doors of its SFO to other families. This has the advantage of providing the career structure, challenge and motivation for talented people that the SFO may not, and of spreading costs and risks across a larger asset base; there is also the opportunity to establish the MFO as a sustainable business. Two prominent examples of MFOs that have transformed themselves into sizeable financial institutions are Bessemer Trust, based in New York, and Glenmede, based in Philadelphia, both owned and controlled by descendants of their founding families, the Phipps and Pew families respectively.[2]

A third model is the multi client family office (MCFO) where existing family office consultants take a few of their best clients and create a more vertical business model of deeper relationships with fewer clients rather than a horizontal one with a large number of clients with smaller assets and a limited level of services. MCFOs are gaining popularity in the USA, but there is little evidence of them being taken up in Europe.[3]

As the sector matures, large institutions like JP Morgan, UBS and HSBC Private Bank are competing more strongly in the family office services market, which has had the effect of cutting margins. This, in turn, has led to a consolidation, resulting in larger MFOs such as Pictet in Europe and Atlantic Trust in the USA. At the same time, services that an SFO can no longer provide economically to its clients are being outsourced.[4]

One of the largest UK MFOs is Fleming Family and Partners, established in 2000. Its origins lie in the investment business of Robert Fleming, founded in 1873, which, as Robert Fleming Holdings, was sold to Chase Manhattan Bank in August 2000. Its target client base comprises family groups, including the Fleming family, individuals, charities and institutions. Another well-known example is Sand Aire, a privately owned MFO. The executive chairman, Alexander Scott, is a member of the family who originally created Sand Aire as an SFO (to manage the family's assets after they sold Provincial Insurance in the mid-1990s), and he believes that, at its best, the family office delivers the purest form of open architecture:[5]

> Its people, often with institutional backgrounds, build custom-made, flexible solutions for families, using skills not normally available for private clients. Services are delivered according to the precise needs of the family.

Sand Aire lists its principal objectives as helping to develop the vision, strategy and structures needed for stewardship of wealth; providing the professional investment management skills needed to deliver investment

When the largest and most successful family businesses set up philanthropic foundations, the result is often a charitable institution with global reach

performance consistent with clients' objectives; and co-ordinating the financial responsibilities and lifestyle requirements of its clients.

Despite Sand Aire's origins, it is not true that only families who have sold their business need a family office. A family office is especially useful as part of the governance structure of multigenerational companies with shareholders who do not work in the business because it focuses on structural and financial responsibilities. It can help improve family harmony and unity, provide wealth management education for the next generation, bolster family members' legal and financial know-how, and enhance their purchasing power.

This educational role is becoming increasingly important. Family offices have traditionally operated around the investment component of wealth management, but today they are addressing broader aspects of family wealth. In particular, there is greater emphasis being placed on human, intellectual and social capital perspectives, and there is much more concern about the ways in which family wealth affects the lives of heirs. Thus many family offices are focusing on the need to create educational programmes for the next generation, giving them the skills required to make independent evaluations regarding the family's wealth. The expertise of the family office can be put to good use in educating the next generation from an early age about the challenges and responsibilities of wealth, investment and philanthropy – and in offering opportunities to gain hands-on experience in dealing with those responsibilities.

Evaluating MFOs

When choosing an MFO, a family should carefully review the services offered and undertake a broad-based assessment of the MFO's attributes. The Chicago-based Family Office Exchange (FOX) has put together some guidelines and a comprehensive list of questions that should underpin the evaluation process.[6] The questions are grouped under seven headings: firm background and ownership; integrated financial services; client relationship management and communications; profile of the MFO's clients and references; growth of its business and personnel; pricing and fees; sample reports (such as organisation charts and performance analysis reports).

The best MFOs share a number of attributes, including stable and committed ownership, compatible clients, an open architecture enabling the conflict-free pursuit of the best solutions for all their clients and transparent fees that match services. They also have exceptional and motivated employees, up-to-date technology, and family and corporate governance systems that underpin integrity, discretion and confidentiality.[7]

Looking ahead, there is evidence that the US-developed model of the diversified family office is taking hold in the UK and Europe. At present, however, growth in the sector seems unlikely to be spectacular, in particular because of the European predisposition to privacy, with the preferred approach based on a closely run family function rather than a willingness to delegate. More generally, transformation in the financial services industry, although creating opportunities for independent family offices, in the short term at least is confusing. Extra challenges will also arise from the more complex family make-up created by extended families.

Family business philanthropy

As we have seen, organising philanthropy can be one of the roles played by a family office. Family business social and philanthropic activities are often a product of family business values, with family members seeking to have their values and vision reflected in the behaviour of their business.

But this is a subject on which it is difficult to generalise. There are huge family companies that give nothing to charity, while some much smaller-scale family firms might donate 10 per cent of their profits each year. Nevertheless, as corporate social responsibility has developed into a mainstream business issue and a global trend, there is growing evidence that many family businesses see philanthropy as a unique opportunity for them to stand out from the crowd. Bruntwood Estates recently won a family business Social Responsibility award, and chairman Michael Ogelsby champions the family business case:[8]

> Corporate social responsibility has become something which every company has got to have – it is part of the tick-list. The trouble is that it comes from the chequebook and doesn't come from the heart. For family businesses, that is what makes us different, that is what we bring to the table. The corporates do it because they've got to do it and we do it because we really believe in it.

Manchester-based Bruntwood Estates, run by the first and second generations, is one of the largest private commercial property investment development and management companies in the north of England. Michael Ogelsby founded the company in 1977. Having witnessed the deterioration of Manchester in the wake of the 1970s property crash, the Ogelsby family and Bruntwood have a strong determination to contribute to the growth and development of the region. The company and family have created a solid profile as benefactors of city regeneration through a wide-ranging programme of charitable activities, including support for the arts in the region.[9]

A debate is taking place within the family business community concerning the extent to which charitable giving should be a personal or a corporate responsibility. Personal responsibility has traditionally won the day because while families are generally supportive of charitable causes, they often prefer (especially in Europe) anonymity and a low profile. The other side of the argument now has serious support though, and there is a cross-over with the broader themes of corporate social and ethical responsibility and corporate citizenship. Many now argue that charitable endeavour can and should take place as a corporate initiative, and that, as well as giving money to good causes, no one should feel ashamed if there is also some benefit for the company. For example: 'We want to support our community, we can do this by sponsoring community events and, as well as the community benefiting, we should be entitled to make the most of the good publicity we receive in return.'

Defining their motives and objectives is therefore an important starting point for families. Graham Davies, head of family philanthropy at

Charities Aid Foundation, has put the broad-based case for family business philanthropy strongly:[10]

> While global corporations can use corporate social responsibility to enhance brand image, these benefits can also apply to family-owned business, satisfying family shareholder objectives for community engagement while also 'giving something back'; organised philanthropy allows family companies to celebrate their success in a meaningful way – while reducing their tax burden, improving their communities, repaying supporters in kind, strengthening family relationships and creating a legacy for successors. As a package, this is very hard to beat.

A key ingredient of this formulation is the role that philanthropy can play in helping to strengthen family bonds. Strong families often share a unifying force that encompasses integrity, honesty, loyalty and high ethical values, and family businesses and their owners are often generous in support of good causes. But as family firms mature, not all family members will be involved in management or ownership, and a philanthropic agenda can become a rewarding way of fostering family cohesion, representing an opportunity for the family to work together and to remain connected to their shared history of achievement.

Organising giving

Often the vehicle for philanthropy is a family foundation or charitable trust, which directs funds to organisations and causes that are consistent with the family's philanthropic objectives and social values. The choice of vehicle will depend on objectives. For example, Ogelsby and Bruntwood Estates channel their giving through two mechanisms: a family charitable trust and a corporate fund. The rationale behind the separation is to avoid the imposition of family interests on the company and to align Bruntwood's giving with corporate objectives. The Ogelsby Charitable Trust's philanthropic objectives are wider than Bruntwood's, encompassing the arts and education. The company's charitable activities are directed through the Bruntwood Community Fund, which is managed in partnership with the Community Foundation for Greater Manchester.[11]

The Oglesby family separates its personal and corporate giving, but many families design an interrelationship of identity and purpose between their business and their foundation that focuses for the most part (or sometimes exclusively) on causes that are aligned with the activities and interests of the business. So we see safety equipment manufacturers directing their philanthropic contributions to research into workplace safety, or educational publishers sponsoring literacy schemes. As a result, the goodwill and values of the business work to underpin those of the foundation, and vice versa.

Of course, when the biggest and most successful family businesses set up foundations, the result is large-scale charitable institutions such as the Ford and Rockefeller foundations that are capable of operating on a global scale and of making a difference in a significant way. The principal European-based example is the Bertelsmann Foundation, founded in 1977 by Reinhard Mohn, a fifth-generation member of media conglomerate Bertelsmann's founding Mohn and Bertelsmann families. On some definitions it ranks as the world's largest charitable foundation and, under its articles, it functions exclusively as a private operating foundation, meaning that it carries out its own project work and does not make grants or support third-party projects. But these famous institutions should not obscure the fact that around the world there are many thousands of other, much smaller private family trusts and foundations supporting good causes in countless communities.

Finally, it is worth remembering that establishing and operating a successful family foundation can be just as problematic as building a successful family business. In each case the first question for the family to address is: 'What are we trying to achieve?' In the case of a family foundation, this means ensuring that its charitable giving is directed to causes that fit in with a mission and strategy that has been carefully defined and thought through. As with a family business, future generations can sometimes find it difficult to identify with the founder's vision, and problems can arise if the original donor's intent becomes outdated and the foundation's objectives fail to engage the passion and commitment of successors. And as with third- and fourth-generation family firms where ownership is in the hands of many cousins and maintaining a unified family approach to the business becomes a major challenge, similar issues can arise with family foundations in the cousin generation, where some family members may feel the foundation is run by enthusiasts more in their own interests than those of the family as a whole. At this stage, leadership skills are required comparable to those needed in the family business to resolve differences among family members, forge a common agenda and re-engage the family behind a vision of strategic philanthropy that helps cement family ties and perpetuate the family legacy.

11

Summary

I t was explained in the Preface that although this book is intended as a guide for those involved in family businesses, or who are contemplating joining one, it is not a how-to book. Each family business is idiosyncratic, shaped by its own set of distinctive personalities, their concerns, objectives and relationships, as well as by a range of other personal and commercial characteristics. This means that there are few if any success and longevity rules that can be applied from firm to firm without qualification and adaptation. Instead, the aim, chapter by chapter, has been to provide some broad frameworks, mindsets, processes and best-practice principles to help shape problem-solving perspectives for family business people, as well as some tools and working guidelines designed to contribute to the efforts of these firms to achieve long-term continuity, growth and prosperity. Here the central themes of each chapter are summarised, with a list of the main conclusions, suggestions and learning points.

1 Why family businesses are special

Chapter 1 provides a broad-based introduction to two fundamental ideas that underpin the book: that family businesses differ in a variety of critically important ways from non-family businesses; and that business families function quite differently from non-business families. If a family business is to achieve its full potential, it is crucial that its owners and managers understand these two distinctions and the challenges they create.

The economic importance of family businesses is also discussed, together with attempts via research to test whether their advantages and disadvantages have a measurable impact on commercial performance. Although family firms are to be found in every sector of commercial activity, their special strengths mean that they flourish best in fields in which their advantages can be fully exploited.

Key conclusions

✳ Family businesses comprise the predominant form of enterprise around the world, yet, until recently, little information or guidance has been available on the unique and complex issues they face.

✳ As well as making the right decisions on the commercial challenges that affect all enterprises, family business people need special skills to help them analyse the complicated dynamics that surround their businesses and their families.

✳ Among a range of advantages, family businesses often foster a unique atmosphere that creates a sense of belonging and an enhanced common purpose.

✳ These firms are also vulnerable to some serious dilemmas and challenges. Family emotions can interfere with commercial decision-making, succession often presents major difficulties and family business people have to work hard to counter the tendency towards a dangerous, introverted atmosphere.

✳ There are no panaceas because every family business is unique. But there are some common patterns of experience, and developing an appreciation of them is important so as to help avoid repeating everyone else's mistakes.

2   Family business dynamics: people, systems and growing complexity

The special status of family businesses derives from their structure, which is characterised by complexity on three levels: a family system, a business system and an ownership system, all linked together by wealth, legal arrangements, employment relationships and emotional/relational bonds. To understand family business dynamics, it is essential to be aware of the interaction of these systems and the way that complexity increases over time.

The other central feature that makes family businesses special is the people who are involved in them, and the background and perspectives of each of the major participants. Two of the main problems that can arise between these people are father–son conflict and sibling rivalry.

Key conclusions

✳ Whatever the size of the business, family members – founders, husbands and wives, the next generation, in-laws and so on – each come to it with their own attitudes, opinions and objectives. An appreciation of these perspectives is a critical aspect of understanding how family businesses operate.

✳ The shared relationships that can help a family firm achieve commercial outperformance also have a potentially negative impact on how the business is organised and how it operates. In particular, there are inherent tensions between the emotional factors that govern family life and the objective nature of business management.

✳ Conflict arising from the overlap of family and business systems cannot be avoided entirely. Successful families devise strategies that help them keep the overlap under control.

✳ Understanding the ownership structure in a family business is often fundamental to understanding the forces at work within it.

✳ Some of the psychology behind both father–son conflict and sibling rivalry needs to be understood before the issues can be managed.

✳ Sons acquiring managerial autonomy within some part of the organisation can secure space in which to grow and mature without appearing to desert their father.

✳ To minimise the scope for rivalry, siblings should try to divide their roles in the family business so that they can focus on their own jobs, not on those of their siblings.

3   The family's relationship with the business: developing a strategic vision and building teamwork

Successful families learn to build a shared vision by aligning individual and family values and goals, and that vision becomes a guide for planning, decision-making and action. The starting point is the simple question, 'What is our business for?' Developing a consensus on this question helps families improve their chances of success when they move on to establishing ground rules for their relationship with the business and in defining the responsibilities of family members.

The aim is to formulate and adopt policies that strike a good balance between the best interests of the business and the well-being of the family; and then to design and establish effective governance structures that help the family develop a cohesive approach to the business and provide organisational focus and accountability.

Key conclusions

✳ Values are what a family and its business stand for; vision is a shared sense of where each is heading. Together, values and vision provide a major source of strength and resilience for the family firm, and are central to long-term family business success.

✳ Times change, families expand, and markets and business cycles move on, so it is important that values and vision are periodically re-examined and refreshed.

✳ A family can significantly improve its chances of success by planning its future together, establishing clear policies governing its relationship with the business and defining the responsibilities of family members. The planning process helps families to approach their businesses in a committed, unified way, rather than as a group of individuals who just happen to be related.

✳ Ingredients of successful planning include establishing open communication, learning to manage differences and adopting strategies that help build family teamwork.

✳ Families need to define policies covering the critical area of family–business relationships, such as the involvement of family members in the business, share ownership and management succession.

✳ Establishing organised procedures and a formal framework in which dialogue can take place is a vital step for families seeking to develop a unified approach to their business. For example, establishing a family council provides an organised forum for family communication, policy-making, planning and the management of differences.

✳ It is a good idea for families to record the conclusions of their planning in a written family constitution (sometimes also called a protocol or creed), which spells out the family's policies in relation to the business.

4 The next generation: human resource management and leadership perspectives

Today's generation is growing up in a commercial culture that is very different from the one in which earlier family members took on responsibility. Increasingly well-educated, cosmopolitan and independent, next-generation family members are taking a much more considered and cautious approach when weighing up the pros and cons of joining the business.

Overlaps and conflicts between the family, business and ownership systems are particularly acute and troublesome in relation to human resource management practices, so clear and explicit management criteria must be drawn up relating to these issues and family members. Family employees should be rewarded and promoted in line with their contribution to the business, and their performance should be evaluated regularly and objectively within a system that applies to all staff.

Key conclusions

✳ Contradictory system forces are best managed by maintaining a distinction between ownership considerations (under which family employees are subject to family norms) and management considerations (under which they are required to submit to the company's principles).

✳ Before joining the family business, the next generation should discuss the prospect as well as other career possibilities with seniors. The decision to join should rest on commitment, not the expectations of others or because it is an easy option.

✳ Obtaining outside work experience helps the junior generation develop an objective view of their own talents and abilities, and will also increase their effectiveness if they do join.

✳ 'Some day son, all this will be yours' is no substitute for a clear and comprehensive entry deal.

✳ Once next-generation members start working in the family firm, they should establish a planned training programme; show they are willing to work hard and provide an extra dimension of commitment; earn the respect of employees through their behaviour and dedication; and reject special privileges.

5 Getting help: making the most of outside resources

As a company becomes larger and more complex, the foundations have to be laid for a more structured, less centralised organisation. The task is significantly more difficult for family than for non-family businesses because there is a strong temptation in many family firms to depend on internal experience and internal judgements. This tendency to introversion can be countered by the effective use of outside talent: non-family managers; non-executive directors; and advisers and consultants.

Key conclusions

✷ The decision to appoint outsiders from any of the three groups may be a difficult one – marking a cultural shift. But it is often an important step in making the company more open to external influence and can help secure its future.

✷ Family companies must work to attract high-quality, non-family employees and (under carefully designed incentive schemes) to reward their contribution.

✷ Motivation of non-family managers is a central issue in the development of family businesses. There must be clear evidence of a career path for such employees and of comparability of reward for responsibility and expertise between family and non-family members.

✷ Non-executive directors can be especially valuable to family-owned companies, providing seasoned guidance, specialised expertise and networking connections.

✷ Skilled family business advisers and consultants are able to probe difficult family business issues and develop discussion of a family's problem areas in a subtle and sensitive way that minimises the possibility of friction and confrontation. Their selection should be based on competence and their performance periodically reviewed, and possible conflicts of interest need to be thought about and avoided.

6   Professionalising the boardroom: the role of a balanced board of directors

The role of the board of directors in the governance structure of a family-controlled company is critically important. Establishing a board that includes independent outsiders is probably crucial for the vast majority of family businesses if they are to achieve long-term success. Such a board brings objectivity and experience to policy and operational deliberations, and imposes important disciplines. When a family introduces board diversity it sends a positive and motivating message to customers, shareholders and employees.

In larger, more mature family companies there is a balance to be struck between the interests of the family as owners of the business and the managers entrusted to run it. No single model works for all, and, instead, a solid set of principles and processes must be drawn up and applied in the unique circumstances of each company.

Key conclusions

✳ Introducing outside directors and thus moving towards a more accountable system of corporate governance does not always come easily to family business founders or owner managing directors, and is sometimes viewed as a threat to the family's culture.

✳ The board can be effective only when the managing director or controlling owner have the confidence to accept a degree of reduction in their power and control over the business, and are willing to subject their stewardship to examination by outsiders.

✳ When establishing a well-balanced board, family business people are often pleasantly surprised at the kind of talent they can attract. The first question is not 'Who might I ask?', but rather 'What am I looking for?', after which the search can begin to find people who fit the bill.

✳ The board's main duties are to protect the interests of the shareholders; to help make big-ticket decisions on major issues affecting the company; to oversee management performance (including that of the managing director and senior management); and to monitor and mediate the family's involvement in the business.

7 Cousin companies: family governance in multigenerational family firms

The ownership structure in a family business usually has a significant impact on the forces at work within it, and ownership of family businesses tends to progress through a three-stage sequence: owner-managed; sibling partnership; and cousin consortium. By the cousin consortium stage, the third or fourth generation is in place, there is a well-established business, and there may be several dozen or more family members who have some sort of stake in it.

By this stage, ownership will have fragmented into the hands of many cousins from different sibling branches of the family, with no single branch having a controlling shareholding. Some of these owners will work in the business, but probably most will not. The potential for friction and dysfunctional behaviour if the large-scale complexity arising with these family and shareholder groups is not controlled and managed is significant. Governance architecture must be tailored to meet the unique needs and circumstances of particular families.

Key conclusions

✳ In a cousin consortium, the powerful family connection that worked for the business in the first two ownership stages may be significantly weakened. Unlike siblings brought up in the same family, cousins often have little in common, and some may never have met.

✳ As family businesses evolve and their owning families become more complex, a migration takes place towards ownership by family members who are increasingly remote from the operations of the business. The needs, expectations and ambitions of owners running the business can be very different from those who are not employed by the firm.

✳ Crucial questions need to be addressed on core family values and the family's vision. 'Why is our business better because the family owns it?' 'Why do we as a family want to stay in business together and what rewards are we seeking?'

✳ Special governance systems and mechanisms are needed to manage the diversity of interests and demands, and to let everyone have their say. Family members who do not subscribe to the consensus vision should be allowed to exit as shareholders.

✳ Policies are also needed on issues such as who can own shares (bloodline, in-laws, non-family, and so on), share valuation and transfer, the expected return on investment and protecting the interests of minority family shareholders.

✳ No single model of family and corporate governance works for all family businesses, and what successful multigenerational companies have achieved is the development of agreed principles and processes that work in the unique circumstances of their family and company.

8   Managing succession: the leadership challenge

The willingness of family company owners to plan for their succession is often a decisive factor, determining whether their business survives or fails. A well-structured, systematic approach to succession planning is required to overcome all the forces that favour doing nothing. The chapter explains why preparation and planning for succession are so difficult and important, analyses the options, and provides practical guidelines on ensuring that transitions are accomplished as smoothly and as advantageously as possible.

Succession from first to second generation is dictated largely by the character of the business founder. All the issues are made more complicated by the founder's dual role as parent and employer, and probably ambivalent attitudes concerning relinquishing control and coming to terms with age and mortality. Later-generation transitions are much more likely to be governed by the size and nature of the company, and by market conditions.

Key conclusions

✳ Doing nothing about succession is often disastrous for family companies. Yet many business owners, reluctant to give up control and preferring ambiguity, decide that avoiding the issue is the best course for them.

✳ Succession is not an event, it is a process. Start planning early to make the most of a crucial family business advantage: the opportunity to solve tomorrow's predictable problems today.

✳ Succession should involve a well-planned partnership with the next generation. Parents must take responsibility, particularly for ensuring their children receive a sound, broadly based education, and that they are well nurtured and develop self-esteem.

✳ Senior-generation members must strike a balance that enables their successors to share their dream, while making sure they are not pressurised into feeling they have no choice but to be part of it.

✳ If they do want to join the business, encourage them to obtain extended work experience in another organisation first. Then provide a training programme that is relevant and worthwhile.

✳ Set a target date for stepping down from day-to-day operational control. This should be far enough ahead so that the successor and everyone else can plan and prepare. Once a date has been set, stick to it.

✳ Succession is not just a question of transferring a tried and tested system for running the firm to the next generation. Rather it is a system change; a transition to a different type of business structure with a different culture, different procedures and different ground rules.

9   Building financial security and relinquishing control

Financial security is important for the family business owners' retirement, yet many neglect their personal finances. They often believe that the business (usually in ways unspecified) itself represents their personal nest egg. This may well turn out to be true, but it involves a number of assumptions that cannot always be taken for granted. Building financial security can be achieved either inside or outside the family business, or, if there are no viable succession options, by selling it. Various sale structures are examined in this chapter.

When passing the family company down to the next generation, continuity of the business, liquidity and family needs are the cornerstones of estate planning. Ensuring ownership ends up in the right hands in the next generation may require treating heirs differently depending on whether or not they are active in the business. Ways of passing on voting control to selected heirs are examined, as are the uses of trusts. Insurance and share purchase agreements can be used to resolve many of the complications arising from multifamily ownership of a business.

Key conclusions

✳ Broadly, business owners can achieve financial peace of mind in retirement either by continuously taking money out of the business during their period of tenure, or by leaving this money to build in the balance sheet so that, on retirement, a restructuring can be arranged to transfer personal wealth to the departing owners. Both strategies have pros and cons.

✳ If selling the business is the best solution, always employ a professional to negotiate and structure the sale, and be prepared for the fact that selling often represents an unexpected emotional wrench.

✳ While some owners can be happy as the employee of the new owner, most find the cultures incompatible and the loss of ultimate control unacceptable.

✳ Rather than drawing up a restrictive will promoting favoured governance structures or share transfer restrictions, it may be better for seniors to focus more on the successful transmission of their values and vision to the next generation via an ethical will.

✳ Owners often do not have a large enough estate to enable them to leave the business to active, interested offspring and other assets to the remaining children. However, structures are available to help achieve a compromise between short-term fairness and solutions that are in the long-term interests of the business.

✳ Owners of family businesses can substantially reduce or delay tax liabilities payable when the business is passed on, but this does require careful forward planning.

10 Wealth management: family offices and philanthropy

Once larger family businesses have established the family governance structures and mechanisms they need to manage complexity and the relationship between family and business, they often look for other ways to help foster their family commitment and vision, and to perpetuate their family's legacy. Opportunities to achieve these objectives can be provided by the family office and philanthropic initiatives.

Key conclusions

✳ The family office should have a formal business structure with a management board (which can consist of family members as well as outside advisers). It should report to the family on investment performance, liquidity and other operating information.

✳ The determination of an appropriate asset allocation and investment management strategy takes place with a comprehensive understanding of the family's financial situation and its risk–return objectives.

✳ A family office is especially useful as part of the governance structure of multigenerational companies with shareholders who do not work in the business, because it focuses on structural and financial responsibilities and can help improve family harmony and unity.

✳ The expertise of the family office can be put to good use in educating the next generation from an early age about the challenges and responsibilities of wealth, investment and philanthropy.

✳ Many family businesses see philanthropy as a unique opportunity for them to stand out from the crowd.

✳ A philanthropic agenda can become a rewarding way of fostering family cohesion, representing an opportunity for the family to work together and to remain connected to their shared history of achievement.

Notes

Preface

1 BDO Stoy Hayward and London Business School (1989) *Staying the Course: Survival Characteristics of the Family-Owned Business*. London: BDO Centre for Family Business. BDO Stoy Hayward and London Business School (1990) *Managing the Family Business in the UK: A Quantitative Survey*. London: BDO Centre for Family Business.

2 See Chapter 1 in John L. Ward (2004) *Perpetuating the Family Business: 50 Lessons Learned From Long-Lasting Successful Families in Business*. Basingstoke: Palgrave Macmillan.

3 This is explained well in Tom Davidow (2006) 'Reshaping – Not Retiring', *Families in Business*, September/October, pp. 71–2.

1 Why family businesses are special

1 Kelin Gersick, John Davis, Marion McCollom Hampton and Ivan Lansberg (1997) *Generation to Generation: Life Cycles of the Family Business*. Boston, MA: Harvard Business School Press.

2 John Ward (2005) 'Keeping the Business Within the Family', FT Mastering Corporate Governance Series, *Financial Times*, 2 June.

3 *The Economist* (1996) 'In Praise of the Family Firm', 9 March, p. 14.

4 Barclays Bank (2002) *A Family Affair: Today's Family Businesses*. London: Barclays Bank.

5 *The Sunday Times* (2005) 'Top Track 100', sponsored by KPMG, 26 June.

6 Manchester Business School and CIIM Business School (2006) *The UK Family Business PLC Economy*. Research led by Dr Panikkos Poutziouris, Visiting Fellow, Family Business Initiatives, Manchester Business School.

7 Sir Terry Leahy (2006) 'Public Companies Can Learn Lessons From Family Firms', *The Independent*, 6 April, p. 62.

8 Jonathan Moules (2005) 'Energy Services Group Draws Power From Ties That Go Back Generations', *Financial Times*, 28 January, p. 19.

9 Melanie Stern (2006) 'Ford: Will Patient Capital Pay', *Families in Business*, May–June, pp. 52–3.

10 Hermann Simon (1996) *Hidden Champions: Lessons from 500 of the World's Best Unknown Companies*. Boston, MA: Harvard Business School Press.

11 Epilogue to Alan Wilkinson (1994) *From Corner Shop to Corner Shop in Five Generations: A History of William Jackson & Son Ltd*. Beverley, East Yorkshire: The Hutton Press.

12 www.coopers.com.au (accessed 15 June 2006).

13 The methodology and findings of this research, which was supported by the Leverhulme Trust and the Stoy Centre for Family Business, have been summarised in *The Management and Performance of Unquoted Family Companies in the United Kingdom*, available from the BDO Centre for Family Business, 8 Baker Street, London W1M 1DA.

14 Manchester Business School and CIIM Business School op. cit.

15 R. Anderson and D. Reeb (2003) 'Founding Family Ownership and Firm Performance: Evidence from the S&P 500', *Journal of Finance*, Vol. LVIII, No. 3, June, pp. 1308–28.

16 Emerald Now (2005) 'Management Learning Into Practice: Spotlight on John Ward', www.emeraldinsight.com (accessed 28 June 2006), quoting John Ward (ed.) (2005) *Unconventional Wisdom: Counterintuitive Insights for Family Business Success*. Chichester: John Wiley & Sons.

17 Barclays Bank, op. cit.

18 NatWest/British Franchising Association (2006) *Annual Survey of Franchising*. Henley-on-Thames, Oxon: British Franchising Association.

2 Family business dynamics

1 Peter Davis (1990) 'Three types of founders – and their dark sides', *Family Business Magazine*, February.

2 Peter Collier and David Horrowitz (2002) *The Fords: An American Epic*. New York: Encounter Books.

3 Peter Davis, op. cit.

4 Sara Carter and Eleanor Shaw (2006) *Women's Business Ownership: Recent Research and Policy Developments*. Stirling: Department of Management and Organisation, Stirling University.

5 In this section we acknowledge especially the work of the business administration authority Harry Levinson and, in particular, his paper 'Conflicts that plague family businesses', *Harvard Business Review*, March–April 1971, pp. 90–98.

6 Harry Levinson (1983) 'Consulting with family businesses: What to look for, what to look out for', *Organizational Dynamics*, Summer, pp. 4–82, American Management Association, New York.

7 Thomas J. Watson Jr and Peter Petre (1990) *Father Son & Co.: My Life at IBM and Beyond*, pp. ix–x. New York: Bantam Books.

8 Adele Faber and Elaine Mazlish (1998) *Siblings Without Rivalry: How to Help Your Children Live Together So You Can Live Too*. New York: HarperCollins Publishers.

9 Harry Levinson (1971), op. cit., p. 96.

10 John Ward (ed.) (2005) *Unconventional Wisdom: Counterintuitive Insights for Family Business Success*. Chichester, UK: John Wiley & Sons.

11 John Ward (1987) *Keeping the Family Business Healthy*. San Francisco: Jossey Bass.

3 The family's relationship with the business

1 Judith Ross (1999) 'A taste of tradition: Kenzaburo Mogi and Kikkoman', *Harvard Business School Bulletin Online*, February, www.alumni.hbs.edu/bulletin. Accessed 21 August 2006.

2 See Randel Carlock and John Ward (2001) *Strategic Planning for the Family Business: Parallel Planning to Unify the Family and Business*. New York: Palgrave.

3 Amy Braden (2003) *Effective Governance: The Eight Proactive Practices of Successful Families*. London: JPMorgan Private Bank.

4 www.axeljohnson.com/AJIPublic/AJI/family/familygenerations. Accessed 18 August 2006.

5 Suzy Bibko (2006) 'The value of family', *Families in Business*, Special Report, Conference Roundtable Discussion, May/June, pp. 23–7.

6 For an interesting analysis of how adapting the family vision can be an antidote to generational conflict, see Jane Zalman (2005) 'Expanding the vision', *Families in Business*, November/December, pp. 70–1.

7 Suzy Bibko, op. cit.

8 Nigel Nicholson (2006) 'The who, what and how of leadership: What's different about running a family business?' Paper delivered at the 5th National Forum Conference of the Institute for Family Business (UK), *Family Firm Leadership: Creating a High Performance Ownership and Management Team*, London, 11 May 2006.

9 Kelin Gersick, John Davis, Marion McCollom Hampton and Ivan Lansberg (1997) *Generation to Generation: Life Cycles of the Family Business*, p. 149. Boston, MA: Harvard Business School Press.

10 Nick Stinnett and John DeFrain (1985) *Secrets of Strong Families*. Boston, Mass.: Little, Brown.

11 John L. Ward (2004) *Perpetuating the Family Business: 50 Lessons Learned from Long-Lasting, Successful Families in Business*, p. 20. Basingstoke: Palgrave Macmillan.

12 Sir John Harvey-Jones with Anthea Masey (1990) *Troubleshooter*. London: BBC Books.

13 Jean L. Kahwajy (2005) 'It's not what's said that's important, but what's heard', in John Ward (ed.) (2005) *Unconventional Wisdom: Counterintuitive Insights for Family Business Success*, p. 147. Chichester, UK: John Wiley & Sons.

14 This was one of the main conclusions of London Business School (2003) *Leadership, Culture and Change in UK Family Firms: BDO Centre for Family Business Research Report*. London: BDO Centre for Family Business.

15 Jean L. Kahwajy (2005) 'It's not what's said that's important, but what's heard', in John Ward (ed.) op. cit., pp. 148–9.

16 Amy Edmondson (2005) 'The challenge for family business teams: Collaboration for excellence'. Paper delivered at the 4th National Forum Conference of the Institute for Family Business (UK), *Success Through Family Teamwork: Working Together Across the Generations*, Birmingham, 19 May 2005.

17 Readers interested in more details of Edmondson's ideas in this area are referred to Amy C. Edmondson and Diana M. Smith (forthcoming) 'Too hot to handle? Engaging relationship conflict to make better decisions and build resilient management teams'. *California Management Review*.

18 JPMorgan (2006) *Family Business Honours*. London: J.P. Morgan Chase & Co.

19 Chris Tighe (2006) 'A lesson from the "family bible" of success'. *Financial Times*, 18 January, p.12.

20 See Asian Institute of Management (2006) *GMR Group: Case Studies*, Manila: The Asian Institute of Management. Also, Suzy Bibko (2006) 'Good Groundwork', *Families in Business*, September/October, pp. 43–6.

4 The next generation

1 Randel S. Carlock and Elizabeth Florent-Treacy (2003) 'Finding a role in the family firm', *Families in Business*, January, pp. 52–3.

2 William Hammond, one of Ernest Betjeman's most skilled workmen, quoted in Bevis Hillier (2006) *John Betjeman: The Biography*, p.164. London: John Murray (Publishers).

3 John Ward (2005) 'Unconventional strategy: Why family firms outperform', in *Unconventional Wisdom: Counterintuitive Insights for Family Business Success*, pp. 13–33. Chichester, UK: John Wiley & Sons.

4 Ibid., pp. 16–17.

5 Ivan S. Lansberg (1983) 'Managing human resources in family firms: The problem of institutional overlap', *Organizational Dynamics*, Summer, pp. 39–46.

6 Ibid., p. 45.

7 Ibid.

8 John Timpson (2000) *Dear James: Secrets of Success From a Management Maverick*, p. 296. London: Caspian Publishing.

5 Getting help

1 The survey, organised by JPMorgan Private Bank and administered by Professor Nigel Nicholson and Asa Bjornberg of the London Business School, was

conducted during the annual conference of the Institute for Family Business (UK), held in Birmingham on 19–20 May 2005.

2 Suzy Bibko (2006) 'The value of family', *Families in Business*, Special Report, Conference Roundtable Discussion, May/June, pp. 23–7.

6 Professionalising the board

1 BDO Centre for Family Business (2003) *Leadership, Culture and Change in UK Family Firms*. Leadership Research Report (research by London Business School). London: BDO Stoy Hayward.

2 J. Richard Hackman and Greg R. Oldham (1980) *Work Redesign*. Reading, MA: Addison-Wesley Publishing Company. See also David W. Johnson and Frank P. Johnson (2005) *Joining Together: Group Theory and Group Skills*. Needham Heights, MA: Allyn and Bacon.

3 John L. Ward (2004) *Professionalising the Board of the Family Company*. Paper delivered to 'Master Class 5', Institute for Family Business (UK) seminar, London, 7 September.

4 Ivan Lansberg (1999) *Succeeding Generations: Realizing the Dream of Families in Business*, p. 296. Boston, MA: Harvard Business School Press.

5 See Chairmen's Forum (2004) *Chairman's Guide to Board Performance Review: A Practical Guide for the Chairman to Organise and Carry Out an Annual Performance Review of the Board*. London: The Chairmen's Forum (www.chairmensforum. org.uk).

6 John Davis (2001) 'Organizing the Family-Run Business', *Harvard Business School Working Knowledge for Business Leaders*, October, http://hbswk.hbs.edu/ item/2536.html. Accessed 21 August 2006.

7 Miles L. Mace (1986) *Directors: Myth and Reality*. Boston: Harvard Business School Press.

8 See Ulrich Steger (2005) 'Good News for Family Firms'. In John Ward (ed.) (2005) *Unconventional Wisdom: Counterintuitive Insights for Family Business Success*, Chapter 10, pp. 183–204. Chichester, UK: John Wiley & Sons.

9 Ivan Lansberg (1999) *Succeeding Generations: Realizing the Dream of Families in Business*, p. 312. Boston, MA: Harvard Business School Press.

10 Drew Mendoza and The Family Business Consulting Group (2003) 'When Good Boards Don't Work', *Families in Business*, January, pp. 61–2.

11 Ibid.

12 John L. Ward, op. cit.

13 Nigel Nicholson and Asa Bjornberg (2005) *Family Business Leadership Inquiry*, p. 53. London: Institute of Family Business (UK).

7 Cousin companies

1 This summary is adapted from Randel S. Carlock (1999) *Becoming a Learning Family: Tools for Growth and Development of Effective Business Families*. Minneapolis, MN: University of St Thomas College of Business Center for Family Enterprise (www.stthomas.edu/cob/centers/cfe/research/growth.html).

2 For a comprehensive review of this topic, see Chapter 6, 'The Complex Family Enterprise', in Kelin Gersick, John Davis, Marion McCollom Hampton and Ivan Lansberg (1997) *Generation to Generation: Life Cycles of the Family Business*, pp. 175–92. Boston, MA: Harvard Business School Press.

3 Ivan Lansberg (2005) *Professionalising Governance in the Family Firm*. Paper delivered to 'Master Class 6', Institute for Family Business (UK) seminar, London, 29 September.

4 Ron Chernow (1993) *The Warburgs: A Family Saga*. London: Chatto and Windus.

5 Dennis T. Jaffe (2003) 'Resolving Family Feuds', *Families in Business*, January, pp. 86–7.

6 Chris Tighe (2006) 'A lesson from the "family bible" of success', *Financial Times*, 18 January, p.12.

7 Tony Bogod, Peter Leach and Rupert Merson (eds) (2004) *Across the Generations: Insights From 100-Year-Old Family Businesses*, Chapter 5. London: BDO Centre for Family Business.

8 Ivan Lansberg (1999) *Succeeding Generations: Realizing the Dream of Families in Business*, pp. 288–9. Boston, MA: Harvard Business School Press.

9 Judith Derbyshire (2004) *Clarks Shoes*. Presentation by the Company Secretary to the Third National Forum Conference of the Institute for Family Business, London, 20–21 May.

10 See Asian Institute of Management (2006) *GMR Group: Case Studies*. Manila: The Asian Institute of Management. See also Suzy Bibko (2006) 'Good Groundwork', *Families in Business*, September/October, pp. 43–6.

11 Musgrave Group (2006) *The Musgrave Family Constitution*. Cork, Ireland: Musgrave Group plc.

12 Amy Braden (2003) *Effective Governance: The Eight Proactive Practices of Successful Families*. London: J.P. Morgan Chase & Co.

13 JPMorgan Private Bank (2004) *Family Business Honours Case Reports*. London: J.P. Morgan Chase & Co.

14 Ivan Lansberg (2005) *Professionalising Governance in the Family Firm*. Paper delivered to 'Master Class 6', Institute for Family Business (UK) seminar, London, 29 September.

15 See Nigel Nicholson & Asa Björnberg (2005) 'Conflicts in the Family Firm: Types, Traps and Solutions'. In *Family Business Leadership Inquiry*, London: Institute for Family Business (UK).

8 Managing succession

1 *The Economist* (2004) 'Family Business: Passing on the Crown'. *The Economist Special Report,* 4 November.

2 BDO Stoy Hayward and London Business School (1990) *Managing the Family Business in the UK: A Quantitative Survey.* London: BDO Centre for Family Business.

3 Jeffrey Sonnenfeld (1988) *The Hero's Farewell: What Happens When CEOs Retire.* New York: Oxford University Press (published in the UK in 1989).

4 Thomas J. Watson Jr and Peter Petre (1990) *Father Son & Co.: My Life at IBM and Beyond.* New York: Bantam Books.

5 Ivan Lansberg (1988) *The Succession Conspiracy: Mapping Resistance to Succession Planning in First Generation Family Firms.* Yale School of Organization and Management, Working Paper A70.

6 Alan Crosbie (2000) *Don't Leave it to the Children: Starting, Building and Sustaining a Family Business,* p.105. Dublin: Marino Books.

7 Jane Zalman (2005) 'Expanding the Vision', *Families in Business,* November/December, pp. 70–1.

8 Dennis T. Jaffe (2003) 'Creating Effective Management Teams', *Families in Business,* April–May, pp. 76–7.

9 Frederic M. Hudson (1999) *The Adult Years: Mastering the Art of Self-Renewal.* San Francisco: Jossey Bass.

10 For an excellent discussion of how demographic changes may impact on succession see Barbara Murray (2005) 'From My Hands to Yours: Retirement as Self-Renewal', *Families in Business,* November–December, pp. 36–9.

11 Nigel Nicholson and Asa Bjornberg (2005) 'Retirement and Succession', in *Family Business Leadership Inquiry,* London: Institute of Family Business (UK), pp. 34–9.

12 Harry Levinson (1974) 'Don't Choose Your Own Successor', *Harvard Business Review,* November–December, p. 60.

13 Suzy Bibko (2006) 'Good Groundwork', *Families in Business,* September/October, pp. 43–6. See also, Asian Institute of Management (2006) *GMR Group: Case Studies.* Manila: The Asian Institute of Management.

14 Stephen J. Dorgan, John J. Dowdy and Thomas M. Rippin (2006) 'Who Should – and Shouldn't – Run the Family Business', *The McKinsey Quarterly,* No. 3, pp. 13–15.

15 See Nigel Nicholson and Asa Bjornberg (2005) 'Shared Leadership in Family Firms', in *Family Business Leadership Inquiry,* London: Institute of Family Business (UK), pp. 18–20.

16 Cited in *The Economist,* op. cit.

17 The approach described in this paragraph is adapted from Penny Webb (2005) 'A Systemic Approach to Responsible Ownership'. Paper presented at the 4th National Forum Conference of the Institute for Family Business (UK), *Success*

Through Family Teamwork: Working Together Across the Generations, Birmingham, 19 May 2005.

18 Joachim Schwass (2005) 'An Effective Successor Development Strategy', in John Ward (ed.) *Unconventional Wisdom: Counterintuitive Insights for Family Business Success*. Chichester, UK: John Wiley & Sons, pp. 109–110 and 114.

19 John Ward (1987) *Keeping the Family Business Healthy*. San Francisco: Jossey Bass.

9 Building financial security and relinquishing control

1 Melanie Stern (2004) 'Sell In, Not Out', *Families in Business*, July–August, pp. 72–3.

2 Irish businessman and family business lecturer Alan Crosbie has particularly strong views about this. See 'When It All Goes Wrong' in Alan Crosbie (2000) *Don't Leave It to the Children: Starting, Building and Sustaining a Family Business*, Chapter 4, pp. 51–67. Dublin: Marino Books.

3 Ibid., p. 63.

4 Ivan Lansberg (2001) 'The Perils of Looking to the Past to Solve the Future', *Families in Business*, Autumn, pp. 54–6.

5 See Barry K. Baines (2006) *Ethical Wills: Putting Your Values on Paper* (2nd edition). Cambridge MA: Da Capo Press.

6 Alan Crosbie, op.cit., pp. 121–2.

7 See the Introduction to Tony Bogod, Peter Leach and Rupert Merson (eds) (2004) *Across the Generations: Insights From 100-Year-Old Family Businesses*. London: BDO Centre for Family Business. Many of the cases in this book illustrate family business people expending a lot of effort trying to be fair.

8 Marshall B. Paisner (2000) *Sustaining the Family Business*. New York: Perseus Books Group / Basic Books.

9 Andrew Drake (2004) 'Keeping It In the Family: The Fear of Outsiders', *Families in Business*, September–October, pp. 41–2.

10 Wealth management

1 Close WINS Investment Trusts (2003) *UK Family Offices: A Research Report Produced in Conjunction with Cass Business School*. London: Winterflood Securities Limited. More recent (informal) estimates among family office experts suggest this figure may now (September 2006) be in the range 35–40.

2 Charlotte Beyer and Timothy Brown (2003) 'Does a Multi-Family Office Make Sense for You?', *Families in Business*, January, pp. 78–80.

3 Lisa Gray (2004) *The New Family Office: Innovative Strategies for Consulting to the Affluent*. London: Institutional Investor Books.

4 François de Visscher (2005) 'Family Offices: An Old Yet Emerging Model', *Families in Business*, January–February, pp. 58–60.

5 Alexander Scott (2006). Personal interview with Alexander Scott, executive chairman of multifamily office Sand Aire.

6 See www.foxexchange.com/public/fox/mfo/mfo_questions.asp. Accessed on 28 September 2006.

7 For a review of factors to take into account when evaluating MFOs, see Charlotte Beyer and Timothy Brown, op. cit.

8 Quoted in Nigel Nicholson and Asa Bjornberg (2004) *JP Morgan Family Business Honours Case Reports*. London: J.P. Morgan Chase & Co., p. 24.

9 Ibid., p. 27.

10 Graham Davies (2005) 'Philanthropy: A Family Business', *Families in Business*, March–April, pp. 49–50.

11 Susan Mackenzie (ed.) (2005) *A Guide to Giving* (2nd edition). London: Association of Charitable Foundations (ACF).

Index